Toward Anti-Oppressive Teaching

Designing and Using Simulated Encounters

Elizabeth A. Self
Barbara S. Stengel

HARVARD EDUCATION PRESS
CAMBRIDGE, MASSACHUSETTS

Copyright © 2020 by the President and Fellows of Harvard College

All rights reserved. No part of this publication may be reproduced or transmitted in any form or by any means, electronic or mechanical, including photocopy, recording, or any information storage and retrieval systems, without permission in writing from the publisher.

Paperback ISBN 978-1-68253-565-3
Library Edition ISBN 978-1-68253-566-0

Library of Congress Cataloging-in-Publication Data

Names: Self, Elizabeth A. (Elizabeth Anne), author. | Stengel, Barbara Senkowski, author.
Title: Toward anti-oppressive teaching : designing and using simulated encounters / Elizabeth A. Self, Barbara S. Stengel.
Description: Cambridge, Massachusetts : Harvard Education Press, [2020] | Includes index. | Summary: "Toward Anti-Oppressive Teaching introduces an innovative approach for using live-actor simulations to prepare preservice teachers for diverse classroom settings"— Provided by publisher.
Identifiers: LCCN 2020027742 | ISBN 9781682535653 (paperback) | ISBN 9781682535660 (library binding)
Subjects: LCSH: Culturally relevant pedagogy—United States. | Simulated environment (Teaching method) | Classroom simulators—United States. | Teachers—Training of—United States. | Minorities—Education—United States. | Multicultural education—United States.
Classification: LCC LC1099.3 .S45 2020 | DDC 370.1170973—dc23
LC record available at https://lccn.loc.gov/2020027742

Published by Harvard Education Press,
an imprint of the Harvard Education Publishing Group

Harvard Education Press
8 Story Street
Cambridge, MA 02138

Cover Design: Endpaper Studio
Cover Photo: fstop123/DigitalVision Vectors via Getty Images

The typefaces used in this book are Minion Pro and Helvetica Neue

Contents

Introduction 1

PART I: The SHIFT Cycle

CHAPTER 1 Why SHIFT? 11
CHAPTER 2 SHIFTing Practice: Guiding Principles 35
CHAPTER 3 Pulled Up Short: Why SHIFT Works 55
CHAPTER 4 The Impact of SHIFT 75

PART II: Start SHIFTing

CHAPTER 5 Infrastructure for the Encounter and the Debrief 97
CHAPTER 6 Crafting Simulations 113
CHAPTER 7 Caring for Actors 133
CHAPTER 8 Learning to Facilitate 153

CODA The Future of SHIFT 173

APPENDIX: Sample Simulation Materials

Daria Miller Simulation 177
Alondra Correa Simulation 184
Phil Duncan Simulation 192
Alexis Jimenez and Matthew Manning Simulation 198

Notes 211
Acknowledgments 221
About the Authors 223
Index 225

Introduction

You are a teacher candidate in an undergraduate licensure program, likely in your second year. You are enrolled in a social foundations course that focuses on the interactions between contemporary social problems and various philosophies of education. Over the last few weeks, you have read articles and chapters written by education philosophers, theorists, and researchers that talk about the purpose of schooling and education, the layers of curriculum, the lived experiences of students, and, most recently, the challenges of school and classroom discipline. All of these readings have focused on students, families, and communities historically underserved in US schools and marginalized in US society. In class, your instructor has facilitated discussion about concepts in the readings, engaged you in tasks to make connections between the broad context of US schools and teacher decisions you may need to make in the future, and asked you to start to look at your own schooling—including what you are receiving now—through the lenses provided by the course.

About a third of the way through the course, your instructor presents a live-actor scenario in which you play the part of a teacher meeting with a student named Daria Miller. Daria is an outgoing fifteen-year-old Black honors student who is creative and hardworking but often talks in class when she is not supposed to. In this simulation, you are to meet with Daria after school to talk about an incident that occurred that day when, in class, you called her out publicly for talking and she left the room abruptly, saying, "This is some bullshit. Why's it always gotta be me?"

What do you think you would do in your ten-to-twelve-minute interaction with Daria? What would you say when you walked into the room?

What would you anticipate she might say or do during the interaction? Would you ask any questions about what happened in class or tell her how you feel about it? Would you claim responsibility for calling her out or even address her walking out? If you are a teacher candidate in the SHIFT Project at Vanderbilt University, you have a chance to find out exactly what you would do in this situation before you ever enter the classroom. And if you are a teacher educator, for whom this book is intended, you have a chance to see what each teacher candidate in your course would do and use those interactions to move future teachers closer toward anti-oppressive teaching.

The Daria Miller case is one of a number of live-actor simulations we have created and embedded in a variety of courses at Vanderbilt's Peabody College of Education since 2013 to prepare preservice teachers for common dilemmas they will face in today's classroom. The simulations are part of the SHIFT Project, used to shift horizons in future teachers to move them toward anti-oppressive teaching, concepts more fully explored in chapter 3. Embedded in a series of tasks we call the *SHIFT cycle*, these simulations reveal a lot about the knowledge, assumptions, and biases of a teacher candidate. They also provide a safe and supportive environment in which candidates are given the opportunity to open themselves up to new learning rather than defending traditional approaches that reinforce the status quo of societal inequities. While we are still researching the effects, we believe from data gathered so far that the SHIFT simulations set teacher candidates down a different path, one of preparing for a lifetime of practicing and learning about anti-oppressive teaching.

Interest in using simulations in teacher education is growing. In addition to using these simulations here at Vanderbilt, we have also worked with teacher educators at other institutions to design and use SHIFT simulations in their programs, which has helped us to refine the principles articulated in this text that help make their use effective within a teacher licensure program. Moreover, it has pressed us to consider the moral and ethical obligations that come with this type of work and that are imperative to address as simulations broadly writ increase in use within teacher education and education research. Thus, this book is written for teacher educators who are interested in using simulated encounters in their own teacher preparation programs, as well as those interested in teacher learning, anti-oppressive teaching, or design-based research. We intend the advice and tools provided in this book to introduce the theory and rationale behind SHIFT simulations and to make it easier for teacher educators to use them in specific courses, as well as to envision and plan for how they might be integrated on a larger scale within a licensure program. We include examples of SHIFT simulations that have been used in teacher licensure courses, including the protocols given to both teacher candidates and actors and a narrative of how we developed the case, how it fit into coursework (with paired readings), how the participants responded, and how the instructor debriefed with the class. We explain what we have done and provide other teacher educators with specific examples to use as models with a rationale that will help them construct their own cases or modify the approach to their needs and program.

Why SHIFT?

Toward Anti-Oppressive Teaching describes how programs can design and use simulated encounters with teacher candidates in ways that contribute to more equitable outcomes for historically underserved and marginalized student populations. The simulated encounters we describe are live-actor, video-recorded, group-debriefed interactions between individual teacher candidates—those who are working toward initial licensure—and actors who play the role of a student, parent, or coworker based on a protocol. Each encounter simulates a situation that is common in teaching and that foregrounds identity, positionality, and systems of oppression in an attempt to make them more visible to candidates. The encounters are part of a cycle of instructional tasks that permit candidates to predict what may happen, reflect on what did happen, and analyze their choices during the encounter in an effort to move toward approaches that support more equitable outcomes for students.

This cycle encourages—and in fact demands—that candidates experience a significant shift in their cultural and intellectual "horizons," philosopher Hans Georg Gadamer's characterization of self-understanding in a given moment in time.[1] When a candidate's horizon has shifted, she can no longer see teaching situations in the same way because she has come to understand herself differently, which makes more and different learning possible for her students. We explain both the "why this" (part I) and the "how to" of using this approach (part II), including the principles and the theories of practice. More than anything else, this book starts a broader conversation about how to design these encounters within the context of a teacher preparation program and use them ethically with learners, actors, and local communities in mind.

The need for new pedagogical approaches is evident in empirical research on education outcomes for minoritized students. Few in the US believe that our schools are educating all children well or are beyond any "achievement gap."[2] Black students are more likely to attend segregated schools, more likely to be taught by novice teachers, and far more likely to be punished for subjective disciplinary infractions than their peers.[3] Parents and families of immigrant and refugee students are less likely to receive communication from schools and are often hesitant to enter school buildings or to reach out to teachers with questions or concerns.[4] Children living in poverty experience significantly more teacher turnover in their schools, which results in a lack of stability in the school culture.[5] Girls, especially girls of color, are still underrepresented in advanced STEM courses, and boys, especially boys of color, are often overrepresented in special education and underrepresented in gifted education.[6] Jewish and Muslim students are more likely to be victims of hate crimes than students practicing other religions.[7] LGBTQIA+ students are also more likely to be bullied at school, which impacts their attendance rates and academic achievement, and they are subjected to greater scrutiny on issues like dress codes and public displays of affection.[8] Students with disabilities are less likely to be fully integrated into class activities and student interaction, even in classrooms that are deemed inclusive.[9]

This considerable but still incomplete list reveals how students feel the impact of societal forms of oppression or experience that oppression in new and even more intense ways in school buildings and classrooms. Moreover, this list (represented here mostly in the passive voice) points to the ways in which systems, structures, and procedures perpetuate oppression by making it less visible. That is, students, families, and communities, with their various identities, are framed as the problem rather than the objects of practices perpetuated by other (dominant) persons or social systems. Thus, it is vitally important to provide future teachers for these and all students—before they are in a position to do real harm to young people—with clear lenses that allow them to see the connections between these systems and their future decisions as teachers, lest they unknowingly reproduce these same systems. This requires a substantive shift in teachers' understanding of their work, recognizing their curricular and instructional expertise as always "partial," as well as a shift in the way they regard their students as knowledgeable resources for the teaching and learning they will engage in together.[10] Understanding this is experiential in a Deweyan sense: it involves direct encounters with these systems *and* those who are impacted by them in ways that invoke thought, feeling, and action.[11]

The approach to simulations explored in this book aims to help future teachers see, know, and value children as knowledgeable individuals, as members of culturally rich communities, and as persons situated within systems of oppression that persist in US society and to respond to them and their needs and resources in a way that interrupts business-as-usual and moves toward more equitable outcomes of all kinds.

Terminology and Conventions

We use various terms for consistency, clarity, and convenience. First, we use *teacher preparation program* to denote any form of teacher licensing program, whether university based, district based, or community based. This includes both traditional and alternative routes to licensure. The term does, however, assume some characteristics of these programs: a core group of teacher educators working together over the years to develop and refine the path to licensure, teacher candidates learning in relatively stable cohorts for at least the course of a semester, and courses or other educative spaces in which the simulated encounters can be used. To this end, we discourage teacher educators from designing and using simulated encounters as stand-alones, separate from other learning that is happening in the program.

We use *teacher candidate* to refer to those who are not yet licensed as classroom teachers and are in a program to become such. At Vanderbilt, teacher candidates are undergraduate or professional students seeking licensure along with their baccalaureate or master's degrees. In other programs, teacher candidates may be pursuing licensure only or are already in the classroom as paraprofessionals, residents, or even teachers with a temporary license. Our experience in the SHIFT Project starts with teacher candidates prior to significant classroom experience, but we have also used simulations with candidates who are in classroom placements. The main point is that simulated encounters are used to shape those whose view is still being formed prior to completing their licensure requirements.

In some chapters, we provide direct quotes from teacher candidates who have participated in SHIFT simulations. As a matter of convention, we use the first names and often provide demographic information for teacher candidates who provided their comments through our survey and gave us permission to attribute them. When quoting from encounters or other simulation materials or describing moments from those interactions, we either use pseudonyms when referring to findings from previously published materials for purposes of consistency or do not use names if permission was given at the time of participation to use the materials for research purposes but with the presumption of anonymity (as identified in IRB consent forms).

Throughout the book, we refer to both *teacher educators* and *instructors*. We have attempted to use *teacher educator* more broadly when thinking about the efforts within teacher education over the last several decades to prepare teachers for anti-oppressive education or when referring to faculty and staff in a licensure program who may be involved in designing or using simulated encounters. We use *instructor* when referring to a specific course or experience in which a simulated encounter is employed.

Finally, our motivating goal in the SHIFT Project is the education and development of anti-oppressive educators. We use this term as Kevin Kumashiro uses it, as an ideal toward which teachers constantly aspire.[12] We argue, with Ibram Kendi, that one cannot be either oppressive or not oppressive—the first is clearly wrong, and the second is not nearly enough.[13] One must be affirmatively *anti*-oppressive, committed to actively working against systems that limit human potential. This is the stance from which this work emerges.

About the Book

Part I focuses on what the SHIFT cycle is, offers principles for how we design and use simulated encounters within our program, articulates the theory of learning that guides it, and documents the impact of the project. These chapters provide a practical explanation of the design as well as its theoretical and philosophical underpinnings.

In chapter 1, "Why SHIFT?" we explain how and why this signature pedagogy came to be developed and how it draws on but differs from similar pedagogies in teacher education, both past and present. We then describe the SHIFT cycle in detail and what it looks like for a specific encounter, the Daria Miller simulation.

Chapter 2, "SHIFTing Practice: Guiding Principles," highlights, explains, and explores the design principles that make SHIFT simulations make sense in and for practice. These principles include building critical incidents that reflect dilemmas of teaching, maintaining complexity, immersing students in richly specified contexts, striving for usefully artificial situations, and attending to dispositions of continuous learning.

In chapter 3, "Pulled Up Short," we articulate the theory that helps explain the design and the power of SHIFT Simulations. We reveal how the simulation cycle leads not to a seemingly simple disruption of habit (or taken-for-granted ways of responding to events) but to a personally and existentially disorienting experience that both prompts *and* requires a reconstruction of the meaning and understanding available to the teacher candidate. We argue that preparing future teachers as anti-oppressive educators requires a continual shift in horizons.

Chapter 4, "The Impact of SHIFT," represents our efforts to document how teacher candidates change as a result of this experience over time and as they enter the profession as teachers of record. The chapter is punctuated by qualitative studies of both the process and the impact on candidates and their teaching performance but is substantively built around teacher candidates' comments and feedback during and after their simulation experience. We do this purposely to suggest that the impacts of SHIFT are neither preset nor static but appropriately diverse based on the positionality of the teacher candidate.

Part II directs attention to the conditions needed for integrating SHIFT simulations into any effort to educate those who would be teachers. As the chapters suggest, SHIFT is not simply a pedagogy to be applied but an approach to the endeavor of preparing teachers.

In chapter 5, "Infrastructure for the Encounter and the Debrief," we walk the reader through the process of assessing their present program to check the dispositions, ideas, and values that motivate what they presently do. We ask the reader to identify their understandings of teaching practices and teaching as a (community of) practice.

Chapter 6, "Crafting Simulations," is a guide for designing your own simulations or choosing to adopt/adapt simulations authored by others. We highlight the need to identify real dilemmas in teaching, to draw out rich characters with whom candidates will interact, to deeply specify the cultural context of the interaction, and to maintain circumstances in which the candidate is forced to acknowledge multiple entry points and possible responses.

Actors play a critical role in effective SHIFT simulations, and it is important that those running simulations pay careful attention to those actors. In chapter 7, "Caring for Actors," we offer those who want to make use of SHIFT simulations advice for how to identify, recruit, and train actors who can work the encounter in ways that maintain tension but offer alternatives for thought and action to teacher candidates. We pay particular attention to finding ways to work with and learn from actors that attend to their psychological and mental well-being as they are, in a way, being learned on by novice teachers.

The point of the final chapter, "Learning to Facilitate," is simple: once you have designed the simulation cycle materials, your work is not done. It is just as important to design the work of facilitation, especially of the group debrief. We discuss in detail a set of approaches to debriefing that are not exhaustive but do present a clear case that different simulations may call for different approaches to the group debrief. We articulate one simple principle available in all efforts to debrief: make use of the candidates' own words and actions to ground and guide any shared sense-making efforts.

The appendix provides materials for four of the simulated encounters referenced in this text. We do not provide complete materials for the twenty or so simulations we have created or even all of those referenced in this text. Instead, we include a sampling of scenarios that have been used the most in our program, and thus we know the most about in terms of how they work, and that represent the breadth of identities, scenarios, and interactions that are part of the SHIFT Project. We do this not just for length but also because we do not encourage teacher educators to simply lift the scenarios we have used and set them down in their own programs but, rather, to derive from the guiding principles and models provided the resources needed to craft in response to their own teacher candidates, their own contexts, and their own needs.

We are delighted to share this work with you and invite you to think with us about it, becoming part of the effort toward an anti-oppressive pedagogy that SHIFT simulations represent.

Part I

The SHIFT Cycle

Chapter 1

Why SHIFT?

Simulations have a long history in education, one that begins well before either of us began using them as teacher educators. Our use of simulations also represents a natural outgrowth of significant work by other critical scholars and teacher educators over the course of decades. Still, SHIFT simulations are clearly something novel in terms of how they engage and motivate teacher candidates to confront their own assumptions, biases, and prejudices and their potential effect on students, families, and communities.

In this chapter, each of us provides the backstory of how this project came to be and our own positionality to the work before moving on to look at how SHIFT simulations have built on prior efforts in simulations of various forms to become what they are today.

Liz's Path to Simulations: From Being Schooled to the SHIFT Project

I (Liz) first began to think about simulated encounters in the fall of 2002, when I was living in Charlottesville, Virginia, earning licensure while already teaching high school English in a county to the north. Much of that first year of teaching was a blur, but I distinctly remember sitting in my apartment with my boyfriend, a second-year medical student at the University of Virginia, pretending to be the patient as he reviewed the steps of a neurological exam. It occurred to me then that nothing I was doing to get licensure seemed quite that practical. I began to wonder about how teachers are educated to do their jobs, a question that would stay with me through my years in Virginia, during several more at a charter school in Chicago, and later into graduate school.

In 2009, when I arrived at Vanderbilt University to pursue a master's degree and then a doctorate, I continued to ponder the question of how teachers are educated—but with a new focus. Having begun to grow in my role as an anti-oppressive educator, but still in the early stages of my learning, I was now invested in how future teachers were prepared to think about anti-oppressive education in their classrooms and in the work of teaching. I recognized that I had been poorly prepared in this regard. Although I had developed an explicit curriculum that was culturally relevant and responsive to my Black and Latina students in Chicago, I had not truly begun to interrogate my own assumptions and mind-sets about what it meant to teach more fully in a way that was anti-oppressive. As a result, while there, I had interactions with students, families, and colleagues that did harm, perpetuated inequities, and reinscribed whiteness. In short, I had failed to recognize my own complicity in systemic oppression. Indeed, at that time I had failed to recognize even the systemic nature of oppression and its many forms; yet by the time I left the K–12 classroom, I did recognize the considerable danger in my own ignorance. Some of those interactions left me raw in ways that, in the short term, caused me to be defensive and show my own fragility and, in the long term, set me up for the learning that would come after I left the classroom.

I spent my master's degree doing the learning I'd really needed before I started teaching and developing questions about how teachers developed as anti-oppressive educators. My early doctoral studies focused on the various efforts that had been made to this end both in teaching and other professional fields. I learned about "critical incidents," those workplace moments that become significant in retrospect, and their role in professional growth. And it was there, in my study of cross-professional teaching, that I returned to those moments of pretending to be a patient. I began to wonder if there was a way to create similar moments for teacher candidates in which they had to manage the kinds of interactions I'd handled poorly in my teaching—ones where my own social identities and positionalities caused me to ignorantly replicate and reinforce existing systems of oppression—to give them the chance to mess up as I had but without the impact on children, communities, and coworkers.

In the years since I started working with SHIFT simulations, my thinking has progressed further, as has my own critical consciousness. In this work, I seek to manage my own partial perspectives as a formally educated, white, straight, cisgender, nondisabled, US-born, monolingual, English-speaking woman. Likewise, I strive to ensure that the work I do is responsive to the identities and lived experiences of the teacher candidates themselves so that they can begin to develop a vision of who and how they can be anti-oppressive educators. My goal is no longer to prevent future teachers from making the mistakes I made, though I hope they will be more prepared as anti-oppressive educators when entering the classroom, but to provide lived experiences that allow them to interrogate their assumptions, acknowledge the systemic nature of oppression and their own complicity in it, and recognize the danger of their own ignorance.

Barb's Background: Simulations as a Response to Long-Standing Challenges

When I (Barb) became aware of Liz's interest in live-actor simulations for the purpose of prompting anti-oppressive pedagogical competence in teacher candidates, I was in a position to help her put this intervention into practice broadly. After thirty-five years as a teacher educator in three different institutions, I was leading teacher education efforts for a relatively small but highly respected program where innovation was expected and welcome. For decades I had been in search of the tools (or cluster of tools) that might move predominantly white, often women, and generally straight and Christian teacher candidates toward more than tolerance of students' identities. I had tried everything, or so I thought: an ever-changing array of readings more critical with each passing decade; simulation games and role-play exercises of all kinds linked to class and cultural difference; case-based and other discussion strategies that encouraged layered deconstruction of assumptions about race, class, gender, and ability; mediated and structured field experiences that focused teacher candidates' attention where I thought it might make a difference; and carefully chosen guest speakers, alone and in tandem, who might describe the shift in their own attention in ways that my students could hear. These efforts were sometimes confined to my own courses (usually in the area of social foundations), sometimes joint efforts with one or two other instructors in a "block" (e.g., an urban teaching sophomore block with two courses grounded in a common field experience), and sometimes coordinated throughout a program. Often there was modest success. Some, occasionally even many, students were moved by these experiences to see, think, and act differently. But success was not universal by any stretch of the imagination. I came to realize that my pedagogical efforts were very useful to those teacher candidates whose assumptions had been disturbed by prior experience. I also realized that *together* these kinds of efforts could have a significant impact if, by chance, something struck a chord with a particular person. But I also realized that nothing in these pedagogical efforts reliably broke through teacher candidates' assumptions. The interruption of assumptions, if it came, was serendipitous (e.g., a particular reading closely tracked some personal experience, or a field experience event was especially disturbing).

When I became aware of Liz's pilot work with SHIFT simulations, I was still on the lookout for that reliable interruption of assumptions, the one that would be sharp enough, both cognitively and affectively, to break through but gentle enough to defuse resistance. I knew that we had tools that could assist in sense-making (readings, discussion strategies, mediated field experiences, etc.) *if* teacher candidates could let go, even momentarily, of what they "knew" to be true—about people, about schooling, about themselves.

I am now convinced that live-actor, video-recorded, group-debriefed simulations can reliably and systematically serve that purpose. In branching out from the undergraduate foundations course, to the graduate foundations course, to pilot efforts in subject-specific pedagogy courses, to the classroom management/ecology courses, culminating in a systematic sequence of five SHIFT simulations over three courses, we have learned a great deal about how to do this to maximize the educational impact for teacher candidates.

Simulations in Other Professional Preparation

While SHIFT simulations are relatively new to teacher education, they are the result of decades of efforts to prepare professionals for the relational aspects of their job and work against fundamentally inequitable systems. First and foremost, SHIFT simulations draw on (but are distinct from) standardized patient encounters in medical education, where they have been used for more than fifty years to prepare physicians-in-training. These face-to-face encounters between physicians-in-training and standardized patients (trained actors or real patients) often feature common interactions, such as taking a medical history or delivering bad news, in an environment that is low stakes for the doctor and low risk for the patient.[1] While the relational work of teachers and physicians varies in important ways, the structure of simulated encounters nonetheless offers a productive space for teacher educators to prepare teacher candidates for the sort of human interactions that will fill their days in the classroom.[2] Because of their standardization, these encounters offer a point for comparison in many fields. Medical education uses them heavily for evaluative purposes, to assess physicians' knowledge, skills, and attitudes at various points in their training, whereas SHIFT simulations seek to leverage the variation in candidates' responses to the standardized scenario to support their learning and are never used as a form of summative assessment. Moreover, while only some standardized patient encounters focus on the sociocultural impact of the scenario, all SHIFT simulations do. Thus, SHIFT simulations differ from both the design and use of standardized patient encounters.

Medicine is not the only profession that has contributed to the SHIFT model. SHIFT simulations follow many of the tenets of the case and problem-based methods developed in law and business schools. The case method, introduced in 1870 by the dean of Harvard Law School, has been a signature pedagogy in legal education for over a century. In its most basic form, this method uses a casebook of "raw material"—in law, truncated versions of appellate court findings—as the primary tool for instruction.[3] Law students summarize the case, answer questions posed by the instructor that are increasingly difficult to conclude from the case materials, and then respond to hypothetical cases, applying relevant principles and precedents from the cases they have studied. In business schools, the problem-based method likewise uses "raw materials" from the field in the form of cases developed by business school professors. These cases are developed to represent problems commonly dealt with in the field or, more recently, come from real organizations and businesses. Rather than summarizing and analyzing the case or problem, though, business students often work in small groups, discussing mainly with each other, and are focused on making critical decisions. The problem-based method in medical education goes one step further, providing small groups of students with cases in the form of patient histories but often with illnesses that medical students are not yet knowledgeable about. Here the problem-based method involves group members working together to figure out what else they need to know about the patient to effectively diagnose or treat them and, in some instances, receiving additional information in stages, and only if requested by the group. SHIFT simulations build on these approaches in several ways: they attempt to provide the "raw materials" of teaching in the form of human interaction, they become a case that can be analyzed individually and by the group, and they often present teacher candidates with situations they have not yet learned how to handle in the hope that facing the situation will intrinsically motivate them to further their learning, especially around issues of identity, positionality, and systematic inequality in education.

SHIFT simulations also draw on cross-professional work on critical incidents. A concept that was born out of efforts to improve pilot training for the US Army Air Forces during World War II, *critical incident* is now used in professional education to refer to a meaningful, revelatory, or significant moment that proves influential to the learner's professional development. Many professions, including teaching, have used critical incidents as an instructional tool to focus on assumptions and feelings as a source of reflection and growth.[4] Because of the focus on assumptions and feelings, critical incidents have likewise been used in professional education to develop practitioners' critical consciousness.[5] SHIFT simulations build on this by trying to create moments in the encounters and ensuing reflection to surface assumptions so they can be critically examined and disrupted as needed.

Finally, SHIFT simulations can be seen as part of the move toward embodiment and affective engagement in teacher education. Such efforts include microteaching from the mid-1960s as well as role-play, rehearsal, and other simulation work happening in programs across the country.

Simulations and More in Teaching and Teacher Education

While SHIFT simulations are not the only form of simulation being used in teaching, or even in teacher education, they are unique in their design and use. Simulations in K–12 teaching are most commonly found in social studies education, where educators have used simulations, role-plays, and games for many years to help students experience the difficulty, challenge, or tension of a social issue; to expose them to perspectives in society on an issue; or to evoke the particularities of a specific historical event (e.g., the plague, historical warfare).[6] Likewise, simulations have been used in teacher education for some time but have been referred to by a wide variety of terms, depending on the particular structure.

Simulations as Microteaching, Role-Play, and Rehearsal

Microteaching in teacher education, from the mid-1960s, was one of the earliest forms of simulation in which teacher candidates functioned as the teacher and provided instruction to their peers serving in the role of the learner. Per its name, microteaching provided an opportunity for both teacher candidates and the teacher educator to look closely at specific aspects of teaching, making it an effective place to practice and receive targeted feedback on elements of teaching.[7] Moreover, when teacher candidates got comments from the instructor and classmates, the learning supported not just them but their peers as well. Now microteaching often includes videotaped lessons from teacher education coursework or from K–12 classrooms, cutting across the traditional divide between university- and school-based teaching. This has led to more recent pedagogies in teacher education, such as video clubs in which teacher candidates share recordings of their classroom teaching to rewatch through different lenses.[8]

Efforts around microteaching eventually led to role-play and rehearsal. Role-play in teacher education focuses on interactional aspects of teaching, preparing teacher candidates to respond to a range of identities, perspectives, and behaviors. Teacher candidates take turns acting out classroom situations that require them to engage in a variety of practices—eliciting and interpreting student thinking, orchestrating whole-class discussion, checking for student understanding. Their peers in the class may be prompted to provide certain understandings or behaviors to reflect likely scenarios in the classroom. Since the early 2010s, teacher educators have also been using rehearsal, which is often focused on more routinized aspects of teaching. Rehearsals are similar to microteaching in that they are a kind of preenactment of teaching, but in rehearsals the teacher educator can provide comments at regular intervals that the teacher candidate can immediately use. Rehearsals are often described as a form of deliberate practice. More recently, teacher educators have used both role-play and rehearsal to focus on vital aspects of ambitious teaching while maintaining the complexity of the work.[9]

While many of the teaching demands found in SHIFT simulations also exist in these formats, the relational challenge in microteaching, role-play, and rehearsal is significantly undercut by having teacher candidates interact with "students" who are known to them. As a consequence, the affective component of the work of teaching is difficult to simulate in these formats. Moreover, while teacher candidates in these forms of enactment are still interacting with real people, it is difficult to put them in fraught situations that deal with forms of oppressions in the work of teaching, especially related to the candidates' personal biases. At a minimum, instructors would be limited to identities present in the class; and even with a diverse range of candidates, the learning would then be happening *on* classmates, which raises ethical concerns.

The SHIFT Project builds on these pedagogies while offering something substantively different. Whereas microteaching and rehearsal tend to focus on content instruction or routinized aspects of teaching, SHIFT simulations enact common problems of practice but in moments that make salient the sociopolitical impact of these interactions. Rather than managing a student who is talking out of turn, as might be rehearsed, a SHIFT simulation enacts the moment that could come after that interaction, when a student has walked out of class after being called out for talking. And by using actors rather than other candidates in the class to play the role of the student, parent, or coworker, SHIFT simulations are able to confront the role of identity, positionality, and systems of oppression more directly while preserving candidates' relationships with each other.

Simulations as a Signature Pedagogy

In the last ten years, teacher educators have begun using simulated encounters in a form more closely modeled after standardized patient encounters in medicine. The simulated interaction model (SIM) was introduced into teacher education by Benjamin Dotger and colleagues at Syracuse University, now called the eduSIM Project.[10] Dotger developed the model, along with a set of cases for teacher candidates and education leaders, to focus on dispositional awareness, sensitivity, and individual uncertainty but not explicitly matters of anti-oppressive pedagogy. Dotger's model includes encounters that focus on Howard Barrows's original framework with design tenets that include prevalence, instructional importance, clinical impact, and social impact. The majority of cases included in Dotger's early work focused on interactions with other adults, namely parent-teacher conferences and meetings with coworkers. This work spread to other institutions, including Vanderbilt, and served as a model from which we developed our current work.

The SHIFT Project builds on Dotger's work by adopting certain structures and adapting them for our purposes. We continue to use the same format for teacher and actor protocols, including verbal triggers that help standardize across interactions, but specify additional demographic information about the role to include aspects vital to the interaction. For example, while Dotger's scenarios include age, sex, and employment, our actor protocols also specify race. If we run the scenario at any point with an actor from a different racial background, we then shape the encounter and other parts of the simulation cycle to reflect that. The general pre- and post-simulation reflections recommended by Dotger were ultimately specified for SHIFT simulations, which we call *prereadings* and *rereadings*, echoing Freireian ideas about "reading the word and the world."[11] While some questions remain the same across simulations, the rereadings in particular are very specific to each encounter, leading intentionally into the planned structure of the group debrief.

The biggest adaptation from SIMs is that SHIFT simulations focus consistently on the sociopolitical impact of the encounter. What marks the SHIFT Project as distinctive from Dotger's original work is less the simulation structure and more its primary purpose—to cause teacher candidates to confront their own biases, assumptions, and mind-sets and to recognize how the unthinking habits that stem from these may harm students, families, and communities—with an explicit focus on systems of oppression and the role of identity and positionality in them.

Simulations for Assessment

In addition to being used as a learning tool, teacher educators have used simulated encounters for assessment, either for education research or as a form of formative assessment. For some education researchers, simulated encounters provide a reliable form of measurement that can be used with fidelity to assess interventions. Cohen and colleagues at the University of Virginia, for example, have used digital platforms for standardized assessments to compare the efficacy of different forms of coaching, looking for changes in candidates' practice.[12] The predictability of the interaction within a stable teaching environment made it possible for researchers to see clearly how candidates' actual interactions changed as a result of the feedback, something more difficult to see in dynamic teaching environments. Other teacher educators, such as Meghan Shaughnessy and Timothy Boerst at the University of Michigan, have used the simulated encounter as a way to formatively assess teachers' learning, especially related to candidates' abilities to elicit and interpret student thinking.[13] The predictable format of the interaction—with live actors who were known to some of the students within the program—allowed teacher educators to gain a clearer sense of what content knowledge teacher candidates had, what they were able to elicit from students, and what they could understand based on what students provided in response to the eliciting.

While the uses of these types of simulated encounters offer interesting directions, they veer from what the SHIFT Project aims to do. Given our focus on anti-oppressive teaching, we feel strongly that SHIFT simulations should not be used for summative assessment, though they always offer informal formative feedback on where students are in their understanding. That formative data is then used collectively to avoid providing feedback to individual teacher candidates in a way that may heighten defensiveness. In addition, while SHIFT simulations yield a significant amount of data that allows teacher researchers to better understand how candidates learn about anti-oppressive teaching over time, the encounters are not used in a way that permits a direct pre/post comparison. The level of uncertainty built into the interactions makes this especially difficult as information revealed during the encounter is known to candidates in a rerun of the same interaction.

Simulations in Virtual Formats

While the simulations described above all involve live actors, another form of simulations being explored involves the use of avatars developed on digital platforms to have specific identities, behaviors, and ways of thinking and interacting.[14] These virtual avatars can then be brought to life by an interactor or puppeteer who animates and gives voice to the avatar based on protocols similar to those used in live-actor encounters. The interactor is able to provide real-time responses, similar to live-actor encounters, but may play the role of multiple avatars in one classroom setting, which limits certain kinds of interactions. For example, avatars cannot talk over each other unless multiple interactors are used. Notably, at present, digital platforms tend to be at least as expensive as live-actor versions, though they potentially offer more consistent scalability.

Still, we argue strongly that virtual avatars are not a viable option for simulations that focus on sociocultural impact in teaching. Because SHIFT simulations address issues of identity, positionality, and systems of oppression, the human aspect of the interaction is vital. Teacher candidates need to see the impact of their words and deeds and reckon with the affective aspects of the encounter. When candidates feel that they can say or do anything in the interaction without dealing with the consequences of those choices, the interaction can contribute further to the dehumanization of persons with marginalized identities, including those that could be made readily visible in a digital platform. Moreover, the use of virtual avatars for minoritized identities raises ethical questions about representation. Because multiple avatars are (inter)acted by one person, it is unlikely that the person bringing the avatar to life shares the identities of all those avatars. They are also having to then impersonate marginalized identities based on race, language, gender, or disability, for example. This makes it more likely that some form of essentializing will occur. While the SHIFT Project also uses actors that may not reflect all of the identities present in a simulation (e.g., a Spanish-speaking actor who is Latinx but not from the nation of origin specified), the ability to vary somewhat across rooms in ways that reflect the person playing the role serves as a strength, rather than a limitation, such that teacher candidates in a class recognize that a given identity may appear or be enacted in many different ways.

The SHIFT Difference

SHIFT simulations differ from most other forms of simulation used in teacher education in three key ways.

First, they put teacher candidates in situations that allow, and even encourage, them to react in their typical way, rather than trying to produce a desired performance. SHIFT simulations are situated in coursework at a point when the broad topics taken up in the scenario have been touched on but not deeply grappled with. Indeed, teacher candidates are reminded that we do not expect them to know yet what to do in these situations (and that we do not use the encounter itself as a summative assessment). By lowering the stakes of the encounter and putting candidates in the situation before they have been given explicit ideas about how to handle it, SHIFT simulations intentionally and reliably surface typified acts, thoughts, and feelings that reflect candidates' existing knowledge and skills as well as their assumptions about a broad host of interpersonal matters. Further, by foregrounding the role of systems of oppression in schooling, and often forcing a moment that may actually play out more slowly in real classrooms, we push teacher candidates to say and do the things that are often behind the silence and hesitation in the assignments and discussion that fill most licensure coursework. This opens up intellectual and emotional space and allows us to go deeper than we would otherwise be able to.

Second, SHIFT simulations fully account for teacher candidates' identities and positionalities. Because we use live actors who are not known to the candidates outside of this interaction, and because the protocols are more broadly constructed than in other professional fields, our scenarios provide space to recognize and respond to a candidate's identity and positionality. Actors often respond to teacher candidates differently, depending on the resources they bring into the interaction (e.g., a candidate speaks the language of an immigrant parent in a conversation about a student's difficulties in class). The variation this introduces across teacher candidates' interactions is then intentionally leveraged as candidates learn from each other and come to see how they are positioned differently in different situations.

Third, the simulated encounters are conceptualized as part of a broader pedagogical strategy that leverages them for sense-making, continuing beyond the encounter itself. All simulated encounters are deeply embedded in coursework such that the interaction, and the extended debrief that follows, carries meaning for the long-term development of teacher candidates. While the end-in-view of each encounter is some moment of discomfort, interruption, or disruption, the ultimate emphasis is on the reflection, revision, and repair that comes from the careful sense-making that follows that moment.

How SHIFT Simulations Work

While a simulation is often thought of simply in terms of the encounter, we mean for it to refer to a series of instructional tasks that teacher candidates complete prior to and following the encounter.[15] Each of these tasks is designed to serve a specific purpose in the teacher candidate's learning, as supported across the series of tasks and beyond. These tasks, broadly writ, encompass five stages: prepare, interact, react, review, reconsider (figure 1.1). We refer to this as the simulation, or SHIFT, cycle.

Prepare

The first task in the instructional sequence directs teacher candidates to read the *teacher interaction protocol* (TIP) and respond to a few prereading questions. The TIP is generally one or two pages long and provides information about the people involved and the events that led up to the live encounter. Each TIP hints at but does not fully reveal diverse and potentially conflicting perceptions, conceptions, and assumptions between the teacher candidate and the encounter actor(s). Teacher candidates receive the TIP the class period prior to the actual encounter and respond in writing to the prereading questions at least twenty-four hours before the scheduled encounter. Instructors typically review candidates' answers prior to the encounter to prepare the actors for any approaches not already covered in actor training.

The prereading questions include three to four prompts to get teacher candidates to speculate about to what is going on in the situation. These prompts usually ask teacher candidates to (1) state what the scenario is

FIGURE 1.1 **The SHIFT Cycle**

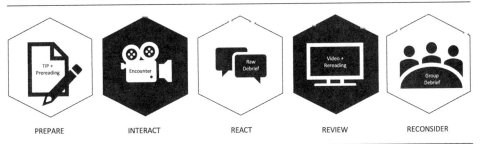

about, based on what they see as the important information in the TIP; (2) envision what they plan to do in the encounter(s); (3) make connections to readings, concepts, or other aspects of their coursework suggested by the TIP circumstances; and (4) explain what other information they would expect (or would like) to have if this were a real situation.

This first task in the cycle is intended to serve as a kind of barometer measure for the instructor and a warm-up for teacher candidates. For the instructor, they reveal, in part, where the candidate's thinking is on a particular topic (e.g., the role of whiteness in subjective disciplinary interactions), how they understand common structures and processes in schooling (e.g., parent-teacher conferences), and what approaches they are most likely to employ in these situations (e.g., one-sided conversations). For the teacher candidates, it is an opportunity to commit to their thinking prior to the encounter so they can compare it with how they see the situation afterward.

Interact

The next task is the actual live-actor encounter, which is video-recorded for individual candidates and instructors to review. Encounters are scheduled in fifteen-minute increments, with ten to twelve minutes for the interactions and a few minutes to turn over rooms between rounds. The live-actor interaction picks up where the TIP leaves off and may include one or more actors with one candidate at a time. Some encounters include the kind of artifacts teachers have in actual classrooms (e.g., test scores, previous work, writing samples), though many have none. Teacher candidates are also permitted to bring in additional materials they find helpful (e.g., a graphic organizer, a rubric, a set of group norms), though few do so.

This stage of learning is intended to reveal to both the candidate and the instructor what they would *actually* feel, think, and do in the face of diversity of persons, cultures, ideas, and emotions. Teacher candidates are asked to stay in their role as the teacher throughout the entire scenario and can use as much or as little of the time they are given, as they see fit. While many candidates start their experience with SHIFT simulations viewing the encounter as the main point of the approach, we see these encounters as a necessary precursor to the kind of learning we want to support. It is usually in the encounter itself that the experience that candidates begin to open up to future learning.

React

Immediately after the live-actor scenario, all the teacher candidates who encountered different actors in different rooms in the same time slot gather in partners or small groups to talk about what they experienced. This raw debrief is unfacilitated; there are no instructors present. Instead, we ask the partners or small groups to record their conversation on an audio-recorder or videotape it with a tablet device for the instructor to review prior to the next class session. In general, we ask three questions: What happened during your encounter? How do you feel about it? What do you want to talk about in the group debrief?

This stage gets teacher candidates talking about the encounter and, notably, causes them to realize that their peers may have handled the interaction differently than they did in ways that have consequences for marginalized individuals. The raw debrief grew out of something the teacher candidates did the first year of the project that we had not anticipated. Because we were running the encounters in a different building than where the course met, teacher candidates were talking in groups after the encounter as they walked back to class after their interactions, and it seemed like this was an important part of teacher candidates' initial sense-making. When we realized this, we began to record the interactions both to better understand the candidates' initial impressions of the scenario but also to see how their reactions to it and understandings of it changed from prior to the encounter until after the group debrief.

Review

At some point between the day of the live encounter and the group debrief, teacher candidates watch the video recordings of their own encounters and respond to a set of rereading questions, which are written in such a way that teacher candidates must watch their videos to respond to the questions. These questions also include three or four prompts asking teacher candidates to restate what the scenario is about, based on what they now see as the important information in the TIP or the video of their encounter; explain whether they changed their approach to the encounters during the interaction, and why; identify key moments or gather specific data from their video, specific to each encounter; and share what questions they still have coming into the group debrief. Responses to these prompts are submitted prior to the group debrief, and ideally with enough time for the instructor to review them to understand the teacher candidates' starting points for group debrief.

The review stage continues the process of sense-making begun with the prereading questions and extended in the raw debriefs, but this time with the video recording as data. The visual evidence of an encounter with sociopolitical impact is powerfully revealing. By viewing one's own responses privately, by being able to self-identify awkward or even disrespectful moments, and by seeing, feeling, and responding to the encounter with a bit of distance, teacher candidates wrestle with the limits of their own recognition and pedagogical responsibility. In short, they can see the places and moments in which they caused harm to another person through their words or deeds in a way that is difficult to perceive, or confront, in daily life.

Rereading questions serves two primary functions: to parallel the prereading questions to compare teacher candidates' understanding of the situation prior to and after the encounters and to draw candidates' attention to aspects of the encounter they may not have attended to in the moment. In some scenarios, we ask teachers to note how much time different people spent talking (including them); in others to list the questions they asked (if any) and what information they gleaned from the responses; and in still others to distinguish what they were thinking at a moment of interaction compared with what they did. These moments or data they attend to in the video recording are intended to cause the teacher candidates to start to question *why* they did what they did, to weigh their choices against other options, and to possibly cause them to see the situation through a new lens. In many instances, teacher candidates are assigned to complete course readings prior to submitting their rereading questions because they provide knowledge, perspectives, or lenses that allow this shift to start to happen. All of this serves as preparation for the richest opportunity for learning—the group debrief.

Reconsider

The final stage of the formalized cycle of tasks is a group debrief, which involves all teacher candidates in the course and the instructor and can also include the actors, other instructors, or guests connected to the scenario. The group debrief is a carefully structured conversation rather than an open-ended one. The instructor at this point has reviewed as many of the videos, raw debriefs, and rereading questions as possible and used that to meet the teacher candidates where they are in their current understanding and move it forward. What this actually looks like varies by scenario and often by class, but the general idea is to leverage the various experiences in the course, the identities and positionalities present (including that of the instructor), and move together toward a clearer understanding of what is happening in this interaction, what can happen, and what must be considered when determining how to act.

The group debrief makes several things possible. First, teacher candidates have a chance to look at themselves and ask, "Is this who I want to be as a teacher?" If the answer is no, the new knowledge and perspectives and lenses provide the teacher with the support necessary to grow. Next, teacher candidates are pushed to confront their own limitations and biases and need for further growth without shaming them for their ignorance or denigrating their efforts. Instead, teacher candidates' responses to the encounter are framed as logical and reasonable within particular framings of the work of teaching, of certain goals for the interaction, or of specific ideologies about school and society. Finally, teacher candidates can be encouraged to feel like they have learned from the encounter without letting them feel like they are done learning from it. Many instructors have teacher candidates end the group debrief with takeaways, remaining questions, or goals for future interactions. But, inevitably, this is not the last time teacher candidates or instructors think or talk about a specific encounter. Instead, the interaction becomes a kind of shared text for the teacher candidates in the room that can be referenced later in coursework or field work to support new application or further learning.

The design of the stages and series of tasks is intended to engage teacher candidates in a process of sense-making that introduces significant uncertainty while expanding the candidates' ability to reason and respond. Moreover, it reflects what we know about learning—that it is often fragmented, not linear, and ongoing and that it is shaped by the tools and resources provided at different points in the process. This cycle of instructional tasks also reflects the principles that guide our design and use of SHIFT simulations.

For Example: The Daria Miller Simulation

So what does this all look like with respect to a specific scenario? The Daria Miller simulation is usually the first simulation that teacher candidates encounter in the SHIFT Program (see appendix). Here we describe what the

SHIFT cycle looks like for this example in the undergraduate program at Vanderbilt, where teacher candidates are likely to be enrolled as sophomores in the Social and Philosophical Aspects of Education course.

Prepare

On the Monday prior to the Wednesday encounter, teacher candidates receive the TIP. At this point in the course, they have read articles and participated in class discussions and instructional tasks related to the purpose of schooling in the US, concepts of curriculum, the work of teaching, and the role of student identity. The course is framed by readings that focus on what it looks like to work against systems of social reproduction and in anti-oppressive ways, drawing on concepts like violence, queering, or teaching paradoxically.[16] In all of this is a focus on "the oppressor in all of us" and the need to recognize, always, our complicity in these systems.[17]

In the Monday class, teacher candidates discuss readings that deal specifically with discipline, including a 2018 review article by Welsh and Little on school discipline and one of several recent articles on the school-to-prison pipeline, restorative practices, zero-excuses policies, the effects of secondary discipline on parents, or the presence of school resources officers as part of "safety" plans in schools.[18] Each of these articles either centers or includes some perspective on the role of race and gender in disciplinary disparities, and some also speak to the role of subjective discipline in those disparities. None of the discussions directly posit what teachers should do, but instead they point to patterns in what they currently do and the impact of that on students, especially those from marginalized and underserved backgrounds.

Along with the TIP, teacher candidates receive the standard prereading questions we use for all of the simulations in the social foundations courses. These include:

1. Complete the following (one) sentence stem in your own words: "This simulation is mainly about . . ." Then make a list of the *three* most important words or phrases in the TIP.
2. What do you expect will happen during the simulation?
3. What does the TIP make you think of
    a. related to the content of this course? Connect to at least one reading or concept from this course.

b. related to your own life? To what extent do you see your own lived experiences present, or not, in this scenario?
c. related to US schools and society? Identify a current event or issue that this situation relates to.
4. If this situation happened in real life, what additional information do you think you would have? What information do you wish you had going into the simulation?

When the teacher candidates read the TIP and respond to the prereading questions, they narrate the scenario as one of respect and classroom management. They either see Daria's behavior as disrespectful or assume that the specific move of calling her out in front of the class was the primary reason she left angrily. They go into the encounter expecting Daria to deny she was talking out of turn or to insist that she was being singled out. Some students note that Daria's positioning as a Black student in the class may play a role, and a few predict that Daria will bring it up in the encounter, but most students specifically attend to neither of these possibilities. Some students connect with Daria in terms of similarities. For the few Black students in our undergraduate population, there is often a sense of connecting around their racial matching; for non-Black students, there is often the idea that they, too, were the "talkative" student without a recognition of the contrast in positioning. Very few teacher candidates note that the behavior seems out of character for Daria or openly wonder about other factors contributing to her response to the teacher's entreaty to quiet down.

React

Two days after receiving the TIP, teacher candidates participate in the actual encounter. Prior to the interaction, the actors playing the role of Daria are coached to be calm but frustrated, resigned but with a bit of hope.[19] They neither engage fully with the candidate at first nor ignore them; instead, they respond as Daria would—polite enough to keep things from getting worse but honest enough to get some things out about how she has been feeling.

Actors are told to provide a three-part disclosure at the first opportunity to share their feelings, either because the teacher candidate has elicited them or because there is a break for them to speak. Otherwise, the candidate drives the interaction. In this disclosure, the actors say something like, "I know I was talking when I wasn't supposed to be, and I'm sorry for that, but so were other kids, and you don't call them out like you did me. And it just seems I'm always being the one getting called out 'cause I'm one of the only Black kids in the room." If the teacher candidate affirms how Daria is feeling or works to learn more about this final comment, Daria shares more about what has been causing her to feel this racial targeting, both in this teacher's class and other places around school. If the candidate gaslights these concerns, Daria tries at least once more to assert her reality but then draws back and simply resigns herself whatever the candidate is asking for. No version of the interaction leads to an easy resolution or things feeling "good" between the candidate and Daria.

In the encounter, teacher candidates overwhelmingly fail to affirm Daria's experience of the classroom, at least at the first pass. In extreme examples, teacher candidates will plainly ignore what Daria has shared and simply move on to assigning consequences for her cursing and walking out (or what will happen in the future if the behavior continues). More commonly, teacher candidates say some version of "I assure you it's not because you're Black." In this version, teacher candidates hear what Daria is saying but feel the fitting response is to assuage her concerns by simply asserting their version of reality. Many teacher candidates tell Daria that they might actually be calling her out more often because they see her as a leader in the class and feel that she can set the tone for others in the class who are also talking after quiet has been called for. In the last few years, more of the teacher candidates apologize for calling Daria out in front of the class, but few (of any race) acknowledge and address the likelihood that their own bias may be playing a role in what Daria is experiencing.

Review

Immediately after the encounter, teacher candidates gather in pairs or groups of three to talk about their experience. Some candidates feel good about the encounter, usually focusing on their own actions ("I said the things I planned to") or the resolution ("She didn't seem as mad as I expected her to"). Others come out unsure of how things went, having expected their efforts to lead to more of a resolution, especially if they apologized, assured the student of their good intent, or encouraged the student to point out when she feels this way. Many of the candidates start to grapple with the difficulty of assuring someone that an action was not motivated by racism. In groups with Black candidates or other candidates of color who have experienced some version of Daria's reality, the process of making new sense of the scenario begins as teacher candidates grapple with how to respond to the scenario from their various racialized positionings.

In the days following the encounter, candidates gain access to their videos and watch them as part of responding to the rereading questions. In watching the videos, some candidates start to recognize patterns in the conversation: that Daria kept bringing up her race and the teacher failed to respond; that Daria seemed to give up in the conversation at a certain point; that they never really responded to Daria's concerns. Many, however, still want to know how to assure Daria that they are not targeting her because of her race *and* how to get her to stop talking.

Reconsider

In the group debrief, which happens five days after the encounter, we lead teacher candidates through a process that attempts to move them from trying to "fix Daria" to imagining how to repair a breach in trust, especially one that has historical and contemporary elements that well exceed the bounds of the interaction. Teacher candidates start with compiling a list of all the problems going on in this situation, from the TIP to the encounter. Inevitably, the first five to seven items on the list start with Daria—"Daria is talking in class," "Daria left the classroom and swore," "Daria is upset."

Once the list is exhausted, we circle all the times "Daria" shows up and then connect teacher candidates to one of the day's readings, W. E. B. DuBois's "How does It Feel to Be a Problem?"[20] From there, teacher candidates engage with a list of anonymized quotes taken from the moment in the videos when Daria makes her disclosure. The list includes versions of ignoring, affirming (if present), gaslighting, apologizing, and eliciting further information. Teacher candidates are then asked to respond to one question: What did Daria hear when the teacher said this? At this point in the debrief, teacher candidates tend to make a turn that allows them to start to see the scenario from the student's perspective rather than their own, which serves as an opening to new learning. In recent years, we have added another step, which involves breaking down the context in which this interaction is taking place—from the legacy of slavery and denial of access to education for Black Americans, to contemporary issues related to discipline covered in our readings, to schools where teachers are predominantly white women, to Daria's position as a gifted Black student in an honors class where she is still one of few Black students.

In this debrief, we also extend well beyond this specific interaction. We talk about what it looks like to approach these conversations from the positions present in the room, based on race and gender in particular. We also describe all the ways that the issues at the heart of the Daria simulation might show up in real life—that many students might feel what Daria does but never say how they are feeling aloud to a teacher, that they may in fact be quite angry and very loud, that some students may feel better at the end of the conversation but others may simply say so in order to please the teacher. We may suggest specific teacher moves to affirm Daria's reality, to honor her courage in saying this openly to her teacher, to elicit more about how she's feeling, to acknowledge the work they have to do in their own classroom in addition to the broader school, to set a time to check in the next week about how she is feeling. But more than anything, we remind teacher candidates that scenarios like these are never fully resolved because of the broader contexts and systems at play. Daria may eventually feel like she can trust her teacher to discipline students' talking more fairly, but racism and white supremacy still exist in her world.

Multiplicative Impact

While we are eager to share the ways in which SHIFT simulations are new and different, we also recognize how this approach builds substantially on previous and current efforts in the field of teacher education and other forms of professional education. In addition to building on past efforts, we state unequivocally that SHIFT simulations will not replace all the other anti-oppressive pedagogies and materials that any particular teacher educator or program currently employs. Rather, the SHIFT simulation multiplies the power of those tools and resources, providing an experience in which other efforts become more meaningful, more applicable, more consequential.

You may find, as we have, that SHIFT simulations can serve as a tool around which other efforts are organized to provide coherence to otherwise abstract and theoretical ideas. The goal, as with so many of these approaches, is to put teacher candidates in situations that require them to see, feel, and do in ways that better prepare them for the actual work of teaching but with greater supports and intentional structures for critical reflection. But perhaps more than any of these approaches, SHIFT simulations take seriously a comment William Keener made in 1894 about the first approach to case method: "We understand most thoroughly and remember longest that which we have acquired by labor on our own part."[21]

Chapter 2

SHIFTing Practice
Guiding Principles

As teacher preparation programs become interested in the SHIFT Program, it is essential that we are able to identify the principles that make SHIFT simulations make sense in and for practice so that they can be effective in new contexts. But we also note that these principles have gone through revision since the start of the project as we have responded to what Rich Milner calls "dangers seen and unseen."[1] When we started the project, we did not fully anticipate how teacher candidates might avoid or sidestep the cultural aspects of a given scenario or overgeneralize these aspects to entire sociocultural groups. Neither did we fully plan for the ways that racially, culturally, and linguistically minoritized teachers might be emotionally triggered by the simulated encounter. Both the avoidance tendencies of the largely white and otherwise privileged candidates and the triggering of candidates minoritized with respect to race, class, gender, sexual orientation, religion, and disability have prompted us to be more explicit in our framing principles to ensure that *every* candidate, whatever their positionality, experience both disruption *and* support through their SHIFT participation.

We offer six design principles. While we would argue that teacher educators can and should enact SHIFT simulations variously based on context, need, and resources, the guiding principles articulated here have evolved over the course of this seven-year design experiment and have helped us make constructive and productive adjustments in practice.

1. Build SHIFT cycles around critical incidents in which dimensions of difference are implicated with respect to power and privilege and in which candidates' and other actors' identities and positionalities become salient.
2. Maintain the complexity of teaching practice in the construction of the protocols.
3. Immerse students in situations in which concepts related to anti-oppressive pedagogy are embodied in richly specified contexts and fleshed out in interaction with a well-prepared live actor.
4. Strive for situations that are usefully artificial, that are safe enough to minimize defensiveness and challenging enough so that candidates are opened up to future learning.
5. Attend to the development of dispositions that ground continuous learning for faculty and students.
6. Locate and sequence your SHIFT cycles to take maximum advantage of the resources of established program elements, or revise your program as needed to ensure that SHIFT simulations make sense.

These principles represent what is distinctive about this project. If you stray from these principles, you may be doing something valuable, but it is not the SHIFT we offer here: these principles are all necessary for the successful enactment of SHIFT simulations and are together sufficient to check the efficacy of your design. It is useful to remember that principles are not rules—as John Dewey pointed out, "Rules are practical; they are habitual ways of doing things. But principles are intellectual; they are the final methods used in judging suggested courses of action . . . The object of . . . principles is to supply standpoints and methods which will enable the individual to make for himself an analysis of the elements . . . in the particular situation."[2] Indeed, these principles don't tell you what to do; they are tools for use in choosing to act this way and not that way.[3]

Principle 1: Build SHIFT cycles around critical incidents in which dimensions of difference are implicated with respect to power and privilege and in which teachers' and other actors' identities and positionalities become salient

Critical incidents are those complex moments that, through reflection, influence professional development by highlighting assumptions and feelings in a way that leads to growth. For teachers, critical incidents can come in the form of interactions—with the whole class or just one student or a few coworkers—that did not go well. The moment often stays with us, laden with confusion, discomfort, and/or uncertainty. We spend time trying to figure out what happened, (re)interpreting the interaction based on conversations with friends or colleagues in a way that shapes both how we see the incident and what we see as a tenable response.

SHIFT cycles take those moments that often arise for teachers in schools and tries to simulate them in a way that allows the growth to happen prior to candidates entering the classroom. As such, these situations have to be both plausible and challenging intellectually, emotionally, morally, and professionally. They have to feel like true dilemmas of teaching, but ones in which there is also something to be learned.

In the SHIFT Project, in our pursuit of an actively anti-oppressive stance for future public school teachers, the focus is on critical incidents in which dimensions of human difference—of identity, values, beliefs, or experiences—are evident and thus have impact with respect to power and privilege. We intentionally complicate teacher candidates' initial reactions to circumstances where systemic oppression causes enough discomfort to call those reactions into question. We seek to replace this self-centered discomfort and uncertainty with "empathy for and desire to better understand the Other" *and* themselves.[4]

It is not surprising, then, that at Vanderbilt we typically begin with a student-focused scenario that has race and racism at its heart (Daria Miller; see appendix) and then move to a family-centered scenario that implicates culture, language, and immigration status (Maryam Sahil or Alondra Correa; see appendix). We finish the initial semester of SHIFT simulations with a colleague-centered encounter that confronts candidates with a range of destructive and damaging stereotypes related to race, language, gender identity, religion, and ability (Phil Duncan; see appendix).

In the first two cases, the protagonist is a person who might well be marginalized based on their identities. In the third case, the protagonist enacts the marginalization by the sloppy use of stereotypes put forward under the guise of "knowing your students."

As we move into critical incidents in subject-specific methods courses, we highlight issues that teachers in that subject area face regularly: planning for difficult discourses in social studies classes when analyzing controversial Supreme Court cases (e.g., *Obergefell*) with a student who is a committed evangelical Christian and a not-yet-out gay student (Alexis Jimenez and Matthew Manning; see appendix); reconciling a bright, responsible student's religious beliefs about creation and intelligent design with the science class's consideration of evolution (Caitlin Jackson); exploring positioning in small-group discussions based on race, gender, and language with respect to competence in mathematics (Matthew Sloan and Luciana Ramirez); and coaching a struggling writer to encourage her effort and while addressing her essentialized misinterpretation of a text about Hispanic families, in a course focused on language and literacy (Riley Adler).

Each of these cases, and others not mentioned here, represents not simply personal difference but group disparities with respect to power and privilege within social and educational systems. They provide a space for unpacking what teacher candidates take for granted about and how they typically react with respect to race, class, gender, and other potential bases for oppressive relations. When teacher candidates are able to see and acknowledge their own presuppositions in action, it clears a space for replacing old habits with a new vision of asset-oriented and anti-oppressive practice.

In play here are not only dimensions of difference but also teachers' and students' identities. We target scenarios in which visible or invisible aspects of identity are raised to surface the question of how school (and) systems are designed with particular groups in mind. The critical incidents we construct are highly contextual, specific even to temporal events and our geographic location, yet they also capture near-universal teaching interactions. Teacher candidates' own personhood can be called into question (e.g., an undocumented student's ability to access education in a time of travel bans and ICE raids, a queer teacher being positioned by a student as a "sinner" in the conservative South). The critical incidents we employ are timely and constructed with both a general target issue and a specific context in mind.

While this provides us with the flexibility to be sure that the critical incident is interesting, challenging, and relevant, it also presents a challenge of fidelity. The scenario can be altered or replaced to update, target, or enrich its impact. In addition, each encounter necessarily changes somewhat based on who the actor is, who the teacher candidate is, and how they come to engage their identities (or not) in the encounter (all of which is interrogated in the group debrief). These aspects of the scenario are always embedded in more general moments of teaching in an effort to consider the affective aspects of teaching and to help teachers see that these concerns are always present, whether we recognize them or not. This is intentional. As we blend the personal and professional elements, candidates recognize that any given scenario in teaching is never merely a matter of "what works" but always also "how and by/for whom." Thus, we prioritize the complexity of teaching practice over the ability to replicate given scenarios in precise terms.

The critical incident is intentionally constructed to disrupt teacher candidates' beliefs, mind-sets, and dispositions with respect to difference, power, and privilege. To ensure that we get it right and do not reinscribe forms of oppression, it is important that critical incidents be designed in active collaboration with individuals or organizations representing the cultural identities being portrayed. This will result in rich backstories for the role that, in turn, give teacher candidates access to the full story behind individual experiences. The richer the information and perspective they have access to as part of the encounter, the more they can understand how such information would be important to them as educators.

Principle 2: Maintain the complexity of teaching practice

Riley Adler

Riley Adler (she/her, age seventeen, white) is one of twenty-three students in your third block, tenth-grade English II Foundations class at Glencliff High School in Nashville. Riley has a history of poor academic performance and high absenteeism and is repeating tenth grade. In your class, her assignments

> are often incomplete or missing. For the last week your class has been reading selections from Sandra Cisneros's *The House on Mango Street*. Because you have a high percentage of Spanish-speaking students in your class, most of whom emigrated with their families from Mexico, you thought the text would be culturally relevant for many of the students. While the class as a whole responded well to the selections, Riley has seemed really disinterested and has not handed in any work.
>
> In class today you assigned your students to do a TNReady (end-of-course, standardized state assessment) writing prompt on the computer using two passages from *The House on Mango Street* that you had not read in class. At first, Riley did not respond to the task, but after some encouragement she began to work. When Riley left for lunch during this split-time class, she was smiling and said she had worked really hard on the assignment. She asked you to look at her essay first so you could conference with her when she came back.

In these simulations, we seek to focus on action in a way that not only guards against a mechanistic understanding of what it means to work in solidarity or teach for social justice but also avoids a mechanistic view of what it means to teach generally. We respond, in part, to Gloria Ladson-Billings's entreaty that we prepare teachers for this work without simply showing them "how we do it."[5] SHIFT simulations are used not to prepare teacher candidates with a set of core actions to use in scenarios like the ones offered but, instead, to help teacher candidates see how particular actions would serve either to reinforce or disrupt existing systems of oppression at play in these scenarios (and beyond). The encounters are not the place of learning but a tool leveraged to support learning.

We are also intentionally prompting the cognitive, affective, and behavioral discomfort of disruption. However, disruption for the practicing teacher does not occur only with respect to issues of social and political difference. It is also part of the everyday practice of teaching. In its least complicated iterations, teaching is an uncertain, even impossible profession, with much of its work invisible to anyone but the teacher herself.[6] The immediacy of every situation puts the teacher's responsibility to the students in high relief while positioning the teacher as insider or outsider, expert or novice, ally or opponent, caretaker or administrator of justice.

The SHIFT Project prepares candidates to live and respond within this complexity.

Illustrative of this is the case of Riley Adler, a SHIFT simulation located in a writing methods course for teacher candidates in the English language arts program. In addition to a longer version of the description provided above, candidates receive a copy of the writing prompt and Riley's essay, which includes significant misinterpretations of the text laid onto deficit ideologies about "Hispanic" families. Here the teacher candidates come up against a very common dilemma with respect to struggling or reluctant writers: how to acknowledge greater effort with the writing and success in writing more than in the past while pointing out the failure to draw reliably on evidence from the texts provided or master specific mechanics.

But there is also the matter of Riley's comments about the family in the passage being "poor," "dirty," and "bad," based, she believes, in evidence drawn from the texts. Riley's case is further complicated by her positioning as a white minority member of a predominantly Latinx class and by the specific prompt employed: musings about family using excerpts from Sandra Cisneros's *The House on Mango Street*, which the teacher has chosen in part as a "mirroring" text for Latinx students in the class.[7] It is also complicated by Riley's regular absenteeism, family background, and past health challenges (of which the teacher is likely not aware).

Before the teacher candidates conference with Riley after lunch, they have to figure out how to engage with Riley, how much to praise the increased production of meaningful words, and how much to acknowledge the problematic aspects of the writing. Before making that decision, they have to take stock of what they know about Riley and how what they don't know might impact their coaching strategy.

The complexity in this scenario is very real, especially when we keep issues of oppression in view. If the teacher does not address Riley's essentializing and deficit comments about Latinx people, they may see that Riley makes more of an effort on writing prompts moving forward, but they also run the most immediate risk of Riley sharing her ideas aloud to classmates whose identities and cultural heritage would be disparaged in the process. If the teacher does address Riley's comments in the conference, they may see Riley shut down again as a writer or feel even further isolated in her class, even if it serves to protect other students in her class. But these are not the only options. As part of this debrief, the instructor talks to candidates about what they might do during the unit that would help draw out students' prior knowledge about the families and communities explored in Cisneros's text, about what they might do instructionally or interpersonally in the face of Riley's comments, and how they should manage Riley's needs as an individual with those of the class.

We complicate this further with more what-ifs—What if students were going to revise and edit this piece of writing after conferencing with you, with multiple rounds of feedback? What if you knew students were going to peer-edit these pieces of writing after conferencing with you? What relevant information might you learn about Riley if you asked some questions about her as well as her writing? What if Riley is not white but a student of color who is not Latinx? We know that learning has occurred when teacher candidates begin to consider this complexity not just within the bounds of the encounter but in situations like it more broadly, especially with this kind of contingent thinking.

SHIFT simulations offer the rare opportunity outside of the classroom to see how students might respond to feedback, questions, ideas, and encouragement during the encounter. Rather than being a place to practice, per se, SHIFT encounters like the one with Riley Adler offer opportunities to learn from common problems of practice. Unthinking habits—modes of reaction that teacher candidates aren't even aware they are likely to enact—are exposed, and candidates must quickly recognize their effect and change their approach as needed. This involves recognizing the limitations of their own knowledge and skills as they garner new knowledge that will enable them to enact what pedagogically responsible practice requires.[8]

Principle 3: Immerse students in situations in which concepts related to anti-oppressive pedagogy are embodied in richly specified contexts and fleshed out in interaction with a well-prepared live actor

Caitlin Jackson

Caitlin Jackson (she/her, age fifteen, white) is one of twenty-four students enrolled in your ninth-grade Honors Biology class at Hillwood High School in Nashville. She lives in Joelton, one of the more rural communities in the district. Caitlin is friendly and outgoing and is well-liked by her teachers and peers. Your relationship is positive, and she is maintaining an A- average in your class as she works toward her goal of becoming a nurse.

In Honors Biology, you engage students in the practice of science through lecture, whole-class discussions, pair or group work, games, and hands-on modeling activities. You also extend learning to outside the classroom. Twice per month you open your classroom to research and discussion of "hot topics" in science, self-selected by students. In the last hot topics sessions, Caitlin asked whether it is moral to conduct research using embryonic stem cells. You redirected the discussion to "focus more on the science" but are now noticing that Caitlin has seemed less engaged in class. Recently, she failed to turn in a proposal for a research project on unifying concepts in science. Knowing how important this class is given Caitlin's career goal, you are concerned about the recent drop in her performance and schedule a time to talk with her.

Each SHIFT simulation cycle is a designed learning environment. That is, we expect that the scenario described in the TIP, the instructional tasks that are part of the SHIFT cycle, and the assigned readings used as part of the sense-making process will have a cumulative and multiplicative impact on each teacher candidate. The quality of the impact depends on the reality of the actor's story. The context and backstory must be both believable and compelling, and the actor has to be able to represent that story with conviction and integrity.

In the reality of SHIFT encounters, teacher candidates cannot avoid grappling with the necessary relations between themselves and the student(s) and among students.[9] Of course, in this circumstance the relations are hypothetical; despite this, candidates tune in to both the importance of attending to the quality of their relations with these hypothetical students and the way those relations dictate what can be learned and how students can grow. Actual and possible relations become visible in the course of the encounter.

The presence or absence of trust and respect, for example, are regularly enacted. The teacher candidates have only what is narrated in the TIP to build on. Nonetheless, they seem remarkably willing to suspend disbelief and to build out the details of their relations in their imaginations. In the most immediately rewarding encounters, they find ways to search out, through difficult conversations with actors, the reality of the hypothetical students' stories. This, the quality of relations, is the reason why we question the effectiveness of using digital avatars rather than live actors. While it is true that avatars can be used to try out a range of professional reactions, something that could be useful in some professional contexts, we are unable to imagine how avatars address the relational challenges when human difference and systematic oppression are at stake.

Relational quality is a function not of the one-on-one attention of the teacher and student but of the shared thinking by teacher and student about some content, the third element in the "instructional triangle."[10] This content may involve the scope and sequence written into the curriculum, the school-level and societal factors affecting learning, or the specific dynamics of the classroom. The inclusion of these factors can only happen in SHIFT-type simulations when the context and narrative thread are richly specified.

Consider the case of Caitlin Jackson. Caitlin is not written as a flat and static character personifying the view of a conservative, white, Christian girl in the South. She is a person with legitimate faith-based and moral concerns about a technology that scientific discoveries have made possible. She is also a solid student of science who has demonstrated her capacity to engage in scientific inquiry. She is a student who intends to pursue a career as a nurse, which demands that she acquire and employ scientific knowledge. Caitlin is a willing participant in a classroom where a range of current issues are regularly taken up, and she has asked the teacher to consider one that is of real interest to her. Her relationship with the teacher is a positive and productive one, and she is surprised when her interest seems to be dismissed without cause or explanation. That she is confused and disappointed is clear. Her race and religious faith privilege her in some ways, which, to the second principle, complicates the situation in a way that is different than if she were a Muslim student of color or if she were from an Indigenous community.

It is easy to understand the challenge presented to a teacher candidate. Stories about science classes being derailed by religious interests abound. In the moment, based on the TIP, the teacher sidesteps the moral questions, trying to simply avoid what might be controversial to return Caitlin and the other students back to "the science." Caitlin has withdrawn from class interaction. Now the teacher candidate has to reach out to Caitlin. And, of course, there is room in this scenario for rich response with regard to the nature of scientific inquiry, the sources of belief, the conditions for the acceptance of facts (scientific and otherwise), the difference between what's worth knowing (the academic) and what's worth doing (the moral), and a host of other important educational concerns. This learning is not simply born out of teacher candidates' reading and contemplating the TIP but, rather, emerges from interactions *with* Caitlin where they must read her posture in addition to hearing her words, pose questions to understand how she is feeling and why she has not submitted her proposal, and get a sense of how she sees aspects of her faith as relevant to a science classroom. In this interaction, candidates find they must pose questions several times, in different ways, to get Caitlin to open up about the concerns underneath the hot topics session and her proposal, in which she outlines a research project that compares and contrasts theories of evolution and intelligent design. They eventually find themselves looking at the outline for a proposal on this project, which then requires them to decide not just whether faith and religion have a place in science class (especially in interaction with other students' beliefs) but also whether Caitlin's proposed topic will work for the goals of the assignment.

Principle 4: Strive for situations that are usefully artificial, that are safe enough to minimize defensiveness and challenging enough so that candidates are opened up to future learning

Alexis Jimenez and Matthew Manning

Alexis Jimenez and Matthew Manning are both enrolled in your eleventh-grade AP US Government and Politics class at MLK Academic Magnet School in Nashville. You are currently covering public policy, civil rights, and civil liberties. Discussions include, for example, whether Colin Kaepernick's decision to kneel during the national anthem, and other athletes' protests past and present, are protected by the First Amendment. The conversation among students has been animated, and you are trying to develop some

> norms moving forward. Lexi (Latina) and Matthew (white) are both solid but generally reserved students, as they have been in recent discussions. Because of this, you don't feel you know either one very well.
>
> On Friday, when you return to your classroom after hall duty, you find Lexi and Matthew in your classroom waiting to speak with you. They ask to speak with you separately. As you meet with each, you begin to understand that they have a similar concern about what's coming—will they be "safe" during the upcoming discussion on the *Obergefell* Supreme Court decision on gay marriage.

Participation in the encounter at the center of each SHIFT simulation intentionally generates discomfort. We know that; we actively seek it. We do so because it is that discomfort that sets us thinking, that clears a space for new ideas, new feelings, and new habits. This is true for whatever we are teaching. If our taken-for-granted ideas and practices are not challenged, we do not grow. However, we also know that discomfort does not always lead to growth. When students are too uncomfortable, they can shut down, or even flee, withdrawing from the kind of engagement that learning requires. So with SHIFT simulations we seek a level of productive discomfort, enough to move students to reconsideration and reconstruction but not so much that they refuse, or are unable, to engage. The simulations are admittedly artificial. These are not actual students in actual classrooms. But they *could* be actual students. Their stories are fully fleshed out and believable. The artifice involved allows us and our teacher candidates to take vulnerability seriously *before* they are in a position to do harm to students in situations like these where identity is at stake, both for the student being enacted in the simulation and their hypothetical classmates.

Consider Matthew and Lexi. Matthew, candidates learn in their encounter with him, is gay but not out to his classmates. Lexi, they learn in a separate encounter, is Catholic and feels that her faith demands she speak out against gay marriage. Some candidates talk with Matthew first, and others with Lexi first. Each student is understandably sensitive to how they will be perceived by their peers, especially given recent "free-wheeling" class discussions. They don't just *feel* vulnerable; they *are* vulnerable. Their peers and their teacher have the capacity to hurt them. Peers might make jokes or speak rudely or insensitively. The teacher may be dismissive or fail to ensure that they can speak and be heard. And so they come to their teacher to preempt either possibility.

This kind of situation is very common in the classroom of any social studies teacher who has the courage and commitment to bring history and government out of the textbooks and into the everyday lives of students. And the dilemma Matthew and Lexi present is all too real: *How can I create safe space for Matthew that is also and at once a safe space for Lexi? And in my effort to reassure the one I speak with first, will I promise something that endangers the other?*

There is a reason why we go out of our way to reassure candidates that there are no immediate stakes associated with their "performance" in the videotaped encounter. There is a reason why nobody else observes them as they engage the encounter in a SHIFT simulation.[11] They must be free to try out the ways of responding to the situation that make the most sense to them in the moment and to see what that actually does to the students in front of them.[12] There is a reason why these encounters are videotaped to be viewed privately by the candidate: *What I have done is inescapable, unavoidable. I must see it. But only I see it. The vulnerability is mine to wrestle with and make sense of.*

Mindful of what Robin DiAngelo calls "white fragility" and what Barbara Applebaum describes as white students' desire to deny the guilt of racism, we are careful in the debrief process to not single out anybody for their in-encounter actions.[13] This is certainly true where race is at issue, but just as true where gender, sexual orientation, or religious commitment play a role. But this does not mean we do not confront candidates with the impact of their words and action. Instead, all quotes or comments are totally anonymous. There is no judgment offered by instructors, even as we interrogate all the comments made in an effort to determine whether they are moving our students toward growth or toward miseducative experience.[14] We take time and energy to help candidates come to see the assumptions, ignorance, and bias that motivate their decisions; but by helping them to recognize it themselves, in themselves, the effect is more educative than defensive.

One might ask, as some of our colleagues have, why do you so carefully steer these initial encounters? Why not simply put students in extended placements in racially, ethnically, linguistically, religiously diverse communities so they can learn naturally the rhythm and quality of positive response? There's no question that simulations are *not* a replacement for long-term immersive experiences. But we recognize that immersion in a community one is not open to can also result in reinscribing forms of oppression and exacerbating stereotypes and prejudices. What is true is that immersion experiences can actually be more effective, more powerful, as a consequence of candidates' participation (and opening up) in SHIFT simulations. They can "practice without penalty."[15]

Broadly, the SHIFT Project relies on the assumption that safe, supported opportunities to make sense of moments of teaching in which teachers' and students' identities are implicated can serve to ground teachers' commitment to anti-oppressive education. These opportunities are outside of actual field experience. Both the teacher candidate and real students and families are safe from the consequences of candidates' early missteps, and candidates themselves are supported in making sense of their decision-making rather than simply evaluated. Moreover, the individual nature of the encounter paired with the shared nature of the group debrief means candidates have all engaged in the encounter but do not have to make that public to their peers to be judged on it. The teacher candidates are accountable to themselves for their own actions, thus minimizing their defensiveness when talking about issues of race, class, gender, etc.

Principle 5: Attend to the development of dispositions that ground continuous learning for faculty and students

Luciana Ramirez and Matthew Sloan

You are a tenth- and eleventh-grade math teacher at McGavock High School in Nashville teaching sections of Integrated II, both honors and regular-tracked classes. This scenario takes place in November of Integrated II Honors. You have been working on growing patterns since the beginning of the year, starting with the Beams task during the first week and moving through other pile pattern–growing tasks. You have noticed that some of your students are able to generalize quickly, while others are not.

Luciana Ramirez (she/her, age sixteen, Latina) is a multilingual student who only recently moved into honors math, where she is developing greater confidence in her mathematical ability. Matthew Sloan (he/him, age sixteen, white) has been enrolled in honors math classes for years and has a level of self-assuredness that rivals only his speed and accuracy.

In today's class you are teaching students about quadratic growth and ask them to analyze, individually and in groups, a growing pattern (a series of stacked horizontal blocks in the pattern 1-2-1, 1-2-3-2-1, 1-2-3-4-3-2-1). You are monitoring during small-group work and decide to start with Luciana and Matthew's group because they seem almost silent at first. You sit with the group for a few minutes to get them moving, and then you move on to other groups. When you glance over during the rest of the class period, the group continues to appear relatively quiet, although everyone seems to be writing on their own papers and listening to one group member speak.

With a few minutes remaining in the class period, you hear Matthew and Luciana arguing. Matthew, sounding frustrated, says, "Why can't you just let it go? It's a group project. You're making this so much harder than it has to be." Luciana then turns her chair away from him and continues to work on her own. You ask them to step into an empty classroom to talk about what happened.

We design scenarios so that teacher candidates not only acquire a willingness to be disrupted in a particularly difficult situation but begin to develop a habit of welcoming disruption. We are teaching candidates to seek out learning and opportunities that push them to continue to grow and question what they think they know, especially around what it looks like to work in solidarity with particular groups. In this encounter, the teacher candidates are aspiring teachers of mathematics.

It can be all too easy for those who think of themselves as social justice educators to begin seeing a "them" and "we" in ways that are (un)intentionally exclusionary. This line not only makes impossible the "we" that may exist through further efforts at solidarity but suggests that there can be an uncritically just cause in a static form. By conceptualizing response to disruption as a thoughtful, socially cultivated habit rather than as a solitary mind-set or personal attitude, we pursue a form of community building and solidarity work in action that is inclusionary in terms of the need for all of us to continue our own learning and growth alongside those for whom we seek justice. Our goal is not to catch out future teachers' "bad habits" and "fix" them. Rather, we are calling out what they take for granted and calling them into direct engagement with students and situations they might rather avoid. In other words, we are teaching them to see their future students and situations as compelling rather than concerning.

Luciana and Matthew, together with their groupmates Alana and Phillip, are working on a mathematical task in the realm of understanding and representing quadratic functions. There are obvious tensions within the group. The tensions could be associated with differences of race, culture, gender, and ability. But they could also stem quite directly from "past histories of association" with mathematics, and those, too, might be associated with race, culture, gender, and ability.[16] Coaching them on the fine points of thinking mathematically together is one of your responsibilities. However, the mathematical thinking does not occur in a vacuum. Identities and histories are always at stake. So you plan to talk with them. They are, of course, not the only group you are monitoring and quite possibly not the only one struggling to find common ground.

Even if you incorporate five SHIFT simulations into your program, as we do with our secondary education program, it is impossible to cover all the dimensions of difference and dilemmas of teaching that one might encounter in a single year of teaching, let alone over the course of a career. The point is to experience disruption, reinterpretation, and reconstruction of habit as a positive and productive event so that the simulation-type situations you encounter in your everyday teaching become the same kind of opportunity to learn in and through practice.

Our graduates will often contact us to say, "I just had a sim moment in my class today" or "I used to be anxious about the simulations, but now I realize that they are happening all the time in my classroom." Teachers are encountering Rileys and Caitlins and Lexis and Lucianas and Matthews every day. Our candidates are learning to see them not as problems but as people presenting opportunities for interpersonal and intellectual growth for all involved. This requires a generosity of spirit on our part as the candidates first encounter these (types of) characters. Our guiding attitude toward the candidates is, "We want to learn with you," which leads candidates to take the same attitude toward their students. As we all come to recognize the limits of particular habits and horizons, we come to peace with ourselves as (often) flawed and as continuously reconstructing new habits in response.

Principle 6: Locate and sequence your SHIFT cycles to take advantage of the resources of established program elements, or revise your program as needed to make SHIFT simulations make sense

SHIFT cycles cannot be effective as a solo intervention. It matters how they are sequenced relative to one another. It matters especially how they are scheduled relative to critical elements of a teacher preparation program and how they are integrated with them. Those elements include coursework with their assigned readings and discussions as well as practicums, field experiences, student teaching, residencies, or other immersion-type experiences.

Social foundations courses are often used in teacher preparation programs to help candidates develop a more complete and accurate vision of the work of teaching and their role in it as teachers, in part to disrupt their own apprenticeship of observation.[17] As such, the course provides an opportunity for teachers to develop a way of being a teacher as well as an explicit professional vision that includes the sociocultural consciousness and cultural humility necessary for anti-oppressive teaching.[18] Social foundations courses, with readings that explore systemic oppression and social inequalities, are an obvious site to situate SHIFT simulations, given their attention to anti-oppressive pedagogy in all its manifestations. For instance, as candidates complete the Daria Miller simulation, they are reading W. E. B. DuBois's discussion of "double consciousness" along with Dorothy Hines-Datiri and Dorinda Carter Andrews's 2017 article "The Effects of Zero Tolerance Policies on Black Girls: Using Critical Race Feminism and Figured Worlds to Examine School Discipline" or Eduardo Bonilla-Silva's "Racism Without Racists."[19] As they debrief on their conference with Alondra Correa, a Puerto Rican mom of a sixth-grade son, they may be reading Mark Warren, Soo Hong, Carolyn Rubin, and Phitsamay Uy's "Beyond the Bake Sale" and one of a set of articles about shifting from parental involvement to family engagement and moving from a school-centric to a family-centric understanding, texts that enable them to make sense of their encounters with immigrant or multilingual parents.[20] And their professional vision gets tested with respect to equity when they read Henry Giroux's vision of "Teachers as Transformative Intellectuals," Kevin Kumashiro's "Teaching Paradoxically," and Nicola Soekoe's essay on engaging as the oppressor, even as they are negotiating their feelings about veteran teacher Phil Duncan, whom candidates love to loathe.[21] These and other regularly updated readings offer instructors and teacher candidates conceptual tools to analyze candidates' experience of the actual encounter. In the group debrief, the focus is on what did and did not transpire in candidates' interaction with the actor in the scenario, but it is also set up to ask candidates to view personal and interpersonal experiences through a theoretical or research lens.

The SHIFT simulations we have highlighted are each situated in a subject-specific course that addresses ways of knowing, communicating, inquiring, and representing understanding in the various subject areas. We call these course experiences "literacies courses," including under that umbrella both academic language and what might be described as disciplinary literacies. Because readings and class discussions take up how we know and how we know we know in a particular subject area, these courses are a fitting location to remind teacher candidates that anti-oppressive pedagogy is integrally linked to content instruction. When Riley Adler struggles to make sense of a Latina-oriented novel, her English teacher might just think that Riley has always struggled and it's happening again. But a closer look at the text may lead her to wonder about the figurative language embedded within cultural referents and the extent to which the lack of background knowledge is playing into or playing up Riley's essentialized misinterpretations of the text. Course readings related to language structures and coaching writing help the instructor guide the teacher candidates to understand these various wonderings. When Caitlin Jackson has the courage to take on the very real moral dimensions of embryonic stem cell research, we can understand why her science teacher might want to sidestep the issue, but also why Caitlin feels dismissed. The science literacies students have already read Cynthia Passmore and Jim Stewart's "A Modeling Approach to Teaching Evolutionary Biology in High Schools," which provides them with tools to understand what is and isn't science *and* what science is and is not capable of telling us but does not give them a script for their conversation with Caitlin.[22] When Luciana Ramirez and Matthew Sloan find conflict around engaging in their assigned mathematics problem with a vision toward finding understanding versus a vision toward finding an answer, we might be tempted to first notice a cultured or gender-based disagreement. A more nuanced interpretation involves the use of critical theory to decipher how "truth" in mathematics is politicized across intersectional dimensions.²³ When Alexis Jimenez and Matthew Manning individually tell the social studies teacher that they are concerned about how the classroom conversation about the *Obergefell* case will go, the candidate feels the pressure of competing identities and ideologies, a very common circumstance for those teaching history and government. The students have already read Diana Hess's and Paula McAvoy's *The Political Classroom* and Barbara Stengel's "The Complex Case of Fear and Safe Space," which provide a solid base for figuring out what might be going on but offer no conclusive answers.²⁴ That class time is spent debriefing the already-viewed encounters as a group highlights the integration of theory and practice, of abstract idea and embodied encounter.

While we have chosen to site our SHIFT simulations within courses, this need not be the case. We know of colleagues at other institutions who have chosen to locate their SHIFT simulations within hybrid practice experiences, in practicums and student teaching.²⁵ While course readings do not play a central role in sense-making that is part of the simulation cycle, the expectations for each practicum experience clearly frame the analysis and discussion. In addition, instructors are able to call on conceptual and research understandings embedded in coursework throughout the program.

Once again, the point is not to do as we have done. The point is to coordinate your SHIFT simulations with already available elements of your program for maximum impact. The SHIFT simulations can open the door to a deeper engagement with other sources of understanding, and those other sources can be used to make SHIFT simulations make sense.

It is also possible that the presence of a particular simulation highlights the absence of something else in the program, driving a need to alter or add to the program design. When we began to do the Maryam Sahlil simulation, a parent-teacher conference with a Kurdish immigrant parent, it highlighted the fact that our program, like many others in secondary education, did not push candidates toward real relationships with families. That push has meant looking, as a team, for other opportunities (in assigned readings, course discussions, field experiences, etc.) to do so.

SHIFT is a critical pragmatist project, an ongoing design study in which the practice shapes relevant theory, the theory informs practice at every stage, and each makes sense to us and to our teacher candidates in light of the other. That we employ these principles going forward does not mean that nothing (including the principles) can change. It does mean, however, that we have settled on a set of guides that will stay in place until future experience and future research demonstrate limits and, like our own understandings and the understandings of our candidates, need to be renewed and reconstructed.

Chapter 3

Pulled Up Short
Why SHIFT Works

The SHIFT Project at Vanderbilt seeks to support the preparation of anti-oppressive educators in substantive ways. Yet, no simulated encounters will accomplish that on their own. Nor can simulations, which lack authentic context, be used to fully assess the preparedness of teacher candidates or provide a satisfactory place to practice. So what do SHIFT simulations do?

SHIFT simulations provide teacher candidates opportunities for new sense-making with respect to matters of equity linked to dimensions of difference. At various points in the cycle, teacher candidates open up to the learning already offered in the form of readings, structured reflections, and class discussions, sources that inform reconstructed horizons and create news lenses for understanding interactions and frameworks for interpretation. This SHIFT process takes teacher candidates deep enough into cognitive belief systems, affective economies, and patterns of practice to shift the sense of self as teacher and shift the habits of attention and regard with which teachers approach students who are stigmatized and minoritized in schools. The candidates see themselves and the situation differently and, as an outcome of the full cycle of interpretation and reconstruction, are able to act differently as well. This is consequential for the kind of educators they can become.

How does this happen?

In this chapter we account for this impact theoretically. We mine the hermeneutic theory of Hans Georg Gadamer (as read through Deborah Kerdeman's educational lens), the pragmatist theory of John Dewey, and the critical affect theory of Sara Ahmed to help understand how and why interruption and reconstruction—embodied, felt, and thought through—is a productive approach to encouraging anti-oppressive teaching practice. Only those teacher candidates who are self-consciously aware of the ways identity, positionality, and systems of power impact their own lives, for better or worse, are able to respond in anti-oppressive and socially just ways toward others. But surrendering our assumptions about the world, allowing our horizon of understanding to be altered, is a challenge to self-understanding. It's difficult. It requires an iterative process of becoming aware of our own position in an unjust world and imagining responses to others that take our own *and* others' experiences seriously. This does not mean understanding the other from *their* point of view; that is not possible. What is possible is to understand ourselves with that other fully within our horizon of understanding. That's the best we can do—and it is what SHIFT simulations both allow and demand.[1]

Admittedly, the iterative process we describe occurs naturally for some candidates and in some scenarios. However, for teacher candidates who have little prior learning related to student identity, their own positionality, or the role of systems of oppression, the process is unlikely to happen without something sparking it. Can such experiences be prompted within a teacher preparation program? The answer seems to be yes, by using critical incidents that unsettle or interrupt candidates' taken-for-granted ways of seeing, interpreting, and responding—that is, by being in the world. To do so, teacher educators must confront candidates with the need to acknowledge the challenge to their self-understanding and offer contexts, guidance, and ideas for reinterpretation and reconstruction of horizons of meaning. As candidates encounter this cycle of disruptive encounter, self-recognition, and reconstruction, they improve their capacity to respond in a fitting way to all students as developing persons, to be pedagogically responsible. They are "pulled up short" but never left without resources for sense-making.[2]

The resources employed to help teacher candidates make sense of these enactments—critical race theory, feminist theory, critical disability studies, or queering—are often difficult to understand separate from personal experience. The simulated encounter offers that experience, becoming a site for interpretation of these theoretical offerings in pursuit of a reconstituted self. The encounter pushes teacher candidates to a space of constructive disequilibrium, which demands that they know more and respond in kind. We refer to this as being *pulled up short* and the learning that follows as a *shift in horizons of understanding*.[3] Being pulled up short is the sine qua non for development as an anti-oppressive educator rooted in pedagogical responsibility.

Below we sketch what happens when teacher candidates participate in the SHIFT simulation cycle. The simulations, set in cycles of activity, move candidates toward anti-oppressive pedagogy because they challenge habits (characteristic ways of acting), beliefs (characteristic ways of thinking), and attitudes or affects (characteristic ways of feeling). In short, SHIFT simulations challenge candidates' understanding of themselves as teachers.

Narrating a SHIFT

Philosopher of education Deborah Kerdeman's reflective analysis of being pulled up short herself illustrates and informs our theoretical grounding. In a 2019 essay, she describes being challenged by students of color in her core graduate class at a predominantly white institution. The students of color were experiencing microaggressions and moments of disrespect and dismissal at the hands of their white peers, and they said so. Kerdeman listened, asked a few questions, and then "suddenly apprehended with gut-wrenching clarity that the problem in my class concerned white privilege. How could I have been so blind to a dynamic that was happening right before my eyes?" This was a moment of significant interruption, and it changed everything. Though her students of color suggested that their concern was not with her actions, she recognized that this could not be the case. She could not escape from the realization her students had provoked: "I stumbled through the rest of the week, shell-shocked but nonetheless clear that I had to address the racial tension in my class. I read the articles my students gave me. I consulted with colleagues at my institution who focus on anti-racist pedagogy. I started monitoring small group discussions and had follow-up meetings with some of the students. The class improved. My life as a teacher and human being also improved, although in ways I could not have imagined at the time." Above all, Kerdeman questioned why and how she could have missed the reality of privilege and the presence of racial injustice of all kinds. A single encounter with a small group of students interrupted her "refusal to acknowledge white privilege" and reoriented her "to try and promote social justice through teaching."[4]

To make sense of her experience, Kerdeman turned to Gadamer, and we followed her lead. In particular, we acknowledge that what Kerdeman experienced, what teacher candidates experience in the course of the SHIFT simulation cycle, is the phenomenon Gadamer describes as being "pulled up short."[5] Kerdeman describes how "when we are pulled up short, events we neither want nor foresee and to which we may believe we are immune interrupt our lives and challenge our self-understanding in ways we cannot imagine in advance of living through them."[6] As for Kerdeman, our teacher candidates do not merely find that their assumptions about the world are interrupted by SHIFT simulations; indeed, self-understanding is interrupted and altered as candidates acquire "insight into one's own existence as a privileged . . . being."[7]

Kerdeman's later-in-life experience of a horizon shift was prompted by an actual, not simulated, critical incident, but one structured similarly to the scenarios we employ in the SHIFT Project. The impact of a challenging encounter she experienced was extended as she sought supports similar to those built into the SHIFT simulation cycle as "a planned instructional experience." As former candidates, now teachers, remind us often, it is not unusual to encounter incidents in classrooms every day, even after years of teaching, that look or feel similar to SHIFT encounters. What is distinctive about SHIFT simulations is the intentional cycle of reflection integrated with related readings and group sense-making.

Note that we are talking about the development of candidates as teachers. Nothing in what we describe and recommend obviates the structural character of inequities nor suggests that structural change is not needed. We do not claim that shifting horizons for individuals is enough to change systemic inequity in schooling or the world. However, we do maintain that shifting horizons is necessary if not sufficient. And we further claim that individuals whose horizons have shifted toward anti-oppressive and justice-oriented stances are in a better place to work for structural change in a similar direction.[8]

The trajectory we sketch for teacher candidates has multiple starting points but no identifiable endpoint. In teaching, there are always opportunities to encounter students who bring new identities, new ways of understanding our positionalities, and new ways of seeing the force of systems of oppression in school and society. A key aspect of the SHIFT Project is that it starts with a focus on race and racism but does not remain there. We recognize the vital need for all teacher candidates to grapple with the importance of recognizing students' racial and ethnic identities, the potential for them to perpetuate racism and whiteness in their classroom, and the need to recognize how our histories of settler colonialism pervade all aspects of school and society. Given the long histories of color-evasiveness and its significant impact on students of color, especially Black and Latinx students, we find it both pedagogically appropriate and useful to begin with an incident that focuses on the role of race and racism, as teacher candidates are opened up to recognizing the myriad ways in which various identities, positionalities, and systems (e.g., Eurocentrism, linguicism, heteronormativity, etc.) play out in (dis)service to students and their learning. This enables discovering new ways of being and doing that push against the status quo. Our goal is to get candidates to the point where they recognize first that discomfort is a site for further learning, not shrinking back, and, second, that their horizons are not as expansive as they think they are.

All of this is situated in the context of a theory of teacher action that we call *pedagogical responsibility*. As teacher educators, we seek to prepare teachers to respond richly, fittingly, and generatively to students situated within past experiences, present circumstances, and future possibilities, all within a broader landscape of societal histories and cultural positioning. In this chapter we describe our understanding of pedagogical responsibility and then take up the experience of being pulled up short by considering both Gadamer's original articulation and Kerdeman's educational extension. We flesh out the nexus of acting, thinking, and feeling that grounds the use of SHIFT simulations, relying on the pragmatist theory of habit offered by John Dewey at the start of the last century and the critical pragmatist/affect theory articulation Sara Ahmed offered at the start of this century.

Pedagogical Responsibility

SHIFT simulations are intentionally disruptive. They employ a pedagogy of interruption or discomfort that prompts a reconstruction of what makes sense.[9] But interruption and discomfort are means, not ends. The point is to make possible teachers' humanizing responses to actual students in complex instructional spaces. As Zeus Leonardo and Ronald Porter note, a pedagogy of disruption calls for "a form of violence, but a humanizing rather than repressive force" that "shifts the regime of knowledge about what is ultimately possible as well as desirable."[10] In Thomas Philip's framing of disruptive pedagogies, "commonsensical" thinking with respect to ideologies of all kinds is both revealed and problematized so that more adequate sense-making is possible.[11]

When pedagogical responsibility is the end-in-view of teacher education, teacher candidates are taught to develop and employ research-based and reliable practices as long as those practices enable all students to flourish. When a teacher encounters students who are not flourishing, or is faced with a problematic or conflict-laden situation, the rhythm of response shifts from effective practices employed as well-formed habits to a more critical and *thought-full* practice of interpretation and response. This kind of *response-ability* was framed by Dewey in both educational and ethical writings and by H. Richard Niebuhr in *The Responsible Self*.[12]

Niebuhr describes how an ethic of responsibility unfolds. We are provoked by some prior action or inaction, something that demands a response (and usually elicits discomfort), and then begin to ask, What is going on here? This is the moment of interpretation as "all things considered" come to the fore. We seek to account for and understand context, history, motivation, guiding principles, personal feelings, and social expectations to move to the third phase of framing options for action and imagining in what Dewey calls "dramatic rehearsal," the consequences of enacting each option.[13] We respond within our community of agents and in light of our constantly reconstructed values, developed and held in those (religious, social, cultural, familial, professional) communities. The goal is a fitting response rather than an ill-fitting reaction.

This is, of course, a complex process that teachers could not possibly enact in each and every moment of their lives. It is too inefficient. Instead, this "method of intelligence" kicks into gear when previously held habits of action fail.[14] To act out of pedagogical response-ability is itself a habit that must be carefully formed in new educators.[15] It requires that teacher candidates learn to recognize provocation—that is, to read their students in ways that allow them to recognize that they are not thriving, to be attuned to their challenges and their flourishing. When teacher candidates' lenses for reading or frameworks for sense-making fail to account for identities and positionalities present in an interaction, they are more likely to fail as teachers. This is especially so in situations in which teachers and students do not share identities or positionings in the world and if the teacher has not recognized those differences and sought to compensate through personal learning or relationship building with the student. This situation has driven, for example, the call for intentional efforts to increase the representation of teachers of color, especially Black and Latinx teachers, in the profession and likely lies behind literature on the benefits of racial matching. It is also possible for challenges of attunement to arise when students and teachers seemingly share minoritized identities, when teachers wrap students in the blanket of the teacher's own identity, unintentionally essentializing students. The key in either situation is provocation: teachers recognize that a gap in understanding is harming a student and/or the student's learning, and they take corrective action.

The very possibility of interpretation is, by definition, shaped by our horizon, by the limits of what we can see. SHIFT simulations are designed to address just this element of teacher candidates' pedagogical responsibility. The simulation cycle subjects candidates' immediate reactions to gentle but direct (and supported) scrutiny so that candidates can fully experience and make (non)sense of them, recognizing the horizon that constrains them. This recognition requires that both horizons and habits of practice are reconstructed without resorting to the defensiveness that warps generative reconstruction of the horizons that constitute the self.[16]

The simulated encounters are not the space of learning but a tool leveraged to support learning. By helping teacher candidates see, for example, how their immediate reaction to a scenario may ultimately disengage a reluctant learner or even recognize that their unthinking response was productive in ways they did not realize, we set them up to keep identities, positionalities, and systems of oppression always in view. We know that learning has occurred if candidates, unprompted, begin to consider unintended consequences of their reactions after the fact, recognize the ways in which their own positionality and that of the student were relevant within the given context, and seek out alternative approaches that align with liberatory and transformative notions of education, whether in future simulations or scenarios they experience in the field.[17]

The sense-making we encourage is a deliberate process that enables teacher candidates to understand where their reactions come from and to understand those reactions as ill-serving habits, misdirected citationality practices, or the unproductive residue of an apprenticeship of observation.[18] In truth, we are enabling them to understand themselves. Rather than labeling teacher candidates' responses as "good"/"bad," we shine light on the many things that influence our individual responses to a scenario to recognize those that are connected to oppressive forces (e.g., whiteness) and consider how habit-based reactions might change if influenced by kinds of recognition and different commitments. The theory here is that when teacher candidates understand their initial reactions as inconsistent with the value and practice paradigms to which they aspire and who they understand themselves to be as teachers, they desire change and can use course resources to fashion a more fitting response, to reground those habits in a more consistent and defensible professional self-understanding.[19]

The Power of Being Pulled up Short

The SHIFT simulation cycle is constructed as a series of multilayered, multimoment conversations that prompt the experience of being pulled up short and provide space and resources for new sense-making. The actual video-recorded encounter puts teacher candidates on alert to look more closely at what they were reacting to and the impact of that reaction. Situating the encounter within a cycle of attention and reflection enables candidates to "break the spell" of what Gadamer calls "fore-meanings" or "prejudices" and then reconstruct more useful understandings, more serviceable prejudices.[20] The SHIFT encounter asks a question of the participants and, in the process, points out the partiality of their understanding and offers an opportunity for what Gadamer calls a "fusion of horizons" and we refer to as a shift.[21]

Humans exist in time and seek to understand the world and ourselves. This seeking after (self-)understanding in the face of finitude is, for Gadamer, what makes us human.[22] There is no separation, no distinction to be made between our selves, our understanding of our selves, and our understanding of the world. What we have experienced delimits what we are capable of understanding and, by extension, who we are. Because our experience is always in some way limited, so too is our understanding bound by prejudices that we cannot completely avoid. The horizons of that understanding extend only so far: "History does not belong to us; we belong to it. Long before we understand ourselves through the process of self-examination, we understand ourselves in a self-evident way in the family, society, and state in which we live . . . *That is why the prejudices of the individual, far more than his judgments, constitute the historical reality of his being.*" In other words, we are our prejudices. Those prejudices can be well-formed or ill-formed. They can be positive or negative. They can be useful or useless. In any case, we do not encounter anything or any person without them. The problem is not that we have prejudgments; it is that they are invisible to us. This "tyranny of hidden prejudices" suggests that recognizing our own prejudices is the precondition to being open to any other.[23] Experience, for Gadamer, is usually an uncomfortable and disruptive process of opening that is dialectical in form and results in the working out of identity and difference. When we live in more homogeneous settings, our prejudices may seem unproblematic. As persons, we move and act within communities of action—from families to neighborhoods to nations—and seamlessly (often unwittingly) forge understandings that serve us well. The limits of our horizons are shared with others in our community and normalized. Our horizons are unchallenged until and unless we are pulled up short by encounters with others whose horizons are different.

Before focusing on the pulled up short moment, we ask, How is the simple act of understanding our self, the world, or others possible? We are always "making sense" of the (social) world into which we have been "thrown," to use Hegel's term, but an individual's sense-making is never untethered. "Drawing on the interpretive legacies we inherit, we construe meaning for ourselves" within an interpretive or hermeneutic circle.[24] If understanding is finite, limited by experience, how do we break out of our own cultural circles of interpretation situated as we are? As Kerdeman puts it, channeling Gadamer, "While understanding is situated, it is neither static nor self-enclosed. To the contrary, understanding is dynamic and porous." Understanding is "a horizon that constantly shifts and evolves to disclose new perspectives."[25]

That understanding is radically finite is not a problem; it is a matter of fact. The problem is what we can do about understanding's limits. And that's our starting point in the SHIFT Project—that any particular teacher's understanding at any particular moment is finite. Teacher education and preparation is largely about pushing back the limits of understanding in targeted and fruitful ways to enable *Bildung*, or formation. The starting point of the SHIFT Project is our capacity to understand differences in understanding itself (self-understanding) with respect to human difference and the ways categories of difference are formed socially and politically.

Sometimes the limits of our understanding prevent us from taking on and fulfilling responsibilities as educators. This can and will occur in any setting that acknowledges difference as meaningful. Teachers in *any* setting will find their understanding challenged by students and their families whose past experiences differ. However, those who teach in communities unlike those that formed them will be confronted over and over again by differences that challenge not only what they think they know and believe but also who they are and understand themselves to be. This constitutes what Gadamer calls "the problem of prejudices."[26] How are teacher educators to prepare candidates for this reality? We start by acknowledging that people "read differently because they [are] moved by different questions, prejudices, and interests."[27] When we read the world differently, how can any of us understand any others? Gadamer describes the process by which we become open to the limitations of our presuppositions. This happens, potentially, whenever we engage in conversation with another about a common concern. It is the common concern that creates the conditions for opening each person's hermeneutic circle.[28]

The primary condition is "a hermeneutically trained consciousness [that] must be, from the start, sensitive to the [other's] alterity."[29] The hermeneutically trained consciousness forms anticipatory ideas consciously "to check them and thus acquire right understanding from the things themselves."[30] When difference is shared and explored in conversation motivated by common concern, though not necessarily common values or goals, a new community of understanding is created. In other words, even though parties cannot escape their own experience in the world, they can come to understand the other's perspective. Both parties consequently realize insights that previously were unavailable to either of them.[31] Horizons can broaden and become more critically reflective. Gadamer calls such interpretation-into-understanding a "fusion of horizons."[32] Fusing horizons results not from some conscious neutrality or from the extinction of our self but from the foregrounding and appropriation of our fore-meanings and prejudices: the confrontation with our biases creates space in our understanding of the perspective (prejudice) of another.

As Kerdeman asserts, "life is full of everyday kinds of shattering."[33] The world presents itself to us such that our assumptions, expectations, and desires are not always met. We do not choose to be pulled up short; but if we're open to it, new understanding emerges. Sometimes, however, as in the case of teacher education, we cannot wait for difference to emerge and openness to be invited. We cannot wait because the likelihood that teachers will encounter diversity and find their assumptions shattered is acute, and the results of the disruption *when* that happens are potentially dangerous.

Jumpstarting a candidate's capacity for encountering the role of identity, positionality, and systems of oppression in ways that build rather than destroy community—developing a hermeneutically trained consciousness—is important for two reasons: disruption without restoration can be dangerous, even explosive, and harms students in the way a novice teacher does not intend or possibly realize; and the future teacher who has experienced SHIFT simulations moves toward becoming what Gadamer thinks of as an "experienced person," one "who is radically undogmatic" owing to multiple experiences of disruption and the knowledge gained therein.[34] The SHIFT experience opens future teachers to more unmet expectations. For the teacher candidates who don't yet know what they need, who can't yet understand what such encounters will prompt in them or demand of them, we SHIFT: we create circumstances under which they will be pulled up short, and then we facilitate the process of fusing horizons, of making sense anew. New pedagogical practices of openness are the result.

When we are pulled up short, we are caught off-guard, left reeling. We experience insecurity—emotional, physical, and intellectual. The insecurity comes from what feels like an attack on our self; cherished beliefs and traits we claim as our own are called into question. As we come face to face with our own limitations, we are humbled. We experience loss.

But loss makes room for learning that is transformative. Kerdeman quotes Georgia Warnke when she claims, "This level of insight does not represent a gradual alteration or expansion of our existing worldview. It is instead a radical transformation."[35] According to Warnke, "What we experience is the error or partiality of our previous views and we experience this in such a way that we are now too experienced or sophisticated to relive the experience of believing them."[36] We never recover from being pulled up short; our horizon, once altered, cannot simply return to its former configuration.

Pulled Up Short in a SHIFT Cycle

What is interrupted in the teacher candidate who goes through the SHIFT cycle? That depends, of course, on the fore-meanings and prejudices that the individual candidate brings into the encounter and reflection. Notably, there is no guarantee, as Kerdeman notes, that all persons will be open to acknowledging pulled up short moments encountered in our everyday lives.[37] Nor is there any guarantee that participating candidates will take advantage of the opportunity that SHIFT simulations afford them. However, several things work in our favor within a teacher education program, despite the personal risk involved.

First, candidates are typically in teacher education programs because they want to understand their students and meet their educational needs. They may not want to acknowledge their own position as privileged or examine their own prejudices or think of themselves as racist, but they do tend to care about their students' well-being. This is enough to get them in, and the cycle supports them through anxiety and self-doubt. The result is understanding another on their terms, within a newly fused horizon, rather than fixing them within the candidate's own prejudices.

The experience of being pulled up short is a particularly valuable one for future teachers. Recognizing that they have been operating under distorted and false assumptions helps ground the habit of checking their assumptions when they meet new ideas and new students. Future teachers are forced to grapple with a sometime painful lack of finality and the constant possibility of unmet expectations. They feel rather than think that the goal is not control of students but mutual understanding of each other and ideas about the world that make more possible. This is what Gadamer has in mind when he insists that the "interpretive consciousness must be awakened and kept awake."[38]

In exploring her own anti-oppressive pulled up short moment with her students of color, Kerdeman analyzes three constitutive elements: a common concern but from different perspectives, being affected (disrupting an understanding of situation and self), and a call-and-response ethical interaction.[39] These three elements are intertwined with each other, and all three surface the affective along with the cognitive and the behavioral. For instance, conversation is not enough as when we use conversation strategies to deflate or defeat. Empathy (or other "right feelings") can simply be a ruse to protect our own feelings. Defensiveness distracts us from the possibility of fitting response.

Habit and Emotion: Unpacking Pulled Up Short

"Pulled up short" seems like a good description of what happens to teacher candidates who participate in SHIFT simulations. Those candidates come face to face with their own limited understanding and engage with heretofore hidden uncertainty. We know this happens from our observations and the candidates' self-reporting. We see them mining readings for explanations of what they are seeing. We notice them linking past experiences with present encounters. We can document resultant changes in teacher candidates' pedagogical behaviors, attitudes, and ideas. But why is it necessary that teacher candidates be pulled up short? Isn't an explanation of systemic inequity or culturally responsive pedagogy enough? Why do our horizons resist simple cognitive recognition in order to shift, demanding discomfort instead? What is it about this relatively modest exercise that uncovers the explanatory power of other sources and resources?

SHIFT simulations are rooted in the recognition that cognition, affect, and disposition to act are always fused in lived experience: *Any idea that I can think has an affective valence and a draw toward behavior. Any feeling I feel is located in an object or idea and tends to move me to some act.* The potential of SHIFT simulations arises from the intentional engagement of cognition, affect, and behavior in one brief encounter. The twelve-minute, video-recorded encounter alone is never enough to shift horizons, but it is enough to elicit thinking, feeling, and behavior that interact (especially when considered in the light of peer experience) to disrupt a candidate's self-understanding, their interpretive horizon.

The recognition that emotion has a cognitive dimension or that ideas carry emotional weight or that we must be moved to action is often given lip service but rarely fully integrated into pedagogical design and planning. This is always problematic, but it seems to be a crucial oversight when the capacity for anti-oppressive pedagogy is the goal. If our prejudices constitute our self, then subjecting them to scrutiny and attempting to overcome them can be cognitively confusing, emotionally painful, and behaviorally bewildering. Teacher educators who encourage this kind of growth in their students have to be prepared to respond to all of it at once.[40]

Dewey on Emotion

More than a century ago, John Dewey responded to ongoing philosophical and psychological debates and anticipated the findings of contemporary neuroscience in an uncanny way.[41] He acknowledged the apparent mind-body dichotomy in theorizing about emotion prevalent throughout philosophical and psychological history and dissolved the correlative dichotomy between affect (the immediate bodily excitation) and emotion (the culturally conditioned recognition) by arguing that every experience, and every concept with which we designate experience, always has an idea, a feeling, and a disposition intrinsic to it. This triadic structure is not distinguishable experientially, though each element may be sorted out for purposes of analysis. Thus, an emotion is the affective face of an experience; no emotion can be experienced apart from the idea and behavioral disposition with which it is associated. In fact, for the pragmatist Dewey, it is the associated behavior, not some quality of feeling, that designates an emotion. It is behavior and its consequences that unify feeling (body) and idea (mind): *I know what I am feeling when and only when I see how I am acting.*

Consider an emotion often associated with encounters with someone or something unfamiliar: fear. Fear is the emotion marked by what Dewey calls "organic shrinkage." Fear is not a feeling, though of course there is no fear without feeling. And particular feelings don't cause actions (of shrinkage, separation, or anything else) in any determined way, though feelings are always implicated in any action: *I act on my feelings, but I don't ever act only on feelings. When I act, both feeling and idea are implicated, and it is the action that determines the meaning of both feeling and idea.* It is important to acknowledge just how contrary this is to our assumptions about the relationship between feeling and action. Whereas we talk as if feelings (and ideas) cause actions, Dewey contends that actions determine (give meaning to) feelings and ideas. What to do (how we act) is always a complicated process of interpretation and response in context, and it is never fully determined: *The fact that I am in the habit of reacting fearfully to a snake does not mean that I cannot revise my perception of a snake either by desensitization training or by learning more about kinds of snakes and recognizing that many common snakes are not at all dangerous.*

Apply this insight to the feelings generated by a SHIFT encounter. Virtually all teacher candidates report feeling excited and interested at the prospect of the encounter. They wonder what awaits them. They may be planning possible responses. If they are honest with themselves, they may recognize some negative stereotypes or prejudices going in to meet the students, parent, or coworker being played by an actor. However, the pragmatist Dewey suggests that definitively naming their thoughts or feelings or actions depends on the result of the encounter. Does the candidate engage the other or dispatch their concerns? Does the candidate focus on acts or interrogate thoughts and feelings? Does the candidate determine the interpretation of the situation or ask questions that might open up shared understanding?

From a pragmatist's perspective, the candidate who discounts or avoids interaction in the encounter *is* fearful. The candidate who is open to questions and otherwise engages the situation *is* caring and confident. Each candidate is excited by the live-actor encounter, and that excitement provides critical energy for the process of shifting horizons. However, the *meaning* of the candidate's affect is based not on the quality of the initial excitement but on the action associated with the excitement. The SHIFT cycle supports candidates as they make constructive sense of their often complex feelings, link actions to feelings in meaningful ways, and take responsibility for those actions. *Any situation where my expectations are not fulfilled, where my self is called into question, is always a situation that excites.* This is why being pulled up short constitutes a potentially productive moment of interruption, the outcome and quality of which is not determined but can be shaped in the process of the SHIFT cycle.

Ahmed on Affect

Why and how each person is excited depends on what Sara Ahmed calls "past histories of association" with the persons, objects, and contexts involved: *I am excited, and I realize my excitement. My feeling of excitement is sensed as positive or negative, as pleasurable or painful, because it is prompted by the perception of some object that I have already conceived in terms of idea, feeling, and behavior.*[42] For example, a candidate with an unsuccessful or uncomfortable past of encounters with multilingual speakers may experience his feelings as painful or unpleasant when encountering Maryam, the Arabic-speaking mother of one of his fifth graders. (The painful feelings are woven into his concept and framed in his experience of the act of trying to communicate with others across language divides.) But the meaning and impact of those feelings in *this* moment are undetermined. This constitutes an educational opportunity for the teacher educator. The candidates' painful associations mean that they are likely to be hesitant to interact, but shared reconsideration can alter this habit of perception and reaction. Will the energy of their feelings become part of an experience of growth, a fusion of horizons? Or will they shrink back from the encounter in a now fearful experience that does not open up to new understanding?

As teacher educators employing SHIFT simulations, we tell candidates in advance that their reactions and responses are not good or bad but are worth careful examination and interrogation. We ask candidates to acknowledge, examine, and even appreciate what they are feeling *and* to refrain from judging what that is. Remember that emotions have behavioral mandates attached, while affects are just bodily states, conscious or unconscious, with no judgment of value or determined action. The candidate who reduces complicated, sometimes contradictory, and often difficult-to-name feelings to a particular emotion commits herself at least loosely to the behavior that the emotion *means*. In the case of fear, this means shrinkage or separation, and the impact of that is educational opportunity lost.

SHIFT simulations are designed to excite, and sometimes those excitations are initially painful. SHIFT simulations are designed to create the gap between expectation (view of oneself as teacher) and reality (automatic reaction based in past experience as inculcated or modeled by others). Once pulled up short, teacher candidates are challenged in a way they can't avoid to name what they think, how they feel, and what the situation demands with respect to action. The SHIFT cycle doesn't abandon them in the space of (possibly negative) excitement but supports each candidate to make constructive sense of the experience in light of the mandate for pedagogical responsibility.

Emotion and Affect in Anti-Oppressive Teaching

When it comes to issues of equity and social justice, we are compelled to go beyond Dewey's analysis of inter- and intrapersonal experience to broader social and political narratives and contexts. This shift from Dewey's microanalysis of the phenomenological moment to the macroanalysis of the metanarrative demands a deconstruction of the ideologies of emotional control operating in twenty-first-century America. What we call *emotions* are tools constructed within social regimes to regulate social interaction and to control the movement of bodies in space, freeing some and constraining others. This is, of course, directly implicated in the pursuit of antioppressive education.

Ahmed's *The Cultural Politics of Emotion* provides a detailed understanding of the way emotions control potential for interaction by keeping people in their place, literally. We return to fear as an example. Ahmed's view is deceptively simple and reinforces Dewey's view that emotions are not independent internal states that motivate action. When a fear relation involves two persons, two bodies, "fear does not simply come from within and then move outwards towards object and others . . . rather, fear works to secure the relationship between those bodies; it brings them together and moves them apart through the shudders that are felt on the skin, on the surface that surfaces through the encounter." Fear, as a sociopolitically constructed and designated emotion, is the name we give to a *relational system* that establishes some bodies as fearing subjects and other bodies as fearful objects.

This relational construction is dynamic. Fear does not reside statically in one person as subject and in another as object; rather, "it slides across signs and between bodies." Fear is expressed in fantasies of danger that establish the other "as fearsome insofar as they *threaten to take the self in*." This means that "the body shrinks back from the world in the desire to avoid the object of fear. Fear involves shrinking the body; *it restricts the body's mobility precisely insofar as it seems to prepare the body for flight.*"[43]

Flight is not the only bodily marker of fear; fight and paralysis are other possible (re)actions. Nonetheless, Ahmed's central insight seems worth considering: "fear works to restrict some bodies through the movement or expansion of others." The function of emotions in general is to "align bodily space with social space," one that is inevitably political. Fear's function, then, is the preservation "of 'me' but also 'us,' or 'what is,' or 'life as we know it,' or even 'life itself.'"[44] This restriction of bodies is antithetical to the demands of education. The teacher who practices pedagogical responsibility may not shrink back from a student who has been othered or restrict their possibilities for "movement or expansion," in an existential sense. A white teacher may be fearful of a Black student, even as the Black student is fearful of the white teacher. An English-speaking teacher may be fearful of a Kurdish-speaking mother, but that mother is surely also fearful of the teacher. Each has the capacity to challenge the other's taken-for-granted reality. However, past histories of association do not necessarily determine present relations. SHIFT simulations are designed to reveal the residue of these past histories, personal and sociopolitical, and offer resources for reconstruction.

Teacher educators seeking to encourage anti-oppressive pedagogy would do well to be on the lookout for the play of power when they detect hints of fearful reaction. We regularly encounter fear—shrinkage or failure to engage initially—in the SHIFT encounters. It is not a simple matter to break the hold of habituated fear when the weight of a sociopolitical system holds it in place. The critical incidents that SHIFT simulations are built around involve people, places, objects, and situations about which teacher candidates are likely to have past histories of association, objects, and actions that are sticky with affect. Juxtaposing them in situations that demand action releases affect and makes shifting of horizons possible and, if well supported, inevitable. As both Gadamer and Kerdeman note, the result is not incremental change but transformation. There is no going back; every reading, resource, and data set is understood differently after the shift of horizon.

Dewey's and Ahmed's insights matter because their theories explain why the SHIFT simulation cycle has the power to pull candidates up short but also to enable their shift in horizon needed to pursue anti-oppressive pedagogy. The SHIFT encounter generates the affective and behavioral reaction necessary to break the hold of prejudices, and the remaining elements of the cycle enable the teacher candidates to make something new and more constructive of that emotion, that energy in motion. Other rich materials, resources, and unmediated experiences stimulate interest but are rarely designed to intentionally interrupt how the candidate feels, thinks, and acts in tandem.

Why SHIFT Simulations Work

The SHIFT Project operates on a theory of careful interruption of prejudices—both in Gadamer's sense of the prejudgments necessary to face the world and in the everyday sense of discriminatory assumptions—designed to occur within a context for deliberation and decision-making that is (relatively) safe and intellectually and emotionally supported. That interruption is linked to equally careful reconstruction. Both phases rely on embodied participation. Leaving the disruption to natural circumstances, such as in formal field experiences, will work to interrupt what is taken-for-granted but in ways that are unlikely to be accompanied by planned support and that may then result in reinscribing or strengthening destructive assumptions. Assuming that engagement with disruptive ideas will be enough is, in our experience, not warranted empirically, at least not for the majority of our candidates. As William James richly describes, the reality that our judgments concerning the worth of things, big or little, depends on the feelings the things arouse in us results in "a certain blindness in human beings."[45] Matters of justice are just such judgments of worth.

The SHIFT design ensures the simultaneous activation of feeling, thought, and act and opens candidates to the reconstruction of habits of pedagogical practice. But this simultaneous activation creates a useful vulnerability that calls for caution. For this reason, live-actor simulated encounters that focus on identity, positionality, and systems of oppression should not be used for assessment purposes. In the context of evaluation, there is no way to privilege vulnerability. Similarly, the blend of individual initiative and reflection and anonymized group debrief (no teacher candidate is required to "confess" their reactions but only their thoughts about a set of reactions raised as common texts) allows the candidate to process the experience in their own time and space. All candidates engage in the encounter, and the instructor has potentially seen them all do so, but teacher candidates do not have to make it public to their peers to be judged on it if they choose not to. This makes candidates accountable to what they actually did in the light of their own vision of themselves as teacher while minimizing their defensiveness.

Some readers may ask whether we have overcomplicated the situation. Why not just tell the teacher candidates to ask more questions, to talk less, as would clearly be effective in working with Daria or Maryam? This is a simple suggestion. Clearly all teacher candidates are bright enough to act on this guidance, right? Except, of course, that they (and we) don't. And our tendencies to assume unhelpful circumstances and to control the conversation are exacerbated in the face of fear or other negative affect. But can't we train them to do so?

This question is both understandable and dangerous. There are elements of teaching practice that can be strengthened by repetition or rehearsal. This is the assumption underlying the efforts of those teacher educators currently focusing on core practices in teaching, and it is worth taking seriously.[46] But anti-oppressive pedagogy involves a prior disposition to take all students as they come and to see those students as both gifted and in need of specific supports. An interpretive horizon that includes all of that is a precondition for being able to effectively enact teaching practices writ small. For instance, when teacher candidates encounter Daria Miller, often in their first SHIFT simulation, they tend to tell her that she "just needs to stop talking" and all the problems will go away. At that point in their experience, few have any other tools for making sense of Daria and the shared situation they are in. SHIFT simulations function as a Deweyan experience (act, result, reflective connection) that enable candidates to discover new conceptual, affective, and behavioral tools for making sense of the situation in ways that enable pedagogical responsibility. More importantly, the SHIFT cycle itself becomes a habit of interpretation for these future teachers. They will be pulled up short again and again in their careers, but through iterative SHIFT cycles they are gradually building not just the capacity to understand diverse others but also a disposition to respond thoughtfully rather than react unthinkingly when their self-understanding is called into question. With respect to the demands of anti-oppressive pedagogy, they will be safe to practice and be ready to learn, always unfinished but still able to carry on.

Chapter 4

The Impact of SHIFT

SHIFT simulations are designed to interrupt teacher candidates' taken-for-granted sense-making about what is effective and equitable in educational interaction and to begin the process of making new sense with respect to the practice of actively anti-oppressive pedagogy by framing new horizons. In this chapter we examine the impact of participation in the program on the teacher candidates with whom we work. We tap our own observations and, especially, the words of the participants themselves to examine observable impacts on teacher candidates as they experience the simulation cycle and self-reported impacts on teachers who have graduated. We are particularly interested in how both observations and self-reports illuminate the developmental trajectory of teacher candidates moving toward anti-oppressive practice. We also note ancillary impacts on participating faculty and the program in general, as well as acknowledge formal research, completed and in process, on how and whether participation in SHIFT simulations results in more equitable and effective practice.

Impacts on Teacher Candidates

With the SHIFT Project, we have seen how candidates learn from the experience over time. Four observations in particular speak to the teacher candidates' experience and how that experience alters their thinking, feeling, and acting: the encounters seem real to them, the experience stays with them, the learning unfolds over time, and the teacher candidates get better at learning from encounters with practice.

The Encounters Seem Real to Them

Despite the artificial nature of these encounters, and the limitations they carry with them when compared to actual classroom teaching, we see evidence year after year that teacher candidates consider the encounters realistic. One consistent point of evidence is that teacher candidates feel nervous before them, anxious during them, and stressed about how it went afterward. In line with findings from studies done on various forms of enactment and simulation, teacher candidates both see how the encounters are unlike K–12 classroom teaching *and* recognize how much the encounters offer in terms of realistically engaging them in difficult conversations and challenging situations.[1] The live-actor aspect of the encounters is critically important. While the actors are willing participants and not people with whom the teacher candidates will have long-term professional relationships, they are nonetheless real people. When candidates make comments that are racist, sexist, or ableist, or when they assume things wrongly about a person sitting directly in front of them, or when they fail to engage with or truly listen to someone telling them hard truths, those things are happening in *real* life, even if it is not happening *for real* in a classroom context. The real nature of the encounters—whether because the reactions they cause are real, because the situation seems realistic, or because the interaction is set up to engage candidates in a way that suspends disbelief long enough for the human-to-human exchange to go from simulated to real—is vital because it becomes an opportunity for further learning. When teacher candidates see the encounters as real, and when they are willing to recognize that they do not yet know how to respond to the situation with which they are presented, they really want to know, *What do I do?*

We have evidence of this from video-recorded encounters, and it's accompanied by a desire for further learning. For example, one candidate who participated in the Phil Duncan simulation was especially triggered by Phil's comment about Cameron, a student in the class whom Phil describes as "flamboyant," one of many (vaguely) coded terms Phil uses in the interaction across dimensions of difference. The candidate became bothered enough at this point in the encounter (about halfway through a typical interaction) that the candidate left. In the individual raw debrief, the candidate repeated several times, "I know it was fake, but . . ." Another teacher candidate in the same round of encounters with Mr. Duncan was likewise flustered by Phil's comments but stayed in the encounter to the end. In the raw debrief, the candidate, recounting Duncan's inflammatory comments, sighed and said simply, "I'm gonna have to deal with this, aren't I? This is real." The candidate then looked at the camera and asked, "What do I do?" Both candidates, who then or now identify as queer, focused much of their raw debriefs and rereading questions on the query, *How do I, identified and positioned as I am, respond in this kind of moment with a coworker?* The realness of the scenario demanded further learning for their own benefit as well as their future students'.

Further evidence that candidates perceive the encounters as real is how they narrate their decision-making during the interaction. This comes up in the Phil Duncan simulation, not during the interaction but in the group debrief. When we prompt teacher candidates, many of whom are at the very beginning of their licensure coursework, to reflect on why they chose not to speak up when Mr. Duncan said things they felt should be challenged, many of them say they are be afraid to lose their jobs or be isolated in their department. While one might argue that these simulated encounters are an excellent place to try out claims candidates might be afraid to make in real life, to take on a bolder, stronger teacher presence in standing up against instances of oppression, the perception of them as real stymies them. For our purposes, this is a desirable outcome. The candidates do what they would likely do during an authentic interaction in a school setting, which provides them with an opportunity to grapple with the very real consequences of their action or, in this case, inaction.

One student who completed the Daria Miller simulation wrote in a follow-up about her inability to acknowledge the potential for racial bias during the interaction with the student, despite anticipating that it might be part of the exchange. She exemplifies the kind of teacher candidate who could have thoughtfully analyzed the situation if given it as a written case. But she also recognized that, when push came to shove, she resorted to doing what she had been socialized to do as a white woman—deny, resist, ignore. Doing what she would likely do in a real-life classroom situation allowed her to recognize the power of that socialization and what it would take to overcome it, rather than leaving her with a false sense of confidence in her ability to address her own racial bias in such a conversation.

Some teacher candidates, however, do appear to keep the artificiality in their mind during the interaction. For example, occasionally Spanish-speaking teachers will conduct a parent-teacher conference with a Spanish-speaking parent in English, despite the parent's willingness to engage in Spanish. These teachers often explain that they were unsure whether the actor was capable of engaging fully in Spanish (though the actors are fluent Spanish speakers and often have spoken Spanish as their first language) or felt like they wanted the encounter to be comprehensible by their instructors or researchers who may look at the video. For virtually all candidates, though, while the layers of artificial and real are both present, the experience is compelling.

The Experience Stays with Them

One of the first impacts we noticed when we started using SHIFT simulations in our program is how teacher candidates talked a lot about their encounters with others and for a long time after the encounter, and even the debrief, was over. Part of the reason the practice spread so quickly in the program is that teacher candidates left an encounter for one course, attended another class soon after in the secondary licensure program, and continued talking about the encounter. Instructors recognized quickly that the encounters held the candidates' interest and kept them thinking well past the end of the interaction and wanted to somehow tie the learning in their class to that level of engagement.

The first place we saw evidence of the staying power of the experience was in teacher candidates' desire to immediately talk to each other about their encounters. In our first several years of running the simulations, we used the simulation lab housed at the medical school across the street from our classroom building. After the very first simulation, when we were still doing raw debriefs individually, we became aware that candidates spent the entirety of the walk back talking about their experience and had to be told to stop talking when they returned to class lest they spoil the experience for those who had not yet completed it. They compared what happened in their encounters, what each person said and did and whether it had the effect they wanted, how their actors were the same or different in their portrayal of the role. The candidates wanted to understand how their experiences could vary so much, given that they had the same information to start with. This figuring out, a process of sense-making that we now realize occurs over a long period of time, seems to be what makes the experience so generative. Likewise, we had candidates tell us they had talked about their encounter, or even shared their videos, with all kinds of people—their friends or roommates, their parents, former teachers, teachers at their field placement. Because of this feedback in the first year, on the recommendation of a colleague, we switched to doing raw debriefs in small groups so that candidates could begin that sense-making process together.

In addition, the encounters themselves and the learning that comes from them serve as a shared text among students in the program. The trajectory of the simulations, when completed in the order anticipated based on a typical course progression, is designed to leverage this. Teacher candidates, for example, encounter Daria Miller in one of their earliest classes and often bring up that encounter when later coursework addresses classroom interaction and ecology. The big understanding in the encounter is not about classroom management, though candidates often read it that way early on. But when they mobilize it within a class focused on classroom ecology, they are reminded that management is inextricably linked to other aspects of classroom life, including teacher positionality and vulnerability, the presence of racism and potential absence of antiracist teaching in a classroom, and the timescales on which harm and repair often occur in teacher-student relationships. The impact, then, is that candidates bring up simulations, much like a concept or a reading, later in class in a way that carries meaning to everyone present. In this way, candidates connect new learning to the experience provided in the simulations, both individually and collectively.

Over the years of the program, the encounters have come to serve for some as critical incidents that define a path of development as an antioppressive teacher. Candidates cite not the people involved in the incident, or even the particulars of the situation, but the ways the experience changed what they could see, how they thought anew about similar situations, and how that might ultimately lead them to act. We see the impact of the simulations most clearly when we ask teacher candidates to talk about the encounter that had the biggest impact on their professional growth. In a recent survey of simulation participants, forty respondents collectively identified ten different simulations as having had the biggest impact, with two (Daria Miller and Phil Duncan) named much more frequently than others. The respondents pointed to how the simulations changed the way they looked at or thought about identities and social issues in classroom practice, often complicating what they thought they knew and surfacing their own complicity in inequitable systems and practices. What follows is a sampling of some participant comments that illustrate these themes.

"I had to think critically about how my own identity [as a white woman] impacted my treatment of the situation and students' perception of my discipline. I thought [one student, a Black boy] was being a bigger jerk but also understood that siding with [the other student, a white girl] might be the result of implicit biases. These are questions with which I am still grappling as a teacher, to which this simulation initially opened my eyes." (Emily, a secondary English candidate)

"Even as a Hispanic, I struggled to connect with [Spanish-speaking mom] Alondra. More is needed than a simple broad ethnic similarity to connect with someone." (Luis, a secondary social studies candidate)

"This simulation really made me stop and think about all of the tiny daily actions I make. Everyone reads about unconscious bias and how it can impact your actions but going through this simulation makes you extremely aware of what impact your biases can have on students. Our class discussion around an article on 'white women tears' brought this simulation to life even more. I used the navigational skills I learned in this simulation when working with other staff and students in my student teaching." (Lindsey, a secondary social studies candidate, on the Daria Miller simulation)

"The interaction with Mr. Duncan and follow-up reflection in the classroom really pushed me to think about my role in the school. In the interaction, I wanted to be nice to my colleague and did not question many of his problematic statements. During the reflection, I realized that by not saying anything, I also contributed to the inequality in our school system. Therefore, I want to become an advocate and lead a meaningful conversation if I do ever become a teacher one day." (Tianling, an ELL candidate, on the Phil Duncan simulation)

For some participants with minoritized identities, the simulations that took up those identities or social issues had a long-lasting impact. It caused them to reconsider values and commitments they thought they had already resolved within the space of actual practice. The following comments came from queer social studies candidates and address the Alexis Jimenez and Matthew Manning simulation and the students' conflicting beliefs on the right to marriage for LGBTQIA+ people:

"The debrief of this simulation brought up conflicting opinions that solidified my beliefs about which student's safety/identities to prioritize in the classroom." (Josh)

"It's certainly the one I think most about—probably due to my own positioning—but it has made me rethink what 'safe' spaces could/should be and for whom and how to have discussions around different types of oppressions." (Karen)

It is worth noting that even students who experience the simulations but are not licensing as teachers find them to be valuable. Over the years we have had students from child studies, education policy, educational psychology, and learning and design programs participate in the simulated encounters as part of coursework in our program. Several respondents noted the relevance of the simulations to their future work in what David Cohen would call "professions in human improvement."[2]

"This is a situation that I encounter almost daily at my medical school. I go to school in East TN where our minority population is <10% and 100% of our faculty are white males. Besides feeling some degree of shock after coming out of the Vanderbilt environment, I have had to put the skills I built in this case into practice constantly speaking with white men who are my superiors both in years and rank while advocating for patients and classmates. The art of speaking up while not causing the opposite party to shut down is still a skill that I am constantly developing in both an academic and clinical setting, but I am thankful for the exposure prior to starting medical school." (Minta, a Medicine, Health, and Society major in premed, on the impact of the Phil Duncan encounter)

"Working in Res Life at a university, I often deal with a lot of parents who are giving a lot of information about their child in a way that is pointing to one specific answer—I regularly have to remind myself not to jump to the first or easiest assumption, and that there might be something else going on. It's also a reminder to keep asking questions." (Lizzie, an education studies major pursuing graduate work in higher education administration)

Respondents had a range of reasons for feeling that one specific encounter had the biggest impact on their learning, but many talked about them in terms of how the simulations moved them out of their "previously learned boxes," whether in terms of how to see a situation or how to respond to it.

The fact that the experience stays with participants is also an important reason to be aware of potential negative learnings from the encounters and to provide teacher candidates with field experiences to counter essentialized learnings. Teacher candidates can and do walk away from the simulations with simplistic takeaways—such as "talk less and listen more" or "ask more questions to start"—which are by themselves helpful but not sufficient to move teacher candidates toward anti-oppressive teaching. Others approached the big understandings built into the simulations but could not quite articulate them with any depth. One student, for example, responded about the impact of simulation that featured a parent-teacher conference: "It gave me the opportunity to think about how we can talk to parents. It was the only situation where we could really preplan, which I think makes it the most useful. There is only so much benefit I can get from a situation that I do not know what direction the conversation will go, but this simulation was much more focused on where I wanted to take the conversation." For this student, who certainly benefited from the practice of talking to parents, there is still a sense of wanting to be in control of these kinds of situations, where the teacher can preplan and then take it in the direction they want. This student missed the big idea of letting go of those plans during conversation to be open to taking the conversation where the other person wants and needs to take it. This is one reason that we argue strongly for using simulations as part of existing approaches in a program. They cannot and should not stand alone in terms of supporting teacher candidates' development as anti-oppressive teachers, in part because they, like almost any experience, can then become representative of what all experiences will be like.

Daniel, a graduate of the secondary math program, made this point thoughtfully:

> The three [simulations] I experienced I felt were all legitimate, and I acknowledge they happen in the real world. But I also think it is worth mentioning they all felt like rather severe, intense cases. Not contrived or fictional, but also like that's very much not the norm, though I feel it was

presented in a way that felt like, "You're going to the battle trenches of education, and here's all the really hard stuff you'll face." Which I think is good—that stuff is out there—but I think the simulation experience should also include some sort of more explicit acknowledgement along the lines of, "You very well may experience this in your career, but (in most cases) this will not be your norm." For example, after the Daria simulation, I felt like I couldn't have gotten that right no matter what. I felt pinned in a sense by the circumstance of the simulation. I honestly left with a perception that I would have trouble having positive relationships with my African-American female students because I felt there wasn't a way to redeem my relationship with Daria. Without legitimate classroom exposure, and just having the single experience, I think I carried this (and in externally processing it in typing now, maybe still do) assumption—that my relationships with African-American girls are probably going to be negative. Which I have not found to be true in my practice so far.

Daniel's comments remind us to consistently attend to the always-partial learnings that the simulations offer, the potential unintended learnings, and learnings that may push teachers away from schools that serve marginalized youth. What is encouraging in Daniel's comments is the level of continuing awareness he developed to monitor those assumptions that are still at play, which is a lot of what the simulation experience is intended to do.

The Learning Unfolds over Time

Data collected and analyzed early in the SHIFT Project, and confirmed through subsequent years of implementation, reveals that the learning that comes from simulated encounters is revealed over time. The simulated encounters do not themselves enlighten candidates to a new way of being or doing but instead provide an opportunity to see the situation presented in the encounter in new ways, which can lead to "enlarging the space of the possible."[3] Candidates may eventually become different kinds of people who act differently in the world because of the simulation experience, but the encounters do not cause this to happen immediately. And when and where that process starts varies by candidate. The SHIFT simulation impacts candidates at different points in the simulation cycle.

In an early analysis of simulation data, using a comparative case study approach, we found that what caused teacher candidates to start the process of sense-making (the shift moment) differed, even among white women candidates who ultimately ended up in fairly similar places in terms of their learning.[4] For one master's-level candidate, Kylie, watching the video of her interaction in the Darius Miller encounter caused her to shift her framing of the interaction from one of respect to one of responsiveness. Kylie used the word *respect* or *respectful* five times in a 476-word response to the prereading questions. In her interaction, she gaslit Darius's concerns about being singled out as a Black student in a predominantly white class and focused again on ideas about appropriateness. Even in her raw debrief immediately after the interaction, she was focused on getting Darius to see things her way—"I couldn't figure out what I would say to him to make him feel like that's not what was happening." But when watching her video, Kylie began to see the situation differently. In her rereading response, she wrote:

> After reviewing my video I realized that I didn't ever address his concerns directly . . . Immediately after Darius expressed his concern about how his race may be the reason why he is being called out in all of his classes, I chose to address his role as a leader in my classroom rather than assuring him that I am not intentionally calling him out for being different than other students. I thought this would be the most appropriate way to address his concerns, but I really think I just didn't want to address the issue of race at all.

While Kylie still had learning ahead around the role of intention in racial bias, she at least recognized the gaslighting that she had been engaging in with Darius. And by the end of the semester, she was also able to recognize that this was a form of defending herself, and that in situations like the one with Darius, she had to be vulnerable to the possibility, even likelihood, that she had done what Darius was accusing her of.

Lisa, another candidate in the same class, also showed a change in how she made sense of the encounter. Focused initially on Darius talking, she did not come to recognize the salience of race in the simulation (her own and the student's) until the group debrief. In her interaction with Darius, Lisa said, in response to his accusation of racial bias, "It's not because you're Black; it's because you're loud." Lisa did not understand how the former framed her perception of the latter, even as she supported Darius's perception of other teachers as racist. And this was especially interesting because she did anticipate the likelihood of race or racism coming up in her prereading responses, unlike most students. Hence, she was willing to acknowledge that other teachers might target Black students because of their race, but not that she might. Toward the end of the group debrief, though, she said plainly, "I think that I devalued the fact that he is a Black student." Moreover, Lisa explained at the end of the semester how important it was to her that she was called out on it: "I'm glad that I was called a racist for the first time in a situation where I could get my bearings a little bit. It was really nice, the simulation part of it pushes you. You can theorize all day long about 'oh, this is how I would react this situation.' But when you're actually thrown into it, and you have to, on the ground, have responses to these people, it comes out of your mouth differently than you intend. And so it was a really valuable practice."

Finally, Miranda was a student who did not make a pivotal shift in her sense-making until the very end of the semester, and then in response to her other simulated encounters. Miranda, unlike most candidates, asked a lot of questions and really listened to Darius for the first several minutes of the interaction rather than assuming she already understood what had happened. Nonetheless, once she had done this, she turned to the same kinds of responses provided by other teachers, ignoring his reality and downplaying the potential that her own racial bias was to blame. When Darius kept going back to his initial concerns, Miranda reflected on it by saying, "I thought we would move past this a lot faster." Miranda stuck with some version of this framing—that they could "move past" his concerns by simply hearing them and providing reassurance—until the end of the semester. By then, she could see how in both of the first two encounters she had failed to truly hear the other person's perspective or make space for it in the conversation, and so she had missed a lot. This approach showed up in her third and final encounter for the semester, when she took a very different approach than other teacher candidates because of this new way of thinking about the reason for such interactions. A comparison of Kylie, Lisa, and Miranda revealed that teacher candidates are impacted differently, at different points in the simulation process and beyond, even among candidates with similar identities and starting points.

We have also studied where teacher candidates end up as a result of their SHIFT experience. In a close analysis of a single class of twenty-three teacher candidates' experiences with the Daria Miller simulation, we found that by the end of the semester the largest group (fifteen participants) clearly recognized the role that race and racism played in the interaction. They understood that the encounter was not just a matter of managing the classroom or interacting with a student who is angry but that the interaction is itself framed by race, theirs and the student's, and shaped by the legacy of racism in the United States. They were making sense of the interaction through a racial lens. A smaller group (five participants) ended up in a place where they attended to the student's concerns and perception of them as teacher but without clear evidence that they recognized how racial positionality played a role. They did not want to seem culturally insensitive, but they also were not obviously sensitive to the role that race and racism played in the interaction. Finally, the smallest group (three participants) revealed a remarkably sophisticated understanding of the situation in terms of what was possible, with clear consideration of the role of power. One of these candidates said:

> The classroom is considered yours where you are the authority figure . . . there's going to be a lot of times where you have to put yourself out of that place to really have any meaningful dialogue. So I guess that's a big takeaway for me, to always have that in mind. If I want to really have a good dialogue with some people about certain things, I'm going to have to get out of . . . [the] view[of] that's my space, and you have to come into my space and tell me. [Instead,] I'm going to go into their space . . . saying, I'm leaving myself open and this is your space so you tell me how you're feeling. And that's going to bring more honest dialogue.

Clearly, candidates experiencing SHIFT simulations don't learn exactly the same things at exactly the same time. Nor do we expect that they would. Nonetheless, the experience stays with them, and their learning seems to continue well past the whole-class debrief, the end of the course, or even graduation from the licensure program.

Shifting from *Should* to *Could*

Over the course of their trajectory of engagement with the simulated encounters, teacher candidates learn what the SHIFT simulations have to offer, which impacts their ability to learn from them. The impact of multiple simulations is clearest to us in how teacher candidates talk about them after a new encounter. While the candidates continue to focus on their own actions, they shift from a framework of "what *should* we do" to "what *could* we do." In addition, they start to engage in contingent thinking, realizing that the point of the encounter is not to prepare them for that situation exactly but to help them figure out how to make sense of a situation in order to respond ethically and defensibly.

Early on in their learning with the simulations, teacher candidates focus on the question *What should we have done?* in whole-class debriefs. Despite our insistence to the contrary, and their own recognition of situational complexity, many teacher candidates feel like there is a right way to do the simulation, and they see that as the intended learning. Over the course of a few encounters, though, teacher candidates start coming to the whole-class debrief with a different question—*What could we do?* They realize that while there are many wrong ways to manage the interaction, there is neither one right way to responsibly handle it nor a way that is without tension. In the whole-class debrief for the Daria Miller simulation, for example, the teacher candidates are often caught up in what to do about Daria's talking. Even when they have explored multiple reasons why the talking should not be the focus of the encounter, they have trouble letting it go—*What do we do to get her to stop talking?* By the final of the first three encounters, however, they start recognizing that there are a lot of options available for how to respond and that different people may have different options available because of their points of connection to the student or parent, to the issue at hand, or to the systemic oppression in play. They develop the ability to see the many moving pieces in these kinds of situations and they want to explore how changing pieces might require a different response. This eventually develops into a kind of if-then contingent thinking.

One place we have seen the contingent thinking that appears later in the trajectory is in the whole-class debrief of the literacy simulation around the challenge of coaching Riley Adler, a struggling writer. This is an interesting place to witness it because the literacy class often includes both undergraduate and master's students. The undergraduates are usually in their junior year and it's been one or two semesters since their first series of three simulations, whereas the master's students are in the midst of them, experiencing both concurrently. So while the master's students have more of many things—years of life, completed degrees, often work experience—they have had less practice in learning from the simulations. In these whole-class debriefs, it is often the undergraduates who move the conversation along. They are excited to debrief a simulation again, and they have often learned the right kinds of questions to ask: *What else could we have found out about the situation? What would have happened if we had tried something different in the encounter? If certain details of the scenario changed, what else would we need to do or try?* In this course dedicated to English language arts candidates and focused on teaching writing, candidates have to decide how to conference with Riley, a student who has written offensive comments about Hispanic families in an in-class assignment. Do they address the student's comments but risk the student shutting down even more in class? Or do they not talk about them for now and then try to do something about them later? In a recent whole-class debrief, the candidates thought about this briefly but then pushed further and thought about how other contexts might shape the way they chose to respond: *What if the students were doing peer reviews? What if this piece of writing was going to be revised?* In this sense, candidates recognized that the intended learning went beyond how to handle this situation well and instead met our goal of moving them toward a more developed level of pedagogical responsibility.

Impacts on Graduates

Our evidence for the impact of SHIFT simulations on graduates from the program is entirely self-reported because we have just begun to frame research in the field that would allow us to make stronger claims. Again, what we share here is what graduates themselves describe as the long-term impact of these experiences: the SHIFT simulations opened them up to future learning, and the SHIFT experience changed the way they now react in the classroom.

The Encounters Opened Them up to Keep Learning

Something we hear again and again from participants, but especially from graduates now teaching, is that the encounters caused them to be more open to recognizing the limits of their knowledge in the classroom and encouraged them to stay open to perspectives they may not have previously considered. "Being so open it hurts" is how writer George Saunders described it, encouraging us to "remain permanently confused"—one of the things we want teacher candidates to learn from the SHIFT simulations.[5] We do not want these future teachers to be unable to act in the classroom, of course, but we also never want them to be too sure they have done the "right" thing in a situation. We want them to remain vulnerable at all times, which *can* hurt.

Ashley, a second-year English teacher at a nearby high school, wrote in a recent survey about what she would not have learned had she not experienced the simulations: "I think I would have been less thorough in my thoughtfulness and consideration of my students. It opened up spaces within me where understanding was lost or knowledge was not present. It caused me to focus more intentionally on growth in those areas."

Simulations Changed the Way They React

Graduates who are now teaching describe the push to assume a stance of openness that they attribute to their SHIFT experience. Some tell us quite plainly that they interact with their students differently because of the simulations. Whether it is listening to a student explain what they think happened before assuming they know, or just slowing down their responses to think it through, teachers sense they have changed the way they respond. A few, like Josh, a third-year teacher in New York City, are able to articulate it:

> I know how differently I would and do respond to students today. During the [Daria Miller] simulation, I remember the feeling of being sort of blindsided by the suggestion of racism by the student and scrambling to a feeble and paternalistic defense and then refocusing the conversation on the child's supposed classroom infraction. In the moment, I think a part of me knew that it wasn't how I should respond, but maybe not. I remember other classmates responding similarly, which was bizarrely comforting. But I remember dwelling on it, in class and outside of it. My professional growth came through teaching these last three years, but the simulation kind of stuck in my mind as a baseline of where I was at when I started. A part of me during that simulation must have believed that classroom behavior was something I needed to control through authority, that feeling was compounded by where I fit within systemic oppression, and the feelings of students were at best, secondary to that aim. As far as the accusation of racism, part of me must have believed that I could reason my way out of that and convince the student with words that her feelings were misguided.

This is all still pretty embarrassing to think about. I was, of course, aware of the common wisdom negating this, having been an undergrad at Vandy for four years, but I guess in some ways I hadn't internalized it fully, because my actions showed a lack of understanding. I had also not yet been a teacher. As a teacher for three years now, I have not had to have a conversation with a student about my actions being racially motivated and prejudiced. We do discuss race, if not every day, a couple times a week. I am a white male teacher in a school of nearly all students of color, and I teach US History. To not speak about race would naturally serve an already oppressive history, and would compound my role in perpetuating that in the classroom. But I also do not force the subject. So at the beginning of the year, I always discuss my background with students, and slowly through the year, students will discuss theirs. If a student ever were to confront me about them feeling discriminated against, that action alone would require incredible resolve and bravery. Just because it has not happened does not mean the thought has never crossed a student's mind, which alone is enough to keep us up at night. Even I as try to make myself completely open to students, building enough rapport where they feel comfortable sharing parts of themselves with me, creating a classroom environment that is inviting and welcomes dissent, I know how much students must fear confronting a teacher about their feelings. This is of course compounded by and shaped by factors of identity and oppression. That is something I learned through teaching that I don't think I recognized at the time of the simulation. If a student were to confront me today, my task would be to affirm their feelings as legitimate and warranted, and not defend myself. Whatever I had wanted to say about discipline (and as a teacher I rarely ask students to stay after class to discuss behavior in that paternalistic way) would likely go unmentioned, because the student's feelings are far more pressing. Later on, I would attempt to show them through my actions that I support them and that I do not have racism in my heart. I hope through the way I teach today that I do affirm this for my students. When you work with kids every day, for hours and hours every day, the humanity of every kid tends to reveal itself in ways that are difficult to imagine as a college student. When you see the humanity in kids, and have a grounding in the role race and oppression play in your environment, the way forward becomes clearer. Part of me might have known as an undergraduate, but part of me was still hardwired in the way that I had been treated by teachers growing up, and the way I had internalized that teachers should act. So I valued having that simulation, not because it truly mirrored the experience of a teacher, but because it shows me in concrete terms how my thinking about kids, and race, and teaching has grown. And it revealed to me in no uncertain terms how much harm a teacher like myself could unknowingly do, if they didn't recognize the humanity in their students, and didn't recognize their own precarious position in an unequal world.

The other thing we hear from teachers is that they have developed the capacity to recognize those moments in their practice "when a simulation is starting." Because the SHIFT simulations simultaneously engage feelings, thinking, and acting, the new teachers connect how they felt in a simulation during the program to their in-practice recognition that something important is about to happen, something consequential for their relationship with the other person. They recognize that if this moment is handled routinely rather than thoughtfully, they could replicate ways of being and interacting that are detrimental to their work as antiracist/anti-oppressive teachers. In short, they could harm their relationship with students or families and perpetuate existing systems of oppression.

Ashley, during her student teaching year, emailed us after responding in the classroom to a student who used the word *gay* as a slur. As a lesbian, Ashley was implicated in this situation not just professionally but also personally, something she had faced in the Phil Duncan simulation during her first year in the program. "When it happened, there was a moment where I internally detached from everything because it felt like a simulation had just begun." She and others have said that at this moment, they tend to slow down and pay attention to different things than they otherwise might have. They open up. Knowing when a simulation "has just begun," to use their words, is important because it allows teachers to avoid reaction, to recognize the risk and potential in how they might respond to a situation that is emerging, and to rethink their habitual responses in turn.

Registering and Researching Other Impacts

SHIFT simulations can be as much about the learning and growth of faculty as teacher candidates. The simulations have led us to be more responsive in our own teaching, especially to candidates' prior conceptions of what teaching and working in schools look like. While we never use the simulations as a source of summative assessment for teacher candidates' knowledge or skills, we do use them formatively to shape our instruction, both within coursework and linked to opportunities for learning through field placements. We recognize what teacher candidates have learned and what they find challenging in order to provide supports in response.

In addition to our learning as faculty, integration of the SHIFT simulations has impacted the program itself, primarily to push the faculty collectively toward greater consistency in addressing the role of systems of oppression in teaching. Expanding the SHIFT Project from just one course to a signature pedagogy over the life of a program means that faculty are addressing the kinds of challenges and dilemmas simulated in the encounters beyond a single situation and in subject-specific contexts. The science literacies simulation (Caitlin Jackson), for example, has ultimately led to an intentional focus on the relationships between epistemologies of science and faith-based beliefs, something that is a consistent issue in our local schools. Because the simulations have to be supported beyond the bounds of the single encounter, our courses, syllabi, and class structures have had to evolve too, moving us in the direction of preparing anti-oppressive educators.

Formal research on the impacts and effects of the SHIFT simulations is ongoing. We are particularly interested in the pathways that teacher candidates take on their way to becoming and sustaining themselves as anti-oppressive teachers. Specifically, how do novice teachers draw on and apply the learning from a simulation to their classroom practice? We are also tracking how teachers' willingness to take on teaching positions in schools with large communities of students from marginalized backgrounds may be impacted by their SHIFT experience.

All of that builds on the impacts of the SHIFT Program on the minds, hearts, and actions of teacher candidates we document here. Based on our observations of candidates' encounters and on candidates' reflections and reports of the impact with students in classroom, we suggest that SHIFT simulations cause candidates to be pulled up short with respect to habitual ways of reacting and responding while moving them toward a new sense of what they *could* do in a given situation. SHIFT simulations push teacher candidates toward a stance we characterize as *pedagogical responsibility*, the capacity to respond thoughtfully rather than react habitually. For a relatively small investment of time (eighteen of 420 program instructional hours) and money (as little as $5 per candidate per simulation to pay actors), teacher candidates are opened up in a way that makes space for anti-oppressive teaching to take root.

Part II

Start SHIFTing

Chapter 5

Infrastructure for the Encounter and the Debrief

SHIFT is not simply a pedagogy to be applied; rather, it represents an approach to the preparation of teachers that involves a commitment to anti-oppressive pedagogy for all students in any school, a belief that teacher candidates can be educated toward an anti-oppressive stance, and a program designed around understanding teaching as a sociocultural practice situated within a community of educators and educational goals. If this commitment, belief, recognition, and design are not part of your practice of teacher education, then it is unlikely that SHIFT simulations will have the same impact. In this chapter we consider the theoretical, professional, ethical, and material infrastructure needed to implement SHIFT simulations and offer some recommendations about how to proceed if you are persuaded that this approach is congruent with your aspirations for your program and expressive of the goals and values you hope to enact.

We employ a set of carefully focused questions to walk you through the process of assessing your present program(s) in order to check the dispositions, belief, values, and ideas that motivate what you presently do. We prompt you to consider the structure and organization of each program (e.g., secondary versus elementary education, undergraduate versus master's level) to identify the opportunities for incorporating SHIFT simulations to enhance or improve your programs. We encourage you to clarify your individual and shared understandings of and commitments to student and teacher diversity as a pedagogical resource. You will need to consider how you can elicit and build on the diversity of ideas, prior experiences, cultural backgrounds, religious commitments, and more that students and teachers bring to develop a constructively critical view of school and society. We also ask you to make explicit your understandings of teaching practices and teaching as a (community of) practice. You will need to do all of this in order to select "sites" for SHIFT simulations within your program. Finally, we urge you to articulate a theory of action or change that can guide your thinking-into-action and maintain motivation when your efforts to implement SHIFT simulations hit the inevitable snag. To inform the questions we ask, we draw on pragmatist theory; critical race theory; culturally relevant, responsive, and sustaining pedagogies; and sociocultural and situative theories of teaching practice.[1] But first we offer more of our own experience developing the SHIFT Project to highlight how each question might play out.

Developing the SHIFT Project at Vanderbilt

After several years of teaching in a predominantly Black school, Liz, a white woman, was acutely aware that she could have been better prepared—though never completely prepared—for the task at hand. She had moved into a doctoral program in part to answer her own questions about equitable educational experience for all and found herself in a position to offer teacher candidates better preparation. But what was it?

The secondary teacher education program she was working in took seriously questions of student and teacher identity and positionality, included coursework and field and community experiences that confronted inequity and systems of oppression in schooling, partnered with the local public school system to ensure that all candidates were prepared to teach in *any* school, and engaged faculty members who seemed to be personally committed to the education of all. Academically well-prepared, ethically open, and sociopolitically aware candidates encountered all the "right" readings; completed field experiences in schools populated by students of color with a diverse array of ethnicities, languages, and religions; and were taught to attend carefully to what students were thinking as a resource for planning instruction. Still, the teacher candidates tended to fall into the trap of seeing pedagogical situations from their own perspectives and perceiving their efforts through a paternalistic or charitable lens. They were used to doing the "right" thing and having their own actions, and perspectives, viewed as "right."

Liz started to investigate the practice of live-actor simulations in other fields and to imagine how that practice might be adapted to teacher education with a focus on preparing the anti-oppressive educator, one committed to and capable of responding constructively to each and all students in contexts of difference, discrimination, and inequity. As an instructor of record in a required undergraduate social foundations course, she piloted simulations taken from Ben Dotger's book but tried to modify them, using them in a way that made identities and systems of oppression more salient.[2] Because she had contacts in the medical school and access to some university funding (and later some small grants), she ran the encounters in the medical school simulation lab (which was set up for video-recording, archiving, and viewing multiple encounters at once) and paid the actors she also trained. The experience piqued her interest in what was possible and revealed a need to construct new encounters that better fit her intended use.

Barb, at the time the director of secondary education, got wind of Liz's efforts and immediately recognized the potential, in part because for several decades she had been actively searching for a tool, strategy, or approach that could break through the good intentions of teacher candidates. Serendipitously, Barb was also teaching a required social foundations course for secondary education candidates at the master's level and made the decision to run SHIFT simulations in that course as well, bringing in Liz and another doctoral candidate as teaching assistants.

In that semester we piloted a sequence of three simulations that fit into concepts and readings explored in the social foundations course: racism and whiteness (Daria Miller), cross-cultural communication with families and students (Maryam Sahil, but later replaced with Alondra Correa), and stereotypical expectations of students with marginalized identities (Phil Duncan). That set of three SHIFT simulations became part of the education of every secondary teaching candidate in the program.

As word spread among program faculty, mostly because of students' comments), Barb shepherded discussions about how the SHIFT simulations impacted our candidates and whether and how faculty wanted to expand their use. Over several semesters we took a trial-and-error approach to placing simulations, driven in part by a "coalition of the willing" among the faculty, which included those who saw simulations as particularly useful for their content (for example, in a classroom ecology course where student identity and systems of oppression obviously impacted classroom culture), those who taught the methods sequences whose own commitment to anti-oppressive pedagogy led them to try *any* potential tool, and those who were willing to try it out but felt unsure whether they were the right person to debrief and make the most of the SHIFT simulations experience. (In cases with willing but not-quite-confident instructors, we utilized excited teaching assistants or helped with debriefing ourselves.)

Barb was also in a position to direct modest resources to the project and to communicate the value of the project to Dean Camilla Benbow. (This was helped along when Liz's work was featured in an *Education Week* article in 2016.[3]) The dean's support was crucial when the costs at the medical center tripled. We were able to secure modest additional funding for the program budget to cover the student work hours, physical space, server space, and video equipment needed to keep the project going, with the promise of a simulation lab as part of a building renovation.

As this was happening, the pattern for the SHIFT simulations was falling into place. We included three simulations in the social foundations course early in the program, two simulations in the classroom ecology course later in the program, and at least one in each subject-specific literacies course. Simulations enacted in the required classroom ecology course build on themes of conflict among students as a result of their identities, shared or differing, and their expectations around classroom engagement, consistent with the focus of that course. The literacies courses take up thinking, reading, writing, speaking, and listening in each subject area, and the simulations, specific to each discipline, are designed to highlight specific challenges of a sociopolitical nature facing teachers in that field. In all, we have developed more than two dozen simulations for different programs and have settled on a sequence of five (four common and one subject specific) that are regularly incorporated into the secondary education program.

It is worth noting that the SHIFT cycle of tasks has not changed since Liz's original design in 2013. Across multiple courses and with multiple faculty members, we agreed that the prereading, encounter, raw debrief, rereading, and group debrief, situated in a space in the course agenda when readings would support the cycle, was the right way to go.

At this point it is hard to imagine SHIFT simulations disappearing from the program at Vanderbilt. They are linked not only to positive impacts on our candidates but also to teacher candidates' expectations. Candidates expect and look forward to (if somewhat nervously) their SHIFT simulations. The word is out that the SHIFT simulations are a tool for understanding what the work of teaching others is really about. As one teaching graduate recently noted, "I used to be a little worried about doing the sims; but now I realize that sims are happening in my classroom every day!"

It is important to note that our successful implementation of the SHIFT simulations has been focused on the secondary education program only and does not incorporate Vanderbilt's elementary and early childhood or special education programs. This is not due solely to lack of interest but, more so, to the different circumstances and priorities within each set of programs. At this writing, the elementary and early childhood master's program is experimenting with SHIFT simulations set in an early social foundations course as well as in math and literacy methods courses. Liz has been asked to teach in the program to give the effort careful guidance. And the faculty are exploring a slightly different enactment (including early encounter, minimal debrief, course learning, and repeated encounter with more extensive debrief later in the semester) to see how it supports other elements of program development. This is not a cause for concern but simply a reflection of the nature of SHIFT simulations and the importance of building them into a program in a form and format that is sustainable. What is not negotiable is the commitment to anti-oppressive pedagogy and the recognition that a horizon shift is needed for both faculty and students to achieve that goal.

Concrete Questions

As we address directly the questions, we offer points of entry with our experience-based guidance built in as commentary, hoping to make our advice concrete but not prescriptive. We press hard on local conditions, reminding you that doing what we did is not as valuable as thinking about things in the ways we did so that the principles, but not necessarily all the practices, remain vital in your program. We are as honest as our perspective allows in shining light on the persistent challenges endemic in trying to make SHIFT simulations a regular and well-integrated feature of any program.

Question 1: Are your personal and programmatic goals already aligned with the affordances of SHIFT simulations? Can the incorporation of SHIFT simulations stimulate interactions among faculty and students that can drive a justice-centered, anti-oppressive shift in program orientation?

If you are pursuing teacher education in a program and with colleagues committed to anti-oppressive pedagogy, but you haven't yet found the right tool to fully accomplish your goals or you are fascinated by the power of SHIFT simulations to bring new dimensions of affect, cognition, and disposition to the fore, then you can begin to think about the material conditions needed. Form a coalition of the willing and move on to the next set of questions. If not, there is other work to be done first.

While SHIFT simulations were clearly appealing to individual faculty members in Vanderbilt's secondary education program, there were plenty of hurdles. The idea of the simulations was not equally appealing to all faculty members. And even where the idea was valued by most, if not all, there was not always a shared understanding of how to use SHIFT simulations. What needed to be stable and what could be flexible? We couldn't know that in advance.

The project proceeded slowly and carefully by engaging in pilot efforts. We were convinced that there was something valuable in a live-actor simulation approach. Trying it out with students enrolled in courses where we had control over the curricular content made it easy, for Liz in her undergraduate social foundations course and Barb in her master's level course, to work out kinks and constraints and highlight the affordances of using this type of approach. The teacher candidates were the catalyst for a great deal of subsequent faculty interest.

The SHIFT simulations interrupted the taken-for-granted pattern of classroom activity and got the teacher candidates talking—about how it felt, about what they expected and encountered, about how they responded and didn't respond. They compared notes as they moved from class to class, and faculty members were drawn into the conversations and moved by the students' engagement. Teacher candidates told their friends who had not yet taken these courses about the SHIFT simulations and began to talk more explicitly about equity in ways that faculty hadn't heard before. These multiple encounters in a single semester created a buzz among the students, and that energy stimulated concrete dialogue among faculty about program goals and structures and a willingness to try SHIFT simulations in other settings, as well as revealing gaps, needs, and points for revision, which we continue to address.

We can, of course, imagine taking a more measured approach to getting such a program up and running. Former Vanderbilt doctoral students Kara Krinks at Lipscomb University and Dan Reynolds at John Carroll University took the SHIFT experience with them to their first full-time academic appointments. They have experimented with individual pilot efforts and are sharing their experience with their new colleagues in hopes of garnering support for some version of this mode of educating teacher candidates. An individual faculty member needs allies for SHIFT to take hold.

Question 2: Is one program more suited than others for beginning a SHIFT Project, whether because of faculty expertise, mission and vision, greater need for revision, congruent curricular content, or course and practicum offerings? Do you have the capacity with respect to project leadership, technological and other material resources, actor pools, etc., to begin with multiple programs, or should you focus your attention in just one program initially?

This is a question of focus, scale, and capacity. It boils down to where and how to begin.

First, there is a need to recognize where a SHIFT project is most likely to flourish. Where can the SHIFT simulations take root—reaching deep to strengthen the program's anti-oppressive commitments and growing upward and outward to impact future teachers? The SHIFT Project at Vanderbilt began in the secondary education program for a whole host of reasons: Liz was working primarily in that program as a former secondary teacher, the secondary education team was quite stable, and the faculty members, operating with a "continuous improvement" mind-set, were open to collaborative changes that blended excellence and equity. Only now is a SHIFT effort being systematically implemented in other programs, with the design adapting to each program's curriculum and structure.

SHIFT simulations require an investment of time and money, though not as much as one might immediately imagine. It is important to remember that SHIFT simulations, well-integrated with course content, will better accomplish some of the instructional and dispositional work of the courses where they are sited. Thoughtful consideration up front about which critical incidents to use and how to sequence them within a course or over courses to take advantage of various readings and curricular foci will streamline planning and emphasize important instruction goals. SHIFT simulations are not an add-on; they are not "something more" in addition to what you already do. SHIFT simulations constitute an intellectual and interpersonal center around which key content and outcomes can be organized. In a social foundations course that takes up questions of systemic racism, equal educational opportunity, and opportunity gaps, the Daria Miller simulation is a centering experience that pushes candidates to take readings and concepts more seriously and understand them more concretely as they imagine themselves as teachers.

It's equally important to recognize that the impact of SHIFT simulations is not substantially different if the administration of the encounters is a "full-package" version or a "budget" version. We have experienced both at Vanderbilt, first operating out of a dedicated simulation lab at the medical school where recordings are seamlessly loaded into a secure storage system, then piecing together video cameras in borrowed offices with video uploaded to a campus document server by a student assistant, and now moving into a new Peabody (College of Education and Human Development) Simulation Lab in a renovated complex on campus. At another Tennessee institution where the SHIFT model is serving as a prompt and guide, the program operates on a modified budget quite successfully, taking advantage of systems already in place for student video-recording (required for the state teacher performance assessment, edTPA): iPads on Swivl tripods capture video that can be uploaded to a Google Drive for reviewing.[4] The kind of digital device you use is much less important than the attention you pay to issues of privacy and security.

The following elements are absolutely necessary to establishing a SHIFT-style program, but they can be configured depending on the resources you have available.

A SYSTEM FOR GATHERING AND REVIEWING CANDIDATES' PRE- AND REREADINGS. This can be as sophisticated as a secure online storage system like Google Docs that directs each student's comments to their own folder or as simple as an email sent to the instructor or facilitator.

A WAY TO VIDEOTAPE THE ENCOUNTERS. If you have access to a simulation lab (with built-in video cameras and secure storage systems), you are all set! Check with your psychology or social work departments or medical school to be sure something like this doesn't already exist on campus. But, as noted above, university video cameras, program iPads, and personal smartphones can be pressed into service. In this case, you will want an upper-level undergraduate or master's student on work-study to serve as videographer (turning cameras on and off and trimming recordings to just the encounter), using conference rooms, faculty offices, practice spaces, or even private hallways as your live-encounter spaces.

A WAY TO STORE VIDEO SECURELY. This is necessary *if* you want to make it available for candidates and *if* you want to view it yourself and *if* you want to use it as data for your own IRB-approved research and/or program development. Most campuses and organizations have use of storage systems or dedicated server space available for program use that are FERPA-compliant. This is not strictly necessary as long as each teacher candidate has the capacity to review their own encounter privately. However, it provides access to data regarding candidate development *and* program development and is a way to hold on to data as new questions surface about the simulations that are ripe for research.

MONEY TO PAY ACTORS OR AN ACTORS' COMPANY (OR BOTH). This is really the only additional funding needed, but it cannot be avoided. One of the ways to ensure the dignity of the actors is to pay them fairly. While the exact figure will depend on prevailing hourly wages in your setting, the compensation should take into account the time spent in training with the project coordinator, rehearsing privately, and engaging in encounters with multiple teacher candidates (typically one to three hours). You may also want to invite the actors to participate in the debriefing and compensate them for their time. Of course, this means finding money in departmental budgets, dean support, program funds, and/or individual faculty resources. It may also mean applying for small instructional grants on campus or seeking larger external funding sources. Because this supports a diversity mission or implicit bias training for teacher candidates, there are potential sources, including community foundations and even local district education foundations. Compensation for actors should cost approximately $900 to $1,800 annually for a program with thirty students, and more for larger programs. If necessary, it is possible to think creatively about in-kind compensation for actors in lieu of cash payments.

BUDGETING CLASS TIME. You can make a decision to use class time for the actual encounters or fold it into candidates' out-of-class requirements. At Vanderbilt, we have left this up to the course instructor, and their choices have been impacted by various considerations. In one course, the class session is constructed in a station format, with the instructor circulating while students come and go to their encounters. In this way, class time is not lost but redirected. In other courses, the instructor holds extra office hours in lieu of class while students line up for their encounters. In still others, encounters are scheduled before and after actual class time. It's also important to budget time for the group debrief. This will typically take sixty to seventy minutes and should be scheduled as (part of) the next class session. Again, it's important to note that this is not an extra or additional session but one that will enable you to weave student experience (and feeling) into critical readings, along with dispositional concerns.

INTERACTION PROTOCOLS. For each SHIFT simulation you choose to incorporate, you will need a generative critical incident transformed into a several-page background story for the actors (actor interaction protocol, AIP) and a one-to-two-page prompt for the teacher candidate (teacher interaction protocol, TIP). TIPs addressing a range of teaching situations and social issues are available and can be adapted for your use under a Creative Commons Copyright, or you can create your own in-house depending on the perceived needs of your candidates.[5]

A PROJECT COORDINATOR. SHIFT simulations can be pulled off without a coordinator, but you are much more likely to have a consistent and sustainable program if you can identify a person who is responsible for logistics, actor coordination, scheduling, equipment management, etc. This may be a faculty member with released time, a faculty member who views this as their service/scholarship, a paid staff member, or a graduate student compensated in work-study hours or tuition support. We emphasize that SHIFT simulations are a possible and potentially important source for scholarship/research. There is much investigation to be done in the area of preparing teacher candidates for anti-oppressive work. Keep in mind that you may be able to attract faculty allies who are interested in this work and allow a team of faculty members to pursue a research agenda together that complements their regular teaching responsibilities. At Vanderbilt, secondary education faculty members have turned SHIFT simulations work into more than a dozen conference presentations, book chapters, and published articles.

Question 3: Who are your teacher candidates, and what are they ready for with respect to addressing diversity and equity head on? Who are your faculty, and how are they prepared, academically and experientially, to facilitate their own learning and the learning of your teacher candidates?

As teacher educators, it is not always easy to assess our own or our teacher candidates' openness to recognizing the play of power and privilege in our/their interpretive horizons or with respect to the strength of our/their commitment to anti-oppressive pedagogy. Ibram Kendi's *How to Be an Anti-Racist* offers a distinction that can be applied to a focus on anti-oppressive teaching, arguing that the opposite of racist is not "not racist" but "anti-racist."[6] That is, it is not enough to claim attitudes and behaviors that are not racist; to oppose racism, we must affirmatively seek policies and practices that are antiracist, that challenge and defeat racism. If we apply the same logic to anti-oppressive pedagogy generally, then the opposite of oppressive is not "not oppressive" but affirmatively anti-oppressive. As teacher educators, do we imagine and implement program practices and policies that challenge and defeat oppressive pedagogies? Have we, in our lives and in our programs, sought and designed experiences that identify and defuse pedagogies that privilege some and not others? Where do our students come from? Is it likely that they have experienced challenges to their privileged status? What can or does this look like with candidates who also carry status as a member of a marginalized group? Reading a book like Kendi's together as a faculty (or, even better, as a program, with faculty and candidates) might be a good way to determine how to begin SHIFT simulations, not just through determining people's receptiveness to the content but their willingness to engage in a true conversation with vulnerability and culpability front and center.

Peabody College at Vanderbilt University is, in many ways, a bastion of privilege. At the same time, the college has a long commitment (dating to its origins) to the education of marginalized populations. The university has recently demonstrated a significant commitment to equity and diversity in the form of need-blind admissions and hiring faculty representing diverse backgrounds and perspectives. As a result, Peabody students expect to take up power and privilege no matter the topic under consideration. Faculty in the Department of Teaching and Learning have been wrestling openly for a decade with diversifying both faculty and programs in the direction of anti-oppressive commitments.

Vanderbilt is located in Nashville, a city where private schools opened in great numbers during school desegregation, where gentrification in historically Black and low-income neighborhoods is pushing minoritized families out, and where immigrant and refugee populations are growing. For these reasons, the first SHIFT simulations we devised focused on racial, ethnic, and linguistic diversity, and the systems that turn these identities into "problems" in schools and society are recognizable to our teacher candidates. We then took up issues related to gender and sexuality, religion and faith, and more. With very few exceptions, candidates dive into the simulations. There is a fair amount of discomfort in the beginning, but this is expected and proves to be generally productive.

Admittedly, this same plan may not be successful everywhere. Vanderbilt is a private, nonsectarian, doctoral-granting university. We acknowledge that the backgrounds of students may be different in state universities or smaller (sectarian) undergraduate institutions. Expectations and assumptions can differ by geographic location or cultural affiliation. If you hope to implement SHIFT simulations, it is important to know your own students and to assess what kinds of challenges will move them along the path to anti-oppressive teaching.

Yet, one of the most compelling aspects of SHIFT simulations is the way they seem to prompt teacher candidates wherever they are. There is an almost uncanny "fit" because of what each simulation offers and what the teacher candidate can handle with some level of openness and vulnerability. Some candidates sniff out the challenge inherent even before the actual encounter; some "get it" when encountered by another live human being; some see it in watching their own video recording; some need the support of the group debrief. Virtually all candidates eventually get the challenge, though not all know where to go with it, even in the end. The SHIFT simulation cycle allows multiple points of entry and apprehension, and that's why it can support learning and development in different candidates whatever they bring to the encounter. Thus, it seems that the question is not *whether* to do SHIFT simulations but *which* simulations and whether you can recycle or adapt those developed elsewhere or you need to write your own. Knowing your students and yourselves enables more defensible choices.

Question 4: Do you understand teaching as a social practice that candidates learn through practice? What are the pedagogical strategies and approaches utilized in the program that make that clear?

You may be inclined to ask what difference it makes whether you understand teaching as a social practice. You may ask what the alternatives are and why situating SHIFT simulations within this kind of context is important. Those are fair questions.

The idea that teaching is a social practice is perhaps best articulated by Lave and Wenger in their 1991 essay "Situated Learning: Legitimate Peripheral Participation" and best exemplified by Magdalene Lampert in her 2001 book *Teaching Problems and the Problems of Teaching*."[7] In these two treatments of teaching as a practice, the complexity of teaching is clearly maintained and the challenges of learning to teach fully respected. In other analyses of teaching, we see teaching portrayed as a technical activity, as a reflective practice, as a (moral) craft, or as a political activity. Today we recognize these elements at work when we focus on core practices and discrete rehearsals, teacher autonomy and leadership, responsible classrooms, and equity-oriented teaching. The point is not that any of these is wrong; it is that each focus is incomplete and, without attention to the material and sociopolitical context, potentially problematic.

Recognizing teaching as a social practice means acknowledging that context matters; that intellect, affect, and habit are always in play and always shaped by prior experience; and that power and value are inevitably part of the exchange. One learns to teach by teaching, by gradually taking on the "legitimate peripheral participation" that Lave and Wenger highlight.[8] The emphasis on *gradually* here cannot be overstated. SHIFT simulations provide encounters that trigger responses of intellect, affect, and habit; enable the interrogation of prior experience and not-constructive habits; and shine light on the play of power and value. But they do so in a loosely controlled setting that generates just enough discomfort to unsettle but not so much that teacher candidates shut down or actively resist the consideration of new ways of thinking, feeling, and doing.

SHIFT simulations are best situated in programs in which the technical aspects of teaching are highlighted and rehearsed; the time, space, and challenging ideas for reflection are provided and coached; *and* the moral and political impacts are surfaced and acknowledged. Is this the case in your program(s)?

We are not asking whether any of us, as individual instructors and coaches or as participants in a program, succeed all the time in integrating these elements into our education of future teachers. Of course, we do not. But we are asking whether these are challenges you, as a program, acknowledge and address.

In the Department of Teaching and Learning at Vanderbilt, the idea that teaching is a social practice is part of our shared inquiry. Researchers pursue studies constructed on this premise; practitioners speak this language fluently. As a result, for us there was no gap between the vision of equitable teaching practice that SHIFT simulations evokes and other discrete practices that frame our secondary education program, such as leveraging student thinking as a core practice developed through the video club, residency experiences, or mediated methods instruction.

Taking the time to recognize the hidden curriculum of your program can make a big difference in whether or not you are able to successfully implement a SHIFT project. Being able to identify those pedagogical strategies and signature pedagogies that capture the assumptions built into your program will help you predict whether, and how, faculty and candidates will respond with understanding to a pedagogical experience that intentionally undoes what they take for granted about teaching.

Question 5: Given your answers to the questions above, what are the courses or opportunities for practice that can house the SHIFT simulations with appropriate reflective power, taking advantage of equity-oriented curriculum, faculty expertise and willingness, and a praxis focus?

Your answer to this question should arise naturally out of the inventory you have taken after answering the first four questions. Still, this may be trickier than almost any other response because it depends as much on faculty capacity and willingness as on the structure of your program. "But that's not how we've always done it" is a powerful barrier to action in the absence of a commitment to regularly reexamining our own social practices of teacher education.

At Vanderbilt, we began with pilot efforts in social foundations classes because we had willing instructors, congruent content, and a contained "experiment space." Teacher educators across the board are more likely to affirm diversity work in social foundations courses (or perhaps in cultural diversity courses, depending on what your program requires/offers). The syllabi were packed with readings that could help us debrief encounters and made it easy to develop a carefully planned sequence of SHIFT simulations that moved teacher candidates from examining their own racial biases and ability to recognize white supremacy at play to seeing how those forces and others interrupt our ability to communicate openly with families and confronting biases and prejudices in a colleague, all with the goal of circling back to their own complicity in the perpetuation of these systems of oppression. The sequence supports not just growth in candidates' thinking and doing but a constant coming back by both candidates and teacher educators to the need for accountability, responsibility, and the desire for more change in themselves as well as the system.

We feel strongly that starting with a straightforward encounter with a student of color is important not just for white teacher candidates but for all teacher candidates. All candidates (and faculty, for that matter) are equally disarmed by the implication that they hold racial bias. With this as an initial simulation, we find that candidates are ready to take other issues seriously without worrying that they will be judged harshly or found wanting morally. Later SHIFT simulations may be designed with particular local challenges in mind. For example, we highlighted the immigrant and refugee populations in Nashville, where we knew candidates would be doing their internships and field experiences.

Question 6: What will (have to) change in individuals and within the program if the SHIFT Project takes hold? What is your theory of how such change occurs?

We ask you to imagine realistically what will have to shift in people and programs to achieve the goal of anti-oppressive pedagogical practices, and how that is likely to happen. Having a clear sense of this up front means that you'll be able to persist when you encounter resistance or struggle to secure needed resources.

At Vanderbilt, we subscribed to an informal wedge theory of program and attitude change. We believed that if we pushed the simulations where we could easily, that these wedges would introduce small movement that would eventually leave room for more substantive shifts. And that's exactly what happened. As SHIFT simulations became part of specific course requirements, candidates talked about them (in both candid and critical ways), faculty became interested and asked to integrate a simulation into their courses, and eventually the program faculty asked, What are we doing about this?

Your approach may depend on the culture at your institution. You may need, for example, to seek a democratic consensus, slowly enabling all program faculty to study the idea and come to a supportive place. This takes more time up front but can result in strong support moving forward.

We urge you to reject any top-down imposition of SHIFT simulations as an add-on feature of a program that is not structured or staffed to enact the practice-based, open-minded and open-hearted, and admittedly risky communication that this requires. However, if you view your program as a kind of "learning organization" where everybody (faculty, candidates, and school partners) is learning simultaneously, though not necessarily the same things, then a SHIFT project may be just the step you need to create new opportunities for learning and development.[9]

We do not suggest a replication of the structure we have enacted at Vanderbilt. Instead, we encourage you to engage in a process of (inter)action that can yield something that fits your context and your capacity. Sequences of experiences and resources employed can be tailored to your institutional situation. We hope to see promising approaches grow in a way that is sensitive to local demands while maintaining a viable commitment to the education of all.

Chapter 6

Crafting Simulations

Once an instructor or program has determined the infrastructure needed to start using SHIFT simulations, your next step is to develop encounters. While not necessarily the main place where learning happens, the encounters do, to some extent, limit what teacher candidates can learn from the simulation. They open candidates up to what comes after the interaction—to watching their videos back in ways that let them notice something different than they did during the encounter, to completing assigned readings that offer new lenses on the interactions, and to entering the group debrief ready to interrogate their assumptions in a way they may not have felt ready to immediately after the encounter ended. So while we will state repeatedly that the encounter is not the only important part of the simulation cycle, it is vital that instructors and designers take great care in how they approach their design, especially given the goal of engaging in this work in a way that is itself anti-oppressive.

Choosing Encounters

In approaching the process of choosing what kinds of encounters to create, the first and most important question to consider is what understandings, of themselves and of their world, our teacher candidates need to have disrupted. As teacher educators, you must consider what disruptions would shift your students' present interpretive horizons. SHIFT simulations are not designed to lead to any kind of final knowledge or endpoint; rather than confirming what candidates think they know, SHIFT simulations unsettle (complicate, nuance, or sometimes upend) whatever certainty candidates may have reached at that point in their learning. So the place to start is to identify those instances when candidates tend to assume some kind of certainty, whether founded in naïve ignorance or prior teaching experience.

In 2019 we designed and used our first simulated encounters in the elementary licensure program. One of the scenarios we developed was the Oscar and Lilliana Martinez simulation, a parent-initiated conference in which the parents communicated their concern about their son's apparent use of Spanish in the classroom and in his coursework. This was not the first parent conference we designed for the SHIFT Project, but the candidates in the elementary program were at a different place in their learning. In the secondary program, candidates encounter their first parent conference before they have had much learning related to parent-teacher conferences or how to engage in them in a way that takes up more relational and two-way forms of family engagement. The simulations designed for the secondary program that focus on multilingual students and families, including Maryam Sahil and Alondra Correa, assume that most teacher candidates will come into the interaction ready to tell the parent about what their student is doing in the classroom and look for the parent's consent with whatever plan they lay out. The teacher candidates, for the most part, are simply replicating the understanding of parent-teacher conferences they bring with them to the encounter, and so much of what we want to disrupt is what parent-teacher conferences are for and, more broadly, who brings valuable knowledge to the work of educating children. These encounters are designed to offer a thick backstory that most teacher candidates are unlikely to learn about in the interaction. This allows us to pull it out in the group debrief as a way of showing how much more useful information teachers might get if they knew to ask for it and how.

The Oscar and Lilliana Martinez simulation presents parents who are reluctant to share a lot of information about the details of their life outside of school, owing in part to their undocumented status. (This population of parents is present in many Nashville public schools where our candidates are placed.) They also push back on the candidate's belief that using Spanish in the classroom is desirable; instead, they share their desire that their son, Francisco, speak only English at school. We designed the scenario in this way not because we want the teacher candidates to avoid asking questions about children's and families' lives outside of school, or because we want them to abandon the idea of multilingualism in the classroom. Rather, this became a place to unsettle their ideas about how a family might react to what can feel like personal questions and to consider the range of reasons some parents might prefer not to talk about it in detail. It also asked them at a broader level to consider how to proceed when parents' express wishes that conflict with what the teacher believes to be desirable or even pedagogically appropriate.

The elementary teachers participating in this new simulation had already taken coursework about parent-teacher conferences and partnering approaches to family engagement. They came into the interaction wanting to know a lot about the child and family and eager to hear what the parents offered in terms of their hopes and fears for their child. They had also been exposed to foundational learning about asset-based approaches to languages, including ideas around translanguaging, and were likely to see the child's use of Spanish in the classroom as a way to engage the whole child, develop his linguistic repertoire in both Spanish and English, and help him feel welcome and capable as a new student in the class. The interaction we designed served to complicate those learned ideas while also providing openings for further learning related to reading and writing development, the coursework in which this scenario was set.

As with each encounter in the SHIFT Project, this was generated in response to the following questions:

- Who are our teacher candidates?
- What do they think they know or understand at this point in their learning?
- And what would it look like to productively disrupt those understandings in ways that move them toward the mind-sets, knowledge, and skills necessary for anti-oppressive education?

Knowing your candidates is an important part of creating encounters because it helps to have in mind what assets and resources candidates bring to the encounters. When we run the Maryam Sahil simulation, we know that few of our candidates speak Arabic, and so we can design the scenario with the assumption that the interaction will be limited by the mother's apparent limited English proficiency. When we run the Alondra Correa simulation, we know that several, if not many, of our candidates will speak some or be fully fluent in Spanish, and so we have to design the scenario with that in mind. While a carefully constructed encounter will offer learning to any teacher candidate, it is also true that at least a first run of a simulation goes best when it is responsive to the specific identities and lived experiences of the teacher candidates who populate a program. Knowing who candidates are also enables the creation of a situation that will get the candidates to open up rather than shut down.

Still, gauging candidates' readiness for disruption is not the only consideration in designing or selecting encounters. It is also important to bear in mind what each specific encounter moves teacher candidates *toward*—more complex, multifaceted, and systemic understandings of social inequity. A general approach is to think about a moment within an existing course when candidates either resist new learning or readily embrace new learning but in ways they are not yet able to apply in a lived experience. The SHIFT encounter can be especially helpful in revealing to candidates how easy it is to replicate what they have experienced, even when they have learned more substantive and more equitable approaches in class. For example, in our social foundations class we spend a week working to change mind-sets from notions of traditional parental involvement to radical ideas of family and community engagement, with particular attention to the experiences of minoritized and marginalized families and communities. We explore the role of communication with parents and families and also with and among students and teachers, especially across power differentials. The Maryam Sahil and Alondra Correa simulations fit nicely at this juncture, giving teacher candidates experience trying to communicate with a multilingual parent who did not experience a US-based K–12 education. This moves them to approach this typical school event with a new gaze and with ways of interacting that break down rather than replicate the power imbalances that still structure these meetings.

There are logistical details that determine what kind of encounters are possible: Which instructors are willing and able to incorporate a simulation cycle in their course? What actors are available and willing to participate? When are teacher candidates most likely to remain open to the kind of unsettling these encounters cause? All of these details of a program can shape what is possible. It is not worth anyone's time to craft a detailed encounter that offers a lot for teacher candidates but cannot be supported within the realities of the program.

Crafting the Encounter

A strong encounter has multiple elements but must include a real dilemma, a plausible narrative, culturally specific details, and multiple points of entry. In disciplinary-specific encounters, an additional consideration is the content being integrated and the desired disciplinary learning. In our experience, teacher educators who write simulations enter the process of crafting the simulation at different points. Some have a real dilemma in mind and have to build in the right people and details to give it substance, whereas others have an actual person or storyline that offers what they want teacher candidates to learn. And some see a need for their teacher candidates to engage with a specific community or identity to reframe how they see those people and groups, whereas others want to push candidates on their need for continued learning. But these four elements must be present in scenarios regardless of where a teacher educator starts.

These elements are woven into the teacher interaction protocol, which the teacher candidates receive prior to the interaction to situate them in the live encounter, and the actor interaction protocol, which the actors receive to help them prepare for and consistently enact the role in the live interaction.

Real Dilemma

Simulated encounters are spaces intended to open up teacher candidates to new learning. They are not opportunities to try to find the "right" way to handle a situation or respond to a given scenario. While there are always better and worse ways to handle the encounters, the simulations should not reflect a situation that is easily resolvable for candidates using specific formulas, frameworks, guidelines, or practices. Instead, simulated encounters should frame a real dilemma, one that resists immediate reaction as settled or simple analysis as obviously accurate. Over the course of the SHIFT cycle, candidates must be able to engage and notice different aspects of the context and interaction and then choose how to act in a responsible way. In our simulations, the dilemma becomes ever more complex as teacher candidates progress through their licensure coursework.

When crafting new simulated encounters, it helps to start by thinking of the kinds of moments in teaching that feel unresolvable. They are either too big or too complicated for there to be a simple solution. (This is especially true for SHIFT simulations because they reveal the role systems of oppression that are broadly situated in society, not just schools, and implicated in historic and contemporary social issues.) As such, no one involved will get everything they are looking for, or at least not right away, and what is right or desirable may be at odds with what seems doable or well aligned with how schools tend to operate. In SHIFT simulations, these moments tend to overlap with situations in which there is some kind of cultural gap—between what the teacher candidate sees and knows and what the student or parent does, between what a teacher candidate needs in class and what the student wants, between how a school or coworker operates and the ideals or ideologies of the teacher candidate. These are the kinds of moments that make for good simulations.

Once you know why you want teacher candidates to be pulled up short, you can then identify a dilemma that will provide some of the complicating or contextual factors to help do that. This becomes what the simulation is about: addressing the potential for racial bias in the classroom while trying to earn the trust of a student of color, partnering with a parent who is mistrustful of the US education system but also feels unsafe in saying why, confronting an experienced coworker whose views are deficit oriented while working as a novice teacher. While the additional layers of the simulation add to the broader story, the dilemma is what is at the heart of it.

Admittedly, real dilemmas often end with dissatisfaction. It is unusual for both the actor and the teacher candidate to finish an encounter feeling like anything has been resolved (and if they do it is often because the teacher candidate has failed to recognize an important aspect of the interaction). We make this design choice deliberately, interrupting both the candidate's desire to feel like they have done "well" and their tendency to rely on the satisfaction of the other person to determine success. While a common final line from the teacher candidate is, *Are we good now?* in a bid for resolution, actors are prepared to circumvent any easy ending. The lack of clear resolution is unsurprising in a brief (ten-to-twelve-minute) encounter, but it is also necessary to support candidates' shifting horizons.

Encounters remain "real dilemmas" at least through the group debrief and typically well beyond. While it is important that you give teacher candidates some idea of better things to do in the interaction they experienced, we caution against providing *a* way to do it well or *a* model or expert perspective of what to do. For example, coming out of the Daria Miller simulation, teacher candidates often feel like they learned things like "Get the student's perspective first" or "Respond to the concerns the student brings rather than just making it about what I need." Those are useful things to come away with from the interaction. These learnings make it possible to approach the long-term project of building teacher-student trust, especially in instances of racial mismatch, but do so without providing an exact roadmap of how to handle the situation that might lead candidates astray were they to try to follow in each similar situation without taking necessary detours.

Plausible Narrative

While all simulated encounters require candidates to suspend disbelief in some way, we make a concerted effort to create a plausible narrative. Many people who have written simulations for our program begin with the narrative. The simulation reflects students, stories, or situations they encountered as teachers, students, or parents in schools or as scenarios they have heard about from others. The story stuck with them because it carries important meaning; they were unprepared for it, they felt overwhelmed by it, or they felt like there was no tidy solution. The situation should be typical enough at a broad level that teachers are likely to encounter it again— talking with a student about an outburst, conferencing with a parent about their child's academic abilities, meeting with a coworker to discuss students they have in common—but then with specifics that ground it in a place and time and help it feel real.

We situate each encounter at a specific school in our local (Nashville) school district. We do this for a few reasons. First, it helps us ground the narrative in a way that reflects what candidates might experience when out at placements and practicums. It also provides some of the broader contextual aspects of a scenario that can be important. Is this story happening at a school that is racially or linguistically homogeneous or more diverse? Is this interaction at a neighborhood school or a selective magnet? Has the local community just experienced a big turnover of teachers, violence in the surrounding areas, or other neighborhood changes? This is information, details, that teacher candidates can look up before or after the interaction to make sense of the broader context. Finally, situating the scenario at local schools ensures that we pay attention to the experience of different racial, ethnic, linguistic, religious, and other groups represented in the city's schools.

In this phase of crafting the encounter, you are becoming a fiction writer, developing characters and storylines. The details typically embedded in TIPs include:

- the grade level and course the interaction is set in;
- how far into the school year the encounter occurs (often early on, because the "feel" of an existing relationship with a student is difficult to simulate);
- what the teacher knows about the student, parent, or coworker they will be interacting with and what that relationship looks like thus far;
- important events that led up to the live interaction, including any prior meetings with coworkers and parents that are relevant to the encounter and what transpired and things that happened with students; and
- a more specific description of what led to the moment that starts the live interaction.

The TIP has to provide enough information for candidates so that the situation feels real, even though it clearly is not. For simulations with coworkers and parents, the information provided might be limited to any prior interactions and the general sense of the person they have. For students, this is more detailed and includes things about their personality, how they interact with classmates, what their general disposition is toward the class and content, and particular strengths, interests, and challenges. Anybody the teacher has spent more than a few hours with is written as a full, "round" character with both general impressions and narrow specifics to help minimize the challenge of interacting with someone the teacher candidate is supposed to know, given the context of the simulation, but in reality is meeting for the first time.

When creating a backstory for the encounters, avoid putting teachers in situations where the TIP has interpreted too much for them or where they are responsible for clearly bad choices. If the teacher candidate has made choices that were not ideal in the situation but not clearly wrong, there is usually not a major issue. But if candidates feel like they were set up to fail in the situation, they can become defensive and reject the possibility for learning from the interaction because they think it could have been avoided all together. For example, in the Daria Miller simulation, the TIP says the teacher has tried to address the student's talking using various methods, all of which are modes we recommend to teacher candidates in our courses; and in the narrated event that precedes the live interaction, the teacher has simply said the student's name in calling for "eyes up here." The teacher candidates did not get to make these choices themselves, but they also are not made to feel responsible for moves like yelling at a student or shaming them. Because of this, candidates are more willing to accept that they would likely handle the lead-up to the live interaction in a similar, if not exactly the same, way.

In addition, TIPs are written to lead candidates to the moment an interaction starts without telling them what they should do during the interaction. They must then decide what the objective or goal for the meeting should be in ways that frame the interaction. The Daria Miller simulation says simply that the teacher feels like they do not want to let the weekend go by without talking to the student. It does not, for example, say that the teacher feels bad about how class ended or note explicitly that the student's response was out of character. This is left to the teacher candidate to infer, as it is an important moment of judgment and noticing we are trying to develop through the simulation.

Specific details go into the AIP as well, including:

- how the actor's character feels about the teacher (candidate) and what has transpired between them prior to the encounter, often with additional information about why;
- things the actor's character must say or might say based on what the teacher candidate does in the interaction;
- a sense of the character's disposition and body language in response to the teacher (candidate); and
- general information about the actor's character, including where they live and spend their time, who their friends or communities are, where they get help or information from, or relevant personal histories.

We generally provide far more details in the AIP than ever come out in the interaction. This extra background provides material for the actor to draw on that makes it more real in the live interaction. It also gives the teacher educator additional information to draw on in the group debrief to help further complicate or contextualize what the teacher candidates did find and let candidates see what they did not learn from the actor. But more important, the thick description of the character gives the actors a sense of how to move or respond, especially in reaction to unexpected things the teacher candidate says or does. Because the list of if-then responses in the AIP are necessarily constrained to what is likely to happen or what the teacher educator can predict, the list is not exhaustive, and actors have to respond to at least some things that are unexpected. Having a picture or vision of the character helps them react in that situation in ways that are consistent with the rest of the protocol.

Culturally Specific Details

Unlike other simulations used in teacher education, SHIFT simulations are very specific about the cultural background of the student, parent, or coworker in the interaction. The level of specificity depends on the goals of the interaction. In almost all of our scenarios, we note the age, race, and gender of the role being portrayed. In some early scenarios, that race and gender varied more because of actor availability, but when we did vary the portrayal across rooms based on need, we then addressed it in the group debrief—How did the interactions vary, based on the portrayal? And how would that aspect of who the student or parent is potentially shape the interaction in the future? When we need to specify a language, we try to attend to language variation. Maryam Sahil, for example, does not just speak Arabic but Mesopotamian Arabic. Her character is Kurdish because of the large Kurdish population in our city and school system. In short, if we are trying to convince our teacher candidates through the interaction that these aspects of who people are matter, then it is important that we specify it in the materials for the interaction and make it meaningful.

In SHIFT simulations, we often engage stereotypes, but always with the goal of complicating them. Daria Miller is an enactment of the "loud Black girl" stereotype whom some may describe as "playing the race card" in the interaction. Maryam Sahil is a Kurdish immigrant mother who does not understand the US education system and is exceedingly deferential to the teacher. Phil Duncan is a culturally insensitive older white man who is also seen by many teacher candidates as "nice." All of these descriptions reflect a level of stereotype that is widely present in the US. The key is that none of the stereotypes is left untouched in what comes after the encounter. The readings students complete after the Daria Miller simulation, for instance, dismantle the stereotype as subjective based on racial bias, and the planned debrief reframes Daria's disclosure as a courageous act that positions her as a "canary in the coal mine," as someone who is able to help us recognize dangers to all of us, but some disproportionately so.[1] Learning that follows the Maryam Sahil interaction repositions her as highly knowledgeable and valuable to her child's learning and raises the question of whether her deference, which is often seen as desirable by the teacher candidates, will work against a real partnership with the teacher if it hides the parent's hesitation about steps being taken. Phil Duncan interaction debriefs are complicated and find candidates trying to tease apart the substance of his comments from their framing and consider the benefit of understanding how he views students in the classroom. While negative learning is always possible, the rereading questions, assigned readings, and group debrief have the potential to not just debunk these stereotypes but also make it possible for teacher candidates to better understand why they might hold the stereotype in the first place and how to mitigate the effects of those viewpoints.

Simulated encounters work well when they are culturally specific. Their value lies in the dilemmas at their core and the thinking that gets expanded as a result of engaging with the dilemma. But the authenticity comes from the narrative and culturally specific details. Without the narrative built out in thoughtful ways, and absent culturally specific details that situate in actual communities, the simulated encounter will feel constraining, with nowhere for teacher candidates or actors to move. We do not have any continuously running scenarios at this point in the program that we could run with the same materials for a culturally different character. Maryam Sahil, for example, has been reimagined as a Puerto Rican mom, once for a licensure program in Connecticut and then again for our program. Liz also made further revisions when we moved the Alondra Correa story from Connecticut to Nashville. The level of cultural and local detail in any story line should require that kind of revision if resituated.

Multiple Points of Entry

A strong simulated encounter provides teacher candidates with multiple points of entry in ways that recognize their various starting points and positionalities. Because SHIFT simulations deal with teacher candidates' mind-sets, ideologies, and self-awareness, it is likely that there will be variability in what they can see and respond to. All simulation designs tend to bet on things that teachers will or won't know or do in a simulation, but the scenario cannot be limited to just one starting point. There has to be something to disrupt for teachers who are entering the scenario past that point. And, in fact, scenarios with staying power, those that have run repeatedly in the program, remain important because they seem to provide points of tension and real dilemmas for *all* candidates. In the early years with Maryam Sahil, many of our teacher candidates instructed Maryam to speak English at home with her son as a solution to his struggle with reading at school. This was a predictable starting point for our monolingual English-speaking teachers but also a low bar in terms of the thinking we wanted to push through the interaction. As the semesters went by, we preemptively taught teacher candidates about the dangers in such advice, which meant that few made this move and instead were able to pay attention to more complex aspects of the interaction, including what tangible suggestions the teacher could potentially make to Maryam, given her lack of confidence in her English.

One way to think about the multiple points of entry is to consider how much information is held back. All teacher candidates enter the interaction with the same information about the scenario, as provided on the TIP, but they leave the simulation with different levels of information based on what they said and did in the encounter. In the Daria Miller encounter, all teacher candidates hear the disclosure in which Daria says she feels singled out in class as one of the few Black students. But teacher candidates only learn about the lunchroom incident that happened right before class or the early incident of tokenizing if they ask and try to better understand why Daria feels the way she does. The information not only serves to help teacher candidates see the importance of engaging the student's viewpoint but, for some, functions as a distraction; some teachers are unwilling to consider the possibility that they have racially targeted Daria but are prepared to assume their colleagues have. All of this opens up the possibility for learning after the interaction.

Moreover, while we do not vary the disclosure based on anything about the teacher candidates, we do vary the way the actors respond to them. Early rounds of the Daria Miller simulation told us that Black teacher candidates felt like the simulation was not "for them" based on how it ran. After talking with some of those candidates as well as the actors, we established that Black teachers may very well target Black students but that the ways they engage to reestablish trust may look different. When a Black teacher says to a Black student that they understand how they feel or hold them to a higher standard, the message sent is different than when a non-Black, and especially a white, teacher does. And varying this response helped focus the intended learning from the scenario: all teachers have racial biases they must attend to in the classroom because of systems of racism and white supremacy in our society. But the resources we bring to build and repair trust with student varies based on who we and the student are, and this is part of the context we must attend to in how we approach the situation.

Content Integration

Discipline-specific scenarios must also integrate content into the situation, ideally in a way that engages it with the cultural specifics. Simulations used in foundations or diversity courses are written to make them accessible for teacher candidates from any subject area. In one sense, this absence hurts the plausible narrative because, as we teach in our program, strong disciplinary teaching informs every other aspect of class, so behavioral issues and family engagement and coworker conversations all should and must center the content. In foundations or diversity course simulations, we background that element of the interaction and then attend to its importance in the group debrief. In subject-specific courses, however, we intentionally foreground this as a critical part of the interaction.

Our English language arts encounter focuses on a writing conference with a struggling student who has produced some text that includes racist and essentialized perspectives on Hispanic people. Our math encounter includes a visual that is often used to launch a unit on the quadratic equation and takes up seriously the issue of gender inequities in STEM classrooms. Our science encounter deals with unitary concepts in science and then layers on religious issues that often come up in our local schools related to intelligent design, similar to the social studies simulation that raises concerns about religious objections to civil rights for LGBTQIA+ people. All of these scenarios could run with just the focus on the content or the critical issues, but the intentional blending of the two helps teacher candidates see how they usually exist together in ways that require attending to both parts. This process always requires working with disciplinary faculty in the department where the simulations will usually run to make sure the scenario reflects the conceptions of the discipline and short- and long-term goals of the interaction, asking them how they could respond to the situation through content in class after the interaction is over In general, though, the content focus of the simulations adds depth and authenticity to the interactions and is only left out of some scenarios used in classes that include candidates from a range of licensure paths.

Shaping the Encounter

Once an encounter exists in some form, whether as an idea or a set of notes or an early draft of the TIP and/or AIP, you need other people to help you shape the encounter, both in terms of the plausible narrative and the culturally specific details. If you are not and have never been a teacher, you will need to work closely with someone who has to make sure the TIP provides enough information for teacher candidates to feel like they can actually attempt to engage in the interaction. That said, what candidates require is often a lot less than what actual teachers would have in a real-life version of the encounter.

More importantly, if you are not a member of the community you are representing in the AIP, or you do not carry the identities of the character you are building, this is the time to engage people who are. In some instances, the dilemma and narrative can come from engagement with communities and individuals being represented. The Maryam Sahil simulation, for example, came from an adult ESL student Liz taught in an evening course at a local high school and an outreach coordinator at the organization that hosted the classes. Liz was able to develop the character based on the adult student's personality and interactions with her, building in details learned about immigrant families in the student's community from the adult student, an outreach coordinator, and online and situating the dilemma in response to asset orientations to language acquisition in scholarly literature. None of these things clearly came "first," and both the adult student and the outreach coordinator supported the development of the simulation at several points. Ultimately, it is people inside a community who get to determine whether a stereotype is being reinforced or disrupted and what kind of situations most commonly occur that are suitable for simulating. More feedback around this often comes from the actors if they reflect cultural specifics of the role being played.

This step in shaping the encounter is when you should pay attention to negative learnings. Even if you are a member of the community you are reflecting in your character and storyline, you want a breadth of perspective on what a teacher candidate may inadvertently take away from the encounter that is not the intended learning. Getting more eyes on what you have planned will help you do that. Share the materials with coworkers, teachers, and more people who are implicated through the storyline. Ask them how they feel about what you have planned in terms of teaching about someone like them, what they want future teachers to learn from the interaction, and what they are most worried about in terms of what could go wrong. This is often a place where the storyline takes a new turn, the dilemma becomes clearer or more nuanced, or the backstory develops further.

While taking in all of the feedback, and as you revise, remember to keep in mind the connections between all the various contextual pieces. Lots of people get excited when they first learn about simulated encounters and have a wealth of ideas about what can happen in them. But there are plenty of things that cannot realistically be done in a live interaction and many that should not be done, and too many different ideas in a single encounter can overly complicate things in a way that distracts from the dilemma and thus diminishes the learning. It is important to take all the feedback and input that people offer, but know that you will have to make the final decision about what is most relevant and useful to the specific interaction, especially anything that community insiders say is essential or forbidden in terms of culturally specific details.

Situating It in the Trajectory

Once a scenario has been developed, the next step is thinking about how it fits into the learning trajectory of your program, if you have not developed the encounter specifically with one in mind. The order of the simulations becomes meaningful to students, even if the teacher educators have not intended them to be so. The encounters are unusual enough to teacher candidates that they see them as moving in the same direction and so try to figure out what that direction is as they move through the series of interactions. While they eventually realize the encounters are not intended to build in a way that lets them intentionally apply learning from one to the next, they are nonetheless engaging in a process of sense-making.

Given our program's coursework, our undergraduate candidates currently start with three scenarios in the required foundations course ordered in a particular way, then complete a disciplinary-specific encounter, and, finally, have one or two in a classroom ecology course. The ordering of the initial three is intentional; the first encounter (Daria Miller) asks the teacher candidate to reckon with their own potential for complicity in replicating structural inequalities in schools and to pay close attention to how they are positioned in these encounters; the second encounter (Alondra Correa) shifts quickly from a situation where the candidate is caught off guard by information to one where they feel knowledgeable about what is going on, doubling-down on the need to go in to these interaction looking for more information; and the third encounter (Phil Duncan) positions the candidate as having little to contribute to the conversation and feeling handcuffed by their status as a new teacher. When candidates come out of the third interaction, they are usually frustrated with Phil Duncan and eager to set him straight, but when nudged in the group debrief they realize his defensiveness in this encounter looks a lot like their own in the first encounter with Daria Miller, bringing the importance of humility, vulnerability, and openness full circle.

Beyond the order of the interactions, teacher educators must consider the story that is told programmatically, with interactions as a part of that. It is important that teacher candidates complete at least some of their encounters before going into practicum placements. The early encounters and coursework enable them to look at the environments they are in with different lenses and push their interactions with students and teachers into a space that positions them as needing to learn rather than being someone to help. Decisions about instructional tasks, assigned readings, and forms of assessment should all take into account what the simulations are contributing to candidates' understanding, because they work together to shape the potential learning.

Revising the Encounter

Over rounds of simulations, it often becomes clear that something needs to be changed in an interaction. The encounter is leaving teacher candidates too comfortable with their assumptions, or they experience too much resolution at the end of the interaction, or the group debrief fails to provide new learning about the interaction. At that point, it can be useful to revise the encounter, rather than write a new one. Remember that simulations are comprised of a set of materials: pre- and rereading questions, the TIP and AIP, and the group debrief.

Changing the Encounter

When we ran our first disciplinary-specific simulated encounter for social studies, we decided to take on the intersection of civil rights for LGBTQIA+ people and conservative religious liberties, which often come into conflict in our local context. In the first iteration, teacher candidates had a single encounter with student Matthew Manning, who was gay but not out in his school and who was concerned about how the class was going to handle the *Obergefell* decision as part of AP Civics and Government. In that first round, teacher candidates overwhelmingly affirmed the student's identity and assured him that a class discussion would be constructed in a way that would allow him to engage while staying "safe." As we looked back, it seemed like nothing had been disrupted. While the teacher educator for the course took pains to point out in group debrief that the candidates could not actually ensure the safety of a student in a class discussion, they clearly had not been pulled up short in a productive way. Hence, in the next iteration the following year, candidates instead interacted with student Alexis Jimenez, or Lexi, who identified as a conservative Christian who felt "convicted" to speak out against gay marriage in an upcoming discussion about *Obergefell* but feared being villainized by her more liberal peers. Again, teachers escaped the potential disruption in this one-on-one encounter by affirming the student's right to their beliefs and committing themselves to a form of student safety in a whole-class discussion that is nearly impossible to provide in complex classroom spaces. The teacher candidates were mostly satisfied with how these encounters went because they seemed to unfold and wrap up smoothly in a manner that belied the messiness that often accompanies these difficult discourses.

As a result, and grounded in a complex view of safe space, we again redesigned the encounter in a final iteration, run in the third year, to include back-to-back interactions with each of these students. Half the teachers met first with Matthew in an interaction that reflected the first version of the encounter with a gay student; the other half of the teachers met first with Lexi in an interaction that reflected the second version of the encounter with a conservative Christian student. Immediately after their first encounter concluded, teachers switched rooms and met with the other student. This version has consistently produced a clear moment of being pulled up short. While the interactions in the first student meeting look similar to the early years of the interaction, those in the second room look rather different, and teacher candidates tend to leave the end of the paired interactions feeling highly dissatisfied with how they handled them. They recognize quickly in the second encounter that they have made promises to a student they cannot keep or that providing the same kind of space for both voices to be heard will necessarily affect the other's sense of safety. Most notably, the raw debriefs following the paired effort became significantly longer, not just because the teacher candidates had more to talk about but because they were genuinely dissatisfied with how they could have handled the pair of interactions in a way that felt productive. This then moved into the classroom for the group debrief, where teacher candidates sought dedicated time to better understand what they could have done with each student. They struggled to manage their (and the students') expectations for safety in a classroom discussion and wanted to explore what structures in a social studies classroom might lend themselves to the kind of difficult discourse that offers learning for both students. In the end, we changed almost nothing about the TIP and AIP themselves. It was simply pairing the interactions that made the difference.

Changing the Group Debrief

Sometimes it is not the interactions that need to be rethought but the group debrief. In our very first year of running simulated encounters, we used the Phil Duncan simulation as the final of the three encounters candidates saw in the social foundations course. While the candidates found the interaction frustrating, they did not question any of their own deeply held beliefs or even nuance their stance coming out of the group debrief. They quickly wrote Phil Duncan off as an old racist white man whom they should steer clear of, which was definitely not the learning we hoped to support. The teacher candidates saw it as an issue of right and wrong, adhering to the good/bad binary that DiAngelo and others point to as a tenet of white fragility: Mr. Duncan was bad; they were not like Mr. Duncan, so therefore they were good.[2]

At that point, we abandoned the interaction for one or two semesters while we tried others in its place. Nothing seemed to fill the void, however, and we eventually returned to it. While the early iteration of the group debrief seemed to focus on having the "right" ideas and beliefs, the second iteration moved toward a focus on whether Phil Duncan was a "nice" man. Part of this was informed by the fact that teacher candidates were encountering him in the wake of the 2016 presidential election. They wanted to acknowledge him as a "nice" man because, for many of them, it meant that he was redeemable in his views and therefore someone they could work to change. This, again, reinforced the good/bad binary: if Mr. Duncan were nice, then he could not be bad and so would be able to learn from the teacher candidates, who were nice *and* right with their beliefs and perspectives on students. This, likewise, reinforced learnings we were trying to disrupt.

It has only been in the more recent iterations of this encounter that we have come to a group debrief that feels productive in terms of our disrupting work. It would be easy to use Phil Duncan only to prepare teacher candidates to confront whom they perceive to be racist, classist, sexist, and homophobic colleagues in their building. It would be useful, to a degree, to give them a chance to practice speaking up in these moments in ways that position them as allies and activists. But it would miss the underlying point that all of us, at points in our lives, will be some version of Phil Duncan—unwilling to question the way we see schools and students in a way that makes us a danger to others. The current group debrief for this encounter focuses on recognizing what Audre Lorde calls "the piece of the oppressor in all of us" and on getting teacher candidates to recognize the need for them to stay vulnerable and accountable for their own biases, to consider how they are different from Phil Duncan if they will not stand up to his comments in some form, and to grapple with the need for persistent action in the face of ongoing injustice.[3] This iteration seems to disrupt teacher candidates' perceptions of not only Mr. Duncan but also themselves. And it pushes them to leave the course (which ends soon after this final interaction) wide open to the kind of learning that our program provides in the subsequent coursework.

Keeping or Losing the Encounter over Time

As teacher educators, you regularly make decisions about what is worth valuable instructional time in a course or program. In some cases, it may feel like a scenario is simply not disrupting anything for the teacher candidates; it may even cause them to double down on previously held beliefs without any additional nuance, or they are so defensive in response to the interaction that new learning cannot happen. While you can attempt to revise or rewrite the interaction, there are certainly instances where you have to recognize that a particular scenario doesn't do the work it was intended to do. There are a handful of scenarios we have written that we no longer use, in some cases because of practical reasons (e.g., the course instructor changed and brought in a new vision for the course), but others because we recognized that the elements were simply not present.

From a practical standpoint, writing new simulations takes a lot of time and effort that, if done well, reaps significant benefits for teacher candidates. Whether you author your own scenarios, adapt ours, or redesign case materials to serve as TIPs and AIPs, remember that it is important to give yourself plenty of time and mental space to develop the core simulations in your program.[4] Only then can you be sure they have a real dilemma, tell a story, provide plenty of entry points, and engage the teacher candidates deeply in context and culturally specific details relevant to learning in your program.

Chapter 7

Caring for Actors

The larger ethical and pedagogical principles that guide the SHIFT Project are also enacted in how we work with and care for actors in the simulated encounters. Specifically, we try to work with actors in a way that honors the emotional and psychological labor they offer in service of teacher candidates' learning and makes it a learning experience for them as well.

Actors are important to simulated encounters. They enact the roles of students, parents, and coworkers, bringing the characters in the scenarios to life. They also offer feedback on the written scenarios, help think through what might happen so that they and we can plan responses, and provide feedback after the encounters on what teacher candidates did well and what they would suggest are places for further improvement. How and when this kind of input is elicited and used depends on the relationship of the actors to their roles, but all actors bring with them a perspective that can expand the potential of a given scenario and extend its life and impact within your program.

Finding Actors

Finding actors is the biggest time cost in running simulated encounters. It is work that takes both time and effort, especially if you need actors who fit a particular demographic. In addition to finding actors, it is vital to care for the actors throughout the simulation cycle, and this, too, requires time and attention. Despite the time and care needed, we find that working with actors is one of the most rewarding parts of the encounters, and finding new ways to incorporate their perspectives and voices can significantly enhance teacher candidates' learning.

You will typically need multiple actors for the same encounter. In our program, for a class of twenty-four candidates we schedule at least two actors and run simultaneous encounters in separate rooms over a three-hour period. If you have larger numbers in your classes, you will need to plan for more actors. While there are both affordances and constraints with having more than one actor interacting with the same group of candidates, we are confident that, on balance, you can preserve the essence of the SHIFT encounter as long as actors are well prepared.

There are many places to turn to when looking for adult actors to play the roles of parents or coworkers, including local theater groups, online sites that post calls for actors, nearby medical schools that employ actors as standardized patients, and even parent organizations in local schools or community organizations or professional and graduate students on university campuses. Adult actors can also work with you year after year; their aging does not usually affect the way they are read in the scenario as much as it does with youth actors. Finding actors through schools and community organizations also offers the possibility of strengthening relationships with groups that can provide additional actors as time passes and give input on the scenarios themselves. For example, when writing the Maryam Sahil simulation, we connected with the Nashville International Center for Empowerment (NICE), a community organization that serves area refugees and immigrants, and where Liz had volunteered as an ESL teacher. Staff members were able to share situations recent immigrants in Nashville were facing in school settings and provide context about the experiences of Kurdish women immigrants specifically. While working with individuals who share the experiences of the roles you are creating is vital, community organizations that include and serve such individuals often have a broader perspective and are able to pinpoint the most common issues for particular groups or in specific communities.

When looking for youth actors, or actors to play the role of adolescents, additional ethical concerns arise. It is important to carefully consider what is worth simulating and how to get teacher candidates addressing issues without doing harm to young people who are still dealing with harm inflicted in and by schools. We have found actors for our youth roles in a variety of ways: recruiting among the undergraduates on campus, reaching out to theater teachers at local high schools, and connecting with theater groups that include youth, especially those with ties to social justice work (e.g., Planned Parenthood's peer educators, the PG-13 Players).

For scenarios featuring secondary education students, it is easy to locate actors who are old enough to legally consent and be paid for their work while still passing for high school students. This is more problematic, however, if you are targeting younger actors to portray elementary students. We are just beginning to use younger actors in SHIFT simulations as we expand the project to our elementary education programs. Based on limited experience and guided by the principles for the care of actors articulated here, we have three important observations with regard to working with younger actors.

- No child under the age of eight should be used as a SHIFT simulation actor. Because actors must understand the point of the simulation, and because the critical incidents at the core of each encounter deal with systems of oppression, we are unwilling to ask younger children, even experienced actors, to try to manage this complexity. As with actors portraying adolescents (often college-age students acting as high schoolers), we have used children that were actually older than the scenario called for. For instance, we had fifth and sixth graders enacting roles for third and fourth graders.[1]
- The nature of scenarios for which we can employ young people as actors is limited by both younger children's capacity for understanding forms of oppression and by the potential for psychic harm. We think it generally inappropriate, for example, to instantiate versions of racism with young children. One simulation that did work well with young actors, and that challenged elementary teacher candidates to be aware of power dynamics in the classroom, involved gender dynamics in group work in which boys (stereotypically) wanted to "go fast" to complete a task while the girls tended to seek understanding through the process and "go slow."
- We only employ (older) children as actors in scenarios when we believe their participation will have positive benefits for them. In the gender-focused simulation example, the boys and the girls

recognized themselves in the scenario. Two of the boy actors acknowledged that "this guy [the character they were portraying] is a jerk" and that "I do that sometimes." The girl actors wanted to talk about how they might respond to boys who tend to want to run the show and even engage in bullying to get their way. Overall, it is important to protect all actors from harm and to construct the experience in ways that maximize benefits for them. When in doubt, don't use any actor in a simulation that doesn't promise to be a positive learning experience for them.

Whenever we use actors who are playing the role of a minoritized youth, we try to work with people who are not in the K–12 setting. While undergraduates are by no means exempt from the kinds of harm done in K–12 (and much could be done with simulated encounters to better prepare university educators around these issues), some distance from the situations we are simulating is desirable for the actors.

In working recently to develop a scenario focused on the experiences of trans students in classrooms, we connected with a graduate from our program who runs the Gay-Straight Alliance (GSA) at her school. She then talked with the students in the GSA about their realities to help us think about situations that could be replicated in a simulated encounter to educate teacher candidates around the needs of LGBTQIA+ students broadly and trans students specifically. However, we quickly agreed that while there was real merit in developing ideas presented by the students, and possibly connecting with the GSA through a student panel, it would be too risky to invite trans students from the school to serve as simulation actors. Because many of these teenaged students faced daily social, emotional, and physical threats at school and sometimes at home, we felt that having students relive those moments in the scenarios, even if they chose to do so, was too risky for all involved. Instead, we used the situations raised by the GSA to think about how we could engage teacher candidates in responding to such issues in a different arena, such as in an interaction with an unsupportive parent or a transphobic coworker. Because some risk for harm is involved in all of our scenarios, though, it is vital that actors are clear on the role they are being asked to play and what will likely happen during their interaction with teacher candidates—which is where the call for actors and their training come in.

Writing a Call for Actors

Writing a call for actors is necessary if you plan to cast a wide net when recruiting, as opposed to developing scenarios around actors who are already available. The wording of the call is important for both you and the actors: you want to end up with actors who can reasonably portray the role you have prepared, but you want to avoid asking actors to disclose private personal information.

A clearly worded call for actors will help ensure you get actors who can fill the role you have prepared and be the "person" teacher candidates are expecting to meet. This requires you to decide what the nonnegotiables are for the scenario and what aspects can vary without distracting from the focus of the interaction. You also want to keep things as consistent as possible across encounter rooms if you're running several simultaneously, as we typically do, so that students feel like they can reasonably share their experiences with each other. For example, several of our roles require the person to be fully fluent in Spanish or Arabic. In these instances, the scenarios focus on what it looks like to work with parents who have immigrated to the US and who might be disadvantaged in a conversation with teachers because of their lack of knowledge of the US school system or due to any discomfort in speaking idiomatic English. In these scenarios, we state clearly that "actors must be fluent Spanish speakers for this role." The actor's fluency becomes important when teacher candidates attempt to communicate with them, whether trying out the few words they know or actually engaging entirely in another language during the interaction. We want to encourage teacher candidates to use the resources they have to navigate the situation and to draw on the resources of the actor to know the kinds of language issues that are difficult for a recent English speaker in the course of conversation.

For interested actors, it is helpful to know the role they are being asked to play. It is important that actors share some perspective with the "character" they are playing, and, depending on the focus of scenario, that means making clear what those shared identities are. When we run the Maryam Sahil simulation, we specify the need for Arabic-speaking actors, but we make clear that the role is for a Kurdish refugee mother. In the past, this role has been played by women who identify with Maryam in a variety of ways, but never all of them. Many of our actors have been immigrants but not refugees. Some are the children of immigrants but were born in the US. None have been Kurdish, and one woman was a Coptic Christian, not

Muslim, as the role is written. In all of these situations, we have talked with the actors and asked them to reflect on how they see themselves in Maryam and how they are different, but we leave it to them to determine what differences they are comfortable portraying and those aspects of the role that they would not feel comfortable stepping into. We also want actors to know when they might have to play a role that does not reflect their personal values and, in fact, may run counter to them. For instance, when we call for actors to play the role of Alexis Jimenez, an evangelical Christian concerned about discussions of gay marriage in her social studies class, we are clear that the role requires actors to argue in opposition to gay marriage and civil rights for LGBTQIA+ individuals. In the past, we have had actors who identified as part of this community play this role, but they came to training aware that this was part of what they would be asked to do. One actor noted that she felt some catharsis in playing the role because she had family members who had directed these same objections at her, and so she could both voice them in a way that she heard them and prepare teachers to respond in a way that made the classroom safer for students like her.

After trying a variety of phrasings, we now call for actors to "play the role of" and then provide a description of that role. For example, with Daria Miller we state that we are looking for someone "to play the role of a Black, tenth-grade girl." This clarifies that the actor needs to look young enough to be read as a tenth grader and should also be someone who is read as a girl who is Black. The actors who have played the role of Daria self-identified in a range of ways—including nonbinary actors comfortable presenting themselves as a girl for the purposes of the scenario and actors who racially identify as African American, Caribbean, of specific African descent (e.g., Nigerian), or bi- or multiracial. In this way, we are careful to let the actors choose what they are comfortable being, for the purposes of the scenario, while making clear what it is we need. As an example, for the Daria Miller role we would not use actors of color from other racial backgrounds because the scenario focuses specifically on anti-Blackness in schools.

Actor Training

Once one or more actors have been recruited for a specific scenario, the next step is actor training, which ideally happens between three and five days before the simulated encounter will run. Whenever possible, actor training should occur with all actors at the same time. This is not just a time-saving measure; it also allows actors to learn from each other in the process of training and gives you a chance to learn from the collective insights of the group.

First and foremost, actors come to training to learn what simulated encounters are and why your program is using them. Understanding how your program uses this tool and to what end will help them determine how to interpret the character and scenario you are providing them. In our case, we talk to actors about the need for teacher candidates to experience very common moments in teaching. A thick backstory not only helps the scenario come alive, but it reveals and makes salient the role of systems of oppression in US schools. In this initial conversation with actors, we make clear the importance of teacher candidates responding to new information, dealing with uncertainty, trying to make sense of short- and long-term goals of the interaction, and feeling potentially uncomfortable and unsure of themselves. Actors often tell us that they want to "help" a teacher candidate struggling during the encounter, so we stress up front that actors should not attempt to do this. We make clear that instructors will do this work to help candidates make sense of their interaction in ways that lead to learning and that their goal as an actor is to make sure there is tension in the scenario and no neat endings. In fact, we practice language for the end of the encounter to make sure actors have available phrases that are not too neat or predictable. We often tell actors that even if the scenario has gone really well, they should use phrases like "I guess so" that are neither confrontational nor confirmational so that teacher candidates feel like they are done but do not necessarily feel like it ended on a high note. In short, your first job in actor training is to help actors figure out what their job is for the purposes of your encounter.

Next, actors come to training to learn the specifics of the scenario. When actors leave the training, you want them to know several key things:

- what you want teacher candidates to get from the interaction and what it is you hope they will learn from this;
- how the scenario is supposed to start and whether the actors or the teacher leads during the scenario;
- which triggers or disclosures (one or more in each critical incident) are "must-dos" that should appear in every encounter, regardless of the teacher candidate, and when and how those should be delivered;

- likely responses from the teacher candidates and how to respond;
- a general sense of the character to help them manage unexpected responses from teacher candidates; and
- how to end the scenario.

Just as it is important for actors to know why you are using simulated encounters in your program, it is helpful to them to know how this specific scenario fits into what teachers are learning. This knowledge is especially important when you are asking actors to be "learned on." In these situations, actors are often hearing teacher candidates say things to them that they have heard from teachers at difficult moments in their own lives or that they hear from other people in society. For example, when Daria Miller actors hear teacher candidates say things like "It's not because you're Black," they are potentially reliving moments when they tried to engage their own teachers around race or recalling a comment someone made to them earlier in the day out in the unsimulated world. Actors tend to feel more prepared to manage these situations, and in ways that are consistent with the character, when they know how we are using the encounters. Knowing this information does not eradicate the potential harm from the situation, but it gives purpose to the interaction in a way that reshapes what the interaction is in terms of a moment of Deweyan immaturity that is necessary for growth. (This reconceptualizing of the interaction is considerably strengthened when actors also provide feedback or participate in the whole-class debrief.)

Once actors know what the encounter is for, the focus moves to their expected actions and reactions. In general, after actors read the TIP, which we send them before training, we talk them through the encounter, starting with how the interaction opens—whether they speak as soon as the teacher comes in or wait for a pause, whether they reveal a lot of information right away or withhold it until the teacher prods them.

We then turn to verbal triggers, especially the must-dos. We never require actors to deliver lines exactly as we've written them, but we do note the reason for what we've written and emphasize what elements needs to be present in whatever they say at that moment. In the Daria Miller simulation, there is a moment in which the actor shares their perception of what happened in class. In the TIP it reads: "I know I was talking when I wasn't supposed to be, and I'm sorry for that, but so were other kids and you don't call them out like you did me. And it just seems I'm always being the one getting called out 'cause I'm one of the only Black kids in the room." This disclosure has three key parts, each of which serves a function. First, Daria admits she was talking when she was not supposed to and apologizes. Daria knows she is a talkative student, she recognizes she should have gotten quiet, and she is sorry for that. She is not mad at the teacher for pointing this out. Second, she feels like she is being singled out and that it happens often. She notes that other students were talking and says she is "always" the one getting called out. And third, she feels that the main issue is racial bias. She also says she's "one of the only" Black kids rather than "the only." This is an important piece of information because the teacher candidates do not know the racial composition of the class, just that of the school and that this is an honors class (in which students of color, especially Black students, are often underrepresented). This is a key part of the Daria Miller encounter that every teacher needs to hear. It is a moment when they must reckon with the realization that the student has experienced this moment in class very differently than they did and then figure out what to do with that information—acknowledge it, probe further into it, or deny and disregard it.

From this opening required verbal trigger, we then walk actors through the rest of the scenario, noting when and how additional information should be made available. This often sounds like a decision tree: if the teacher candidate says or does this, then you say or do that. The recommended responses to teacher candidates include both words and tone as well as body language. To prevent actors from trying to help teacher candidates, we make clear when they should reveal information and how much they should share in one conversational "turn." A lot of this is connected to the general sense of the character, what they would say or do in a given situation, how they would react, and when they would resign themselves to not being heard. Daria Miller, for example, never gets overtly angry. She never yells or really even raises her voice, which is intentional. While we are embodying the stereotype of the "loud Black woman" in this scenario, we only do it in an attempt to undermine it. Daria is angry, and she might be someone we hear above others in the classroom, but with the teacher she is calm and does not want to get into more trouble. Our actors, who may themselves have experienced such a moment, need to know why we do not let this character get angry in the moment as we try to avoid reifying the stereotype.

As part of this process of revealing the character, and in practicing the interaction at the end of training, we also model for actors "good," "likely," and "bad" versions by playing the part of the teacher candidate. We often start the practice rounds with a "likely" version, what we think we will see from most of our teacher candidates, including the strengths we have come to see in the group along with the missteps and mistakes we think they will make that are part of their learning trajectories. This process of enactment lets the actors see what it feels like to be in character and to practice the verbal triggers and responses. After each practice round we debrief with all of the actors to reinforce any uncertain aspects of their performance. Next, we usually give them a "good" round, what we think a really strong teacher candidate might do. This step is important because it ensures that all teacher candidates will feel pushed in the encounter in ways that allow this to be a learning experience, not an assessment. Finally, a "bad" round often involves the trainer talking a lot without providing a chance for the actor to speak or includes more provocative responses (but that are still in the realm of possibility) that may push an actor off-script, especially in terms of laughter. This helps actors figure out what to do if a teacher candidate struggles or pushes them in ways that feel uncomfortable. The practice rounds also give us a chance to talk about how to close the encounter without ending it too neatly in ways that are unlikely to happen in a tense situation such as this.

When actors leave the training, it is our hope that they have a general sense of how to "play" the encounter from start to finish and respond to what they are most likely to see. They are then asked (and paid) to spend at least one hour at home reviewing the written protocol and practicing their lines out loud so they can feel comfortable saying them in the encounter.

During actor training, you may also need to adapt the scenario to best fit the needs of the actors you recruited. In this way, the encounter also learns from the actors. This process engages the perspectives and realities of the actors, insofar as they align with the identities being portrayed in the scenario, and ensures their co-collaboration in the design of the encounter. For example, several years ago, when working with some Muslim actors on Vanderbilt's campus, we had one woman actor who, for cultural and religious reasons, did not shake hands with men. We had not encountered this before with our other actors in this role, and it is a cultural norm that varies among Muslim women. The TIP at that time included a note on how to shake hands with teacher candidates if proffered, in line with what we had learned about greetings among Kurdish adults. However, it was an easy switch for us to simply write in that Maryam Sahil does not shake hands with men and make that consistent across the actors. This then opened up an opportunity in whole-class debrief to discuss whether to consistently assume someone will not shake hands with them and what to do if someone declines in the way Maryam does. Another semester, the actors we recruited for Maryam were not Muslim but were Arabic speaking. As such, none of the women covered their heads, something we had always done for Maryam's role. As a result, that semester we removed this from the protocol and then engaged in a conversation in the whole-class debrief about variations in cultural practices among Muslim women. None of these adaptations substantially changes the scenario, and, in implementation, many of them create openings for increased cultural awareness among teacher candidates and questions about how to navigate an unexpected situation.

In many instances, actors are also learning from the scenario. This is true in situations where actors identify closely with the character they are portraying and where there is significant difference. In the Alexis Ramirez/ Matthew Manning scenario, we often recruit queer-identifying actors for either role, in particular gay, lesbian, and bisexual actors. During actor training, we frequently hear from actors how a teacher should handle Lexi's comments, which express moral disapproval of LGBTQIA+ identities and relationships and call their civil rights into question. The actors often find themselves facing similar comments in their everyday interactions or have heard them in the classroom, and they want to know what their teachers could have done or what they might be able to do moving forward. This is especially so if it is not an issue they have yet resolved for themselves.

In situations where the actor aligns with the role in identity but not perspective, a different form of learning is happening. For example, in the math literacies simulation, Matthew Sloan is a white student arguing with a Latina classmate about a math task. When we run this encounter, we find ourselves explaining to actors why the interaction between Matthew and Luciana plays out as it does and how forms of masculinity and whiteness replicate themselves in the classroom, especially in STEM fields. Other times the questions that arise during actor training are just general learning related to the actors' own positionality in the world. At a recent training, one man, an older, white, cisgendered actor, heard us narrate how some previous queer teacher candidates had experienced the scenario in an attempt to explain how teacher candidates may either be triggered by the scenario or see it as an empowering experience, or both. The actor finally inquired about the use of the term *queer*, which led to a conversation about the term's use historically and currently within the LGBTQIA+ community and in academia especially.

Finally, actors very commonly help each other make sense of the scenario and give a broader response as a group to what is planned. After a few semesters using the Daria Miller simulation, it became clear that we had not designed the scenario well enough to attend to the racial positioning of Black teachers, especially Black women, in the interaction. That semester we consulted with the group of actors to get a sense from them how they might respond differently to a Black teacher candidate, someone who racially matched the character being portrayed. Based on their feedback and that of subsequent rounds of actors, we kept the protocol in place but changed the way actors respond to teachers based on their racial positioning—as a teacher of color and then as Black teachers, with even more specifics for Black women. By working with the actors as a group and having them confer with each other before giving us feedback, we avoided relying on just one person's perspective on the situation and instead got a sense of what a (still small) group of actors thought about the situation. Moreover, when returning actors are present at training, the goal is to let them do as much of the talking as possible, prompting them with questions about what they saw, heard, did, and felt during the interaction. Because our actor pool changes each semester, especially for youth roles, we do not have the chance to reemploy the same individuals as trainers, but, depending on your situation, this might be a possibility. It would give as much control as possible to those playing the role, and who ideally identify with the role in some way, and also reduce the time and energy required of instructors to make this work possible.

While we strive for in-person training as much as possible, there are situations that require us to find alternative means for training. If we have recruited actors late and cannot find a time that works, we send the materials, some notes, and sample videos to actors to review and then meet before the encounter starts to review it together. Doing a synchronous online training is another possibility. And it may be possible to provide actors with annotated videos that pause to point out important points in the interactions, the must-dos, and moments where the actors can bring in their own interpretation. Regardless of the mode of training, the goal is to ensure that the actors have a general sense of the character they are portraying to help them handle unexpected turns and that they know what triggers should show up in every scenario, what they will likely see from teacher candidates and how to respond to them, and where they can use their own discretion to decide how to proceed. We have especially relied on sample videos and additional notes when retraining actors who have worked with us before. This reminds them of key aspects of the scenario without requiring them to come to campus for a short training. In these situations we usually also make notes on their prior encounters to help them see where they need to strengthen the portrayal, dial back certain aspects of the character, or respond more directly to things the teacher candidate is saying.

During the Encounters

When actors are engaging in the simulations, it is important to continue to attend to their experience as well as that of the teacher candidates. In general, we try to touch base with our actors briefly between encounters, as time allows, and to regroup at the end. Our goals in doing this are multifold: to make sure the actors are cared for in the midst of living out tense and sometimes oppressive situations; to get and provide feedback that is consistent with the protocol or that can be added later to ensure that actors are prepared and standardized across rooms around the important issues; and to get a sense of how the teacher candidates are engaging both collectively and individually.

Checking with actors regularly during the encounters is important for your relationship with them and for their relationship to the work. It is good to remember that actors are engaging in draining work. When possible, schedule breaks during long stretches of encounters. Make sure they know where restrooms are and have water available for them. And for scenarios where you know things can get difficult, make sure actors know that they can ask for a break or debrief with the instructor or a simulation coordinator if needed. Much of this work is made easier when the instructor or simulation coordinator can see the encounters as they happen, whether through a one-way window or some technology. Since we have been running encounters in offices and classrooms, project staff has needed to step in and out of the room between each round, which gives them a quick chance to check in with the actor, ask how things are going, let actors ask questions. This opportunity to interface outside of the role also serves as a humanizing moment, and the interactions continue the co-collaboration role established during actors' training.

Even when actors are feeling good about how the encounters are going, they often have questions or want to share situations that arose during the encounters that they were not sure how to respond to. This is especially important with new scenarios, when you do not know what is likely to occur based on previous rounds. In some instances, actors need to know how to answer questions a teacher candidate has asked and they did not know how to answer, or they make impromptu decisions about how to handle something the teacher has said or done and want to know if they did it correctly, or they notice logistical issues that can be resolved between rounds (e.g., camera placement, teacher candidates who do not know how to leave the room). In one of our early rounds with the Maryam Sahil interaction, we found that many teachers were encouraging the mother to speak more English at home with her son in an effort to help with his language development (something that, as we explained, is neither culturally appropriate nor likely to help with the difficulties this particular student is facing in middle school). Actors were not prepared for how to respond to this recommendation, given that the Maryam lacks confidence in her English abilities. We were then able to plan a response and share that with other actors between rounds and later build it into the protocol for actors. In other instances, when the setup for the encounters does not lend itself to watching them while they happen, actors are the first to note teacher candidates who may need follow-up. This communication is especially important in scenarios where teacher candidates may feel triggered. In one instance, the actor's immediate feedback allowed us to find a candidate before they even left their raw debrief and chat a bit about the scenario in a way that allowed them to both process what had happened and get some encouragement about how they had handled things.

Finally, checking in with actors at the end of encounters allows them to give more general feedback to teacher candidates without singling anyone out. Broad commentary from actors tends to be more useful than getting their thoughts on individual teacher candidates because it provides a chance for candidates to hear the learning being provided rather than looking for an assessment of their performance. More general feedback also avoids replicating what people have come to expect in schools.

One surprising finding in our interaction with actors is that they often have much lower expectations than we do for what a "good" encounter looks like. Especially when working with youth actors or actors playing the role of an adolescent, actors are looking for teachers to replicate things they came to expect in their own secondary schooling. They are more likely to affirm teacher candidates who ask questions or try to see the student's side of things, even if they miss other important aspects of the interaction. One Daria Miller actor noted that a teacher candidate had done a good job in the interaction because she had been "strict" with the student, which runs contrary to what we seek to explore in the interaction. While these actors' feedback can be generally helpful, when it's given to individual teacher candidates it can run the risk of affirming approaches that we seek to complicate or disrupt through the whole-class debrief, thereby potentially closing off the teacher candidate to further reflection and learning.

Yet, while there is potential danger in providing individual feedback to actors, there are times when it can be helpful. Creating individual feedback forms for actors to complete between rounds is most useful when you have run the scenario several times and have a sense of what is important for candidates to hear. The only interaction where we have done the individual forms is with the Daria Miller encounter. Because we heard from a lot of teacher candidates who felt immediately afterward that the encounter had "gone well," we wanted to compare their perspectives with those of the actors, hopefully drawing out the divide where it existed. We also wanted to encourage those who *had* delved into Daria's concerns about racial bias but who may have felt unmoored by that experience and thus were questioning themselves. In short, we wanted the teacher candidates who avoided the issue to recognize how a student might experience that moment, and we wanted candidates who did address the question of racial bias head on to hear how that went for the student.

That said, we are thoughtful with how we use these forms. We always scan and save them to see how actors are perceiving the encounters compared with our own perceptions. In addition, we do not provide the form to the teacher candidate unless they request it at the end of the whole-class debrief. Some teacher candidates need more time to process the learning experience of the encounter. We may pursue more of these feedback forms moving forward, if only to manage our own expectations of candidates' performances compared with what the actors' experiences, but it is an option that may be useful in your program.

Honoring Actor Engagement

To honor actors' involvement in creating these encounters, you will want to formally acknowledge them at the end of the simulation cycle to make sure they are seen, recognized, and appreciated for this significant contribution to teacher candidates' learning. There are several ways to do this, depending on your time and financial resources.

No-Cost, Minimal Time Options

Programs using simulated encounters should, at some point after the encounter, make sure the teacher candidates know who the actors are. One of the things we heard early on from undergraduates who worked with us as actors is that when they encountered teacher candidates on campus, they would sometimes greet them as if they were actually the character. We saw this as a problem and sought a way to allow the actor to step out of their character's role and back into their own personhood. There are two easy ways to make this happen: invite actors to the whole-class debrief and make short introductory videos of the actors, letting them share a bit about themselves and possibly giving general feedback to the class. We highly recommend inviting actors to debrief when they are playing the role of a minoritized individual and identify in some way with that role. For example, we often have Daria Miller actors attend the whole-class debrief because it allows them to speak from their own perspective as well as from what they saw in their role as the student. We found that when actors were given the opportunity to come to the debrief, and especially when they were able to participate, they saw the goals of the encounter and felt better about how forced certain aspects of the encounter are.

If actors do attend the whole-class debrief, we recommend stipulating several things to the teacher candidates: do not ask questions directed at the actors (they can pose a question about how a student might perceive something and permit the actor to respond if they choose); do not ask for specific feedback on their interaction; and do not apologize for the interaction (which is often an effort to restore themselves as a "good person"). In addition, we recommend that the actors speak up whenever they want to share something, knowing the instructor may complicate or add on to what they share, and that they not speak about a specific student in their commentary. Such expectations minimize the defensiveness we seek to reduce through the design of the simulation cycle.

If actors are unable to attend the whole-class debrief, or if there are actors whose personal perspective is not especially pertinent to the learning that you are working toward, we recommend that you make a short video allowing the actors to introduce themselves, who they are and what they do outside of their role as a simulation actor, and to share general feedback with the group. You can then show these at the start or end of the whole-class debrief so that actors are able to distance themselves from the words and perspectives of the role as they wish and re-establish their true identity in relation to the teacher candidates.

Low-Cost, More Time Options

In addition to these simple acknowledgments of an actor's individuality, there are other easy ways to value actors in the process that are neither expensive nor hugely time consuming. One approach that could be easily worked into any program is a highlights video or newsletter that captures teacher candidates' learning across a semester and thanks the actors for their involvement. This would require culling teacher candidates' reflections at the end of simulation cycles, comments from whole-class debriefs, brief interviews, and/or video reflections at the end of the course. Sharing this with all the actors who participated, along with a note from the instructors and/or simulation coordinator, goes a long way toward letting actors see the effect of their labors and even encourages them to continue working with the program if they are able.

A second approach is working with actors who are interested in presenting about the work at local events or academic conferences. Such a collaboration allows actors to be seen as the experts they are and to speak to the realities of what this work looks like. Liz had an opportunity to present at an academic conference together with the original Daria Miller actor, even securing funding for part of the actor's travel to the event. The presentation focused on the codesigned nature of the simulation and guiding principles for collaboration between professors and actors, but actors could easily be engaged around a wide variety of topics. And for actors who are not interested in academic conferences, there is a wide variety of events that could be beneficial spaces to explore. Actors who play the role of parents or coworkers could present at events geared toward school parents and employees to talk about what it looks like to work in anti-oppressive ways or to be subjected to oppression in those spaces, depending on their positionality to the interaction. Finding opportunities for actors to speak to their experiences amplifies them both agency and voice that can otherwise be obviated in the churn of simulation work.

High-Cost, High-Time Options

Whenever possible, simulation actors should be paid for their work. Financial compensation involves different processes across program, so how this works varies, as does what is considered reasonable pay. In our program, we pay actors well above minimum wage ($20/hour) and include two hours of training time along with actual encounter time (usually three hours). Due to Vanderbilt's restrictions, however, we cannot pay actors in cash and instead must pay them with a gift card to a major retailer.[2] We are also limited in whom we can tap, since actors must provide information about their citizenship and residency in the US. This, of course, excludes actors who may be interested in participating but are not legally able to be paid by our project. In addition, expectations by your IRB may come into play. Many medical standardized patient programs have actor pools; this helps with recruitment but requires actors to be formally employed by the institution and hired in ways that restrict the ability to pursue actors who fit a specific demographic description. Once you have a sense of what this process looks like, make sure your actors are aware of how they will be paid and when before they agree to participate in the program.

If your program does not have funds to pay actors outright, consider other forms of remuneration, at least at the start. You may be in a position to offer your actors free admission to on-campus speakers or other cultural events. You may be able to offer them access to library resources or to include them, with other community supporters, in end-of-semester festivities. You might offer your own services in an "in kind" swap with an actor, giving a talk or providing consulting services to an organization to which they belong. When funds are low, you can be creative in emphasizing the learning goals of these collaborations. That said, as your program develops, you should continue to push for institutional support that will allow you to pay actors whenever possible. The work they are doing makes these simulations possible, and the actors deserve to be compensated for that work.

While writing the scenarios is both intellectually and creatively demanding, working with actors, especially a culturally and linguistically diverse group, is a reminder of why we do these simulations. Each time we hear an actor say, "This was me" or "This is just like my little brother" or "I want teachers to know how to handle this better than mine did," we are reminded of the significant work we have to do as teacher educators and for whom we do that work. While we have more work to do to figure out how to best support and sustain our actors through these efforts, we do know how important it is to attend to their experiences along with those of the teacher candidates.

Chapter 8

Learning to Facilitate

You have designed a SHIFT simulation and run the encounter with teacher candidates—but your work is not done. The next step is the vital work of preparing for facilitation, especially the group debrief, where candidates learn the most from each other's experience. If SHIFT simulations become an integral part of a teacher education program, it is inevitable that multiple faculty members will be involved in authoring the protocols, skimming videos of the encounters, reviewing pre- and rereadings, and debriefing the experiences, most likely in a course setting. It is important to ensure that course instructors share an understanding of the process and purpose of the SHIFT cycle.

Here we take up questions of preparation—how to prepare oneself as well as plan for the debrief. We discuss in detail a set of approaches to debriefing that are not exhaustive but do demonstrate how different simulations, and perhaps instructors' different identities and strengths, may call for different approaches to the group debrief. We also address how the facilitator can prepare for the possibility of being confronted before, during, or after the encounter by candidates who are experiencing resistance to uncovering the limits of their own horizons or are otherwise triggered by the experience.

This discussion is based on our own experiences as facilitators of SHIFT simulations as well as on reflections we solicited from nineteen other faculty who have served the project in various ways, but especially as course instructors who debrief simulations located in their courses.[1] This included tenure-track faculty members, practice faculty, lecturers whose focus is teacher education, and doctoral students who took on roles as both teaching assistants and instructors of record, largely in the secondary education program but also in the elementary licensure program. These multiple perceptions have broadened our vision of the joys and difficulties of doing this work. We asked these faculty how they thought about their qualifications to take on the SHIFT simulations, the preparation they did receive and what they might have welcomed or needed, their negotiation of the process with their students and as part of the course, and their contributions to revising both the TIP/AIP and the approach to facilitation and debriefing. We also asked them how they could tell when a simulation was "working." This is not formal research, of course. It might be more accurate to say that we crowd-sourced this chapter to speak with and through voices and from perspectives that all our readers could appreciate. We spoke with five instructors of social foundations courses (in both secondary and elementary programs), three instructors of classroom ecology courses, and eight instructors of secondary subject-specific literacies courses. In addition, we spoke with three faculty teaching subject-specific courses for future elementary teachers. This represents a cross-section of teacher educators with different content foci.

Facilitating a SHIFT simulation is a learned skill, as are all pedagogical moves. There is no question that in teacher education, as in other settings, we learn to teach by teaching. But that can't happen without time for reflection and resources, both colleagues and texts, to bounce experiences and ideas off of. As we have included more faculty in the SHIFT Project, we have worked to support and initiate them while also inviting their focused suggestions for improvement. In general, this has resulted in a better and more meaningful experience for our teacher candidates.

Any discussion of facilitation raises issues of quality control and fidelity. We take these seriously because SHIFT simulations do have a particular purpose and process; however, neither the encounters nor the debriefs are scripted. The guidance we provide here is just that—guidance in the service of an encounter and a debrief that will encourage teacher candidates to recognize the limits of their taken-for-granted horizons and to reconstruct them using the resources of personal experience and peer feedback. We attend to quality control in that we want to forestall mislearnings, unintended and potentially destructive and limiting lessons.

Still, the substance of any particular debrief depends on who is in the class and their reactions as well as on the purpose of the class. It depends, too, on which simulation encounter is being debriefed and on how instructor-candidate relationships have developed during the semester. Above all, the debrief is about disrupting previous ways of thinking to make space for new sense-making that serves anti-oppressive pedagogical purposes.

Throughout the discussion of the questions around preparation, we address instructor and teacher candidate identities and the ways those identities impact, complicate, and enhance the SHIFT cycle's potential.

Question 1: What do I (and my colleagues) need to do to be prepared to administer a SHIFT cycle and, especially, to conduct a debrief that is faithful to the process and purpose of SHIFT simulations?

It is a truism to suggest that you can't teach what you don't know. What, then, is the knowing at the heart of SHIFT simulations?

Each simulation cycle has a substantive focus that engages the content of that particular course (e.g., elements of racism and the privilege of whiteness in a social foundations course, the capacity to conduct difficult social and political conversations in social studies) such that preparation is linked to content in the same way for all teaching. However, the SHIFT simulations demand something different. All of the SHIFT simulations challenge teacher candidates to (1) recognize their own complicity in oppressive societal structures by acknowledging the limitations of their understanding at any given moment, while also understanding that systemic forces exert a powerful pull on our horizons; (2) experience a shift in their horizons toward explicitly anti-oppressive understandings; and (3) realize that this kind of shift is only possible when they listen more and better, actively seeking perspectives, experiences, and affects that disconfirm their present and prior assumptions and opens them up to thinking anew. The sine qua non for facilitating SHIFT simulations is having had experiences around oppression that mirror this set of knowings. In other words, each of us who would facilitate SHIFT simulations must ask, *When, in moments that have shifted my own horizons, have I been pulled up short to incorporate and fully recognize, though not inhabit, the horizons of others?*

Nearly all the instructors we spoke with recounted experiences of being pulled up short in their careers as K–12 teachers and, later, as teacher educators. They described, often in detail, what happened and what it felt like. The affects were far from comfortable, but they were clearly motivating. One of the regular instructors in the master's social foundations course, Nicole Joseph, was clear about the way teaching the course with SHIFT simulations shifted her horizons. Joseph, whose research focuses on math identities in girls and women of color, said, "Before I came into this class, I thought I knew a lot about teaching and education. This experience has flipped me on my head, and opened me up to my role [in the classroom] . . . You've got to be pulled up short so that you can pull your own students up short."

Dan Reynolds, a doctoral student who taught a course on reading instruction, described his own pulled up short moment when he tested the Daria Miller simulation for Liz when she was developing her dissertation work. Reynolds expressed wonder at the way his "eyes were opened" when he encountered Daria and then viewed his reactions. He interpreted his experience against his years as a disciplinarian and dean of students in a parochial school, realizing that his own prejudice had been reinforced by the institutional setting in which he worked. The SHIFT encounter gave him the time and opportunity to reconsider how he had interacted with many young people. He exited that experience with a desire to do and learn more about the pedagogical strategy and jumped at the chance to help create a TIP to be used in his own teaching of an English methods course. Since completing his doctorate, he has taken the concept on the road with him. His own pulled up short experience has convinced him of the efficacy of a SHIFT-like cycle, and he is currently sharing his experience with his new colleagues.

Part of being prepared to facilitate SHIFT simulations is knowing firsthand what it means to be pulled up short on the way to anti-oppressive pedagogy and having felt the discomfort and even embarrassment that goes with that, while still recognizing the power of shifting horizons. If you have never internalized this kind of experience, it seems unlikely that you will appreciate how delicate a process this can be. Setting up the circumstances in which students are inevitably confronted with their own ignorance and limitations without invoking active defensiveness and resistance is difficult. Teacher candidates must feel like they can confront their complicity and shortsightedness in private, while their new sense-making is a shared public endeavor they can then attend to with vulnerability. SHIFT simulations cannot be used for evaluation or assessment. They cannot publicly reveal a teacher candidate's failures. Only the candidate can do that. Only the candidate can out their self. And when they do, the effect is powerful.

There is, admittedly, a certain amount of inauthenticity involved in SHIFT simulations. It can be argued that it is more powerful to have this pulled up short moment occur with real students in actual K–12 settings. But that misses the way the relative safety of the SHIFT simulation (for the teacher candidate and their future students) better reveals the candidate's actual mind-set and dispositions. One of our colleagues, Michael Neel, who used the simulations in his classroom ecology courses, quoted a former candidate in likening teacher candidates to sponges, noting that the impact of the SHIFT simulation is like what happens when a sponge is squeezed. What is inside the sponge comes out; it has to. A candidate may "know better" and be able to respond appropriately when asked about how to react to this or that abstract situation, but when faced with a real person accusing them of racism, or asking for safety in a way that makes others less safe, or talking about students in ways that ignore the realities of their marginalized status, teacher candidates revert to type. Their knowledge about the broader issues, the need for advocacy, and even patterns that they risk perpetuating in their response is lost in translation because it's not actually embodied and embedded. SHIFT simulations generate authentic (if ineffective and even unjust) reactions that can be compared and confronted, and in so doing they open up space for reconstruction as an anti-oppressive educator. Preparing someone to facilitate SHIFT simulations will probably not work if they have never come face to face with their own limited horizons and sought to incorporate a richer understanding of the reality of others. The good news is that most teacher educators have such experiences in their backgrounds. Finding ways to elicit, draw on, and engage with those experiences will be an important element of your shared preparation for taking on a SHIFT project.

A second element of facilitating SHIFT simulations is having some degree of comfort and competence with "difficult conversations." The conversations may be difficult because they involve individual differences and conflict or because they surface deeply held values and beliefs or because they elicit strong feelings. Many educators have translated caring for their students into a respectable version of "being nice" to students-turned-teacher-candidates. This default reaction is problematic.

Pedagogical action that leads to growth is virtually always linked to some form of disruption or discomfort. The point is not to avoid the discomfort but to invite it into contexts that allow it to be part of the learning. That means not just always asking what teacher candidates think and how they feel but also exploring and respectfully addressing why this or that is easy or uncomfortable. It relies on a context that values both radical candor and infinite compassion. It means avoiding judgment and, as doctoral student instructor Laura Carter-Stone noted, "honoring imperfection." Faculty members who facilitate SHIFT simulations competently are not thrown by difficult conversations.

Beyond knowing what it feels like to be pulled up short and being able to engage in difficult conversations, the faculty members tasked with facilitating SHIFT simulations must be clear about what they are and are not trying to accomplish with the particular encounter within the program and the course. This begins when planning for the encounter in the syllabus, especially with respect to related topics and readings. Having a sense of both the course content and the prior learning and experiences of teacher candidates within a particular course, along with how and where instructor-candidate relationships develop through the course, is important for scheduling the SHIFT encounter at a time when candidates trust both the instructor and what the process will offer to their learning. Early attempts to site SHIFT simulations in the elementary education master's program resulted in scheduling an encounter earlier in the semester than either the content or the instructor-candidate trust level warranted. That was an object lesson in what not to do, a lesson that is shaping future efforts.

Part of knowing what we are trying to accomplish is to understand that different encounters in different course settings are moving candidates toward specific understandings. For instance, when the SHIFT simulations in foundations courses address anti-Blackness, conceptions of family engagement, and deficit orientations to student identities, they do so directly as part of a course that is focused on teaching as relational but always political work. The topics and issue raised through the encounters are all part of the content of the course. When discipline-based simulations take up the nature of science, the possibilities of civic disagreement and dialogue, the very meaning of math literacy, and the qualities of good writing, assumptions about cultural difference are always in play, but those differences are not the ostensible issue at hand. Instead, they are embedded in visions of how to teach well. What all the SHIFT simulations have in common is a sense that teaching is a praxis, a dialectically structured and politically inflected practice. How we teach, how we structure interactions with and among students, always impacts what we are teaching in ways that should be obvious but are often missed.

To ensure that this is not missed, SHIFT simulation instructors should be clear—for themselves and within a program—about what they hope to accomplish. And they need to be clear that it is not their job to "fix" any particular candidate. As teacher educators, we can create the conditions for candidates to do this work, but we cannot do it for them. Further, SHIFT encounters set apart from thoughtful debriefing in the light of well-chosen readings cannot and will not result in the change of horizon and concomitant understanding we seek in service of anti-oppressive teaching. They can only create an opportunity and encourage a willingness to reconstruct horizons.

Only with this understanding will an instructor be able to integrate the critical incident and encounter into the content and resources of the course. There are several procedural guidelines to keep in mind, no matter the specific focus of the simulation. Having structures or norms in place for real and productive learning among students in different places in their learning, being clear that no candidate did the encounter right, and moving intentionally from judgmental or binary language to descriptive and analytic language are important elements that constitute being prepared to facilitate the full SHIFT cycle and the debriefing that is its final formal moment.

Of course, this means that any instructor must be clear about the process of the SHIFT cycle. The TIP that provides some but not all relevant information, the prereading that captures first thoughts, the actual encounter, the immediate raw debrief, the written rereading that asks candidates to watch their videos, and the group debriefing are designed to prod each candidate gradually but insistently to face the issue at hand. Having a sense of this process and how it builds is what enables an instructor to schedule the simulation most effectively within the flow of the target course. It's also worth keeping in mind that candidates will be talking among themselves along the way, effectively if unintentionally pushing each other to examine their own reactions and to try out new ways of thinking and responding.

So, how might you prepare new instructors to take on this pedagogical responsibility? Probably the same way we prepared to do it. After all, we were learning as we went. We learned from our practice in interaction with each other. Initially, Liz (whose vision this was) played a significant role in both guiding and assisting individuals who agreed to give this a try. Her task was to help the rest of us see what SHIFT meant and could be. You will likely have a similar experience—one person who takes the lead, especially in the beginning.

Even after you have a full slate of SHIFT simulations up and running, you will not be able to simply train others to implement the simulations or facilitate a debriefing. As our colleague Jessica Watkins pointed out, the SHIFT simulations are themselves "productive artifacts for conceptualizing shared pedagogical vision." The collaborative work done to prepare for the SHIFT simulation "provides opportunities for community-building and developing shared values for programs." While we happily provide some initial technical and moral support, through a project leader or other experienced faculty, to those who are willing to take this on, the actual experience of preparing for and facilitating the simulation in conversation with others is the only training that makes a difference.

Question 2: How do I prepare and facilitate a generative debriefing experience?

Probably the most indispensable work toward making a debrief effective occurs in the first few course sessions when basic classroom culture is co-constructed and candidates are encouraged (and pushed when necessary) to engage with each other in a forthright but thoughtful manner. It is here that the context for radical candor and infinite compassion is seeded. This is especially important because peer feedback is the primary mechanism by which the friction necessary for challenging one's horizons arises. That possibility for peer feedback, both direct and indirect, is what you are planning for. We describe several versions of debriefing sessions that allow each candidate to think about their initial reactions and more considered responses in the light of others' reactions and reflections.

Before planning the actual discussion, and even before scheduling the encounter, there are things to think about.

- Be sure that you are cognizant of and comfortable with the core issue in the critical incident.
- Recognize the limitations of the simulated storyline. Be realistic about how much control the candidate has over the situation they are facing.
- Anticipate likely teacher candidate responses, including what they are least likely to notice.
- Be prepared to remind candidates that there is no course consequence attached to the quality of their engagement in the simulation. Remind teacher candidates of that throughout the SHIFT cycle, but particularly prior to the encounter and before beginning a debriefing.
- Realize that there may be little carryover in awareness from one SHIFT simulation to another. You may even need to encourage candidates to let go of past experiences as they try to process the encounter at hand.
- Be prepared to listen to what teacher candidates have said, done, and written in their initial reactions to the experience generously and without judgment. Encourage them to approach their own and their peers' comments with the same generosity.
- Consider the time frame for a productive debriefing. We have spent anywhere from forty-five minutes to three hours, depending on the timeliness of the critical incident, the level of discomfort the candidates are experiencing, and the quantity and quality of readings to be integrated with discussion of the experience.

These considerations address two big concerns: that we attend to the identities, experience, and current understandings of the teacher candidates with whom we pursue the SHIFT experience and that we face honestly the tension inherent in delving into these issues as individuals with specific social histories and as educators who recognize that this is not work we can do *for* the candidates.

Teacher candidates vary from person to person, and perhaps from program to program, in their capacity to interpret and respond to situations that seem to them like straightforward interactions but in fact reveal individual (sociocultural) identities, exclusion and inclusion, control and resistance, and all of the power dynamics that trip teachers up as they work with their students toward growth. Depending on their past histories of interaction with individuals whose stories are different from their own (in terms of race, class, gender, sexual orientation, able-bodiedness, etc.) and lived habits of inclusion and exclusion, some candidates may be naïve about the ways their taken-for-granted reactions can make a situation worse. Other candidates will draw on experiences with differing ideas and cultural mores, encounters that they may or may not have integrated into a well-formed habit of pedagogical responsibility. This means that we have to be prepared to talk directly about how individual identities and positionalities interact with the situation and those involved in it, especially within the sociohistorical context of the encounter. We have to be prepared to unpack how the situation changes as the interaction progresses. So when Daria Miller suggests I am racist for singling her out, and I assure her that she is wrong and she resists my dismissal of her concern, the situation changes. No longer can I simply explain my actions to a student (while asserting my authority) and assume she will accept that. She is challenging both my interpretation and my authority to make that interpretation. This is a challenge to *all* teacher candidates but a different kind of challenge depending on each candidate's past experience, racial consciousness, and view of themselves as teacher. The complexity for a white woman is different than for a Black man, but the challenge is potentially the same.

As teacher educators, we are called to understand candidates' prior conceptions of their role and work as educators. By the time a SHIFT simulation occurs in a course, as the instructor you have likely formed a sense of the identities that candidates bring with them, along with resources and needs in terms of sense-making, and you will need to keep that in mind in anticipating what may emerge in the course of the debriefing. The demographic mix of students who will debrief a SHIFT encounter will also be a factor depending on the content and characters in the encounter. It is important that no minoritized student feel isolated in the debriefing. When there is just one Black student or one LGBTQIA+ student in a class where issues of racism or homophobia are taken up, you will need to plan to elicit or provide perspectives that will support that candidate's voice.

If candidates' identities and views of themselves as teachers complicate the task of debriefing, so do our own as teacher educators. The primary tension worth some exploration is how you think about yourself as educator versus debriefing facilitator. As instructors in social foundations courses primarily, we have not personally experienced this as a tension. Because the content of the social foundations experience always involves contested social and political issues—macro-, meso-, and micro-level—we recognize that virtually every discussion we facilitate demands that we integrate the roles of teacher as expert authority with teacher as guide.[2] This is not the case, however, for our colleagues who are methods course instructors. If you expand the sequence of SHIFT simulations throughout your program (we recommend that you do that), then you will have to take into account the sensibilities of those instructors focused on the pragmatics of practice.

Several of our colleagues pointed to other, related tensions. Andy Hostetler, who teaches social studies literacies, worries about whether withholding his informed opinion with respect to SHIFT simulations diminishes his authority when he recommends and coaches best practices. Melanie Hundley, who teaches writing methods to future English teachers, collaborates on the debriefing to ensure that the emotionally fraught encounter with Riley Adler is fully explored and that candidates also remain open to ways of teaching writing that challenge what they have taken for granted. She does a tag-team debriefing with Liz, a skilled debriefer and a former English teacher.

Most of our colleagues who have participated in the SHIFT Project at Vanderbilt have figured out how to manage the tension of being an expert on pedagogical strategies yet remaining always open to the continual reconstruction of horizons of understanding. It is important to recognize this tension and sort through what difference it might make in the debriefing and then structure the debriefing so that what is a tension for you as the instructor does not become a problematic tension for the teacher candidates.

Question 3: What are some sample debriefing plans?

The key to debriefing SHIFT simulations is to surface a representative but provocative sampling of candidates' in-encounter reactions to mutually reconstruct more reflective responses. Teacher candidates engage with their own and each other's words and/or actions spoken/exhibited during the (recorded) encounters, in the immediate reactions after the encounter, and in the rereading reflections before attempting to make any generalizations and to reconstruct their own ways of thinking, feeling, and acting in the light of the critical incident. Candidates' initial reactions are typically quite predictable, so you will be well prepared if you look for a set of comments that offers a range of observations, some more constructive than others.

In determining the debriefing format you are most comfortable with and/or best fits the simulation you are facilitating, you will want to consider the following questions:

- Should I start with the collection of comments and observations that I gleaned in advance or invite candidates to select the elements they want to discuss from their own recordings and commentaries?
- If I invite candidates to select the elements for discussion, when, if at all, do I introduce the elements that I found most compelling?
- How should we take up those elements—as a list, so they can come to grips with all at once, or as individual objects of consideration to be taking up one at a time and compared gradually?
- Will I conduct the debriefing with the entire class or allow them to pursue some part of the discussion in small groups without a facilitator?
- Will I have one facilitator or two, or more?

We have facilitated debriefings for the social foundations courses in similar ways, sometimes working with the whole group (as few as twelve students and as many as thirty) and sometimes, if we have a coteacher or teaching assistant, splitting the group in half. Typically, we take responsibility for curating a set of comments and observations prior to the debriefing. We then offer these to each teacher candidate, one at a time, for their consideration and comparison over a seventy-five-minute debriefing experience. (Sometimes we have a printed or projected list available to all at one time.) Each comment or observation is interrogated but never denigrated—Is this a positive or constructive reaction? Is this negative or destructive? How might it be either or both? What does the comment reveal about what you were feeling? How was it likely heard by the actor in the encounter? Is that what you intended, and does that matter? The cumulative effect of this interrogation is that ignorance and limitations are revealed and alternative responses are brought to light. It is never a question of right reactions or wrong answers but always a question of what is more or less fitting in the situation—and that judgment is made by the teacher candidates in the process of their collective unpacking. We don't mean to suggest that there is always an easy resolution. But there is a surprising degree of agreement about which kinds of interactions generate and which obstruct further communication. More gentle questioning and careful listening, less professing, fewer assumptions, and greater humility mark generative interactions. Sighs and "oh, shoot" kinds of reactions when candidates realize that the thing they said or did indicate obstructive interactions.

The facilitator's role in the early phases of the debriefing is generally limited to distributing the comments and starting the comparative questioning. But as candidates hear what others did and said and how they are now feeling about it, that role shifts to framing pointed questions. Consider our experience debriefing the Maryam Sahil simulation. Asking candidates a simple question—What do you know about Maryam and her son?—reveals that a few of them elicited many details about Maryam and Aran during the encounter while others came away knowing very little beyond what was in the TIP. In response to that question, many, if not most, candidates offer different versions of the same observation: Maryam does not know much English; Aran doesn't read at home; the parents want him to do well but can't help him. Then, invariably, one person in the class will reel off a significant number of details about Aran and his family—that his father was a former university physics professor, that his mother is not formally educated, that his family watches the evening news together, that they have lived in Nashville for two years, and that Maryam knows a lot more English than we were giving her credit for. The other candidates are astounded. "How do you know all this?" they want to know. "I asked and I waited while she formed an answer," the student responds. It turns out that when the "teacher" in the simulated encounter at least temporarily withholds their own assessment of the situation and stays open to the framing of the protagonist, it pays off in expanded information. A well-placed question offered by the facilitator can uncover how important information can and will expand understanding. The candidates' recognition that they might have asked, listened, and waited for this expanded information is priceless.

Not all debriefings look exactly the same, and fidelity to the SHIFT concept does not demand that they do. As long as the focus is on the candidates' experiences, and as long as the work of surfacing questions and tensions rests on the candidates' shoulders, the conditions needed for being pulled up short will be served.

Mariah Harmon, a doctoral student who has cotaught several sections of our social foundations courses, has students start debriefing within their "support groups," set up early in the semester and used primarily for debriefing difficult topics of various kinds, to allow them to articulate their individual positioning relative to the simulation topic. As a Black woman, Harmon is highly attuned to the importance of acknowledging identities that impact reactions and responses at every phase. Only after this does she move to the whole group, intentionally sequencing candidate quotes from various stages of the cycle. She sees her role as facilitator as walking the candidates through the development of their awareness of the issues that challenge their horizons. Typically, she spends a full three-hour class session considering individual actions, cross-roughing these individual experiences, surfacing what they did and what they come to wish they did, and calling on course readings and other resources to situate candidates' actual and desired moves historically and politically within systems of oppression.

Nicole Joseph prefers to focus her social foundations debriefing on the following questions: What did you learn about yourself as a result of this experience? Do you have better understanding, more confusion, both? What kind of critical, conscious thinking is happening? Only then will she ask, "What did you learn about the other (the actor in the encounter)"? While Joseph's focus question is slightly different, her goal is the same as all who debrief the social foundations set of simulations: to confront candidates gently but insistently with their own words and actions to shift horizons in ways that push beyond critical reflection to pedagogical action that can be characterized as anti-oppressive. It's important to remember that this is a critical pragmatist project, one that acknowledges the ways we carry oppression as part of our selves but refuses to simply accept that.

Yet, there is a danger in pushing to action too soon. This is an important reminder for all who debrief any SHIFT simulations, but especially the initial ones. Reconstructing horizons takes time; it does not happen in an instant. The pulled up short moment does sometimes happen in an instant (or at least the recognition feels instantaneous), but that moment is embedded in a process of sense-shattering and sense-making that takes time, that requires interaction with others and with ideas. What we as facilitators can do is give candidates the time and space to feed each other lines about the kinds of responses that constitute anti-oppressive interactions with all students.

There are additional considerations when SHIFT simulations are placed in methods courses, where the practice of teaching is front and center, where *what to do* is uppermost in candidates' minds. It remains important, nonetheless, to focus on the deconstruction of taken-for-granted assumptions about students as learners and the nature of teaching that prompts the pulled up short experience. This suggests that the debriefing of practice-based courses might require a sequencing of foci.

When Andy Hostetler debriefs SHIFT simulations set in social studies literacies courses, he typically begins not with the teacher candidates' own comments and observations but with small group discussions of the week's readings. He does this as a warmup and a grounding exercise before asking candidates to rewatch their own videotaped encounter in class and select one moment that is uncomfortable and one that seems smooth or feels easy. Candidates then form small groups to share their chosen moments. They come back together as a whole class to share insights, challenges, and tensions that they noticed in their small groups. Only after discussing readings and reviewing selected moments does Hostetler allow candidates to think about pedagogical moves. In a sense, the readings and the explicit discussion of pedagogical moves "sandwich" the debriefing of the encounter.

Melanie Hundley made a pedagogical decision to tag-team the debrief to deflect "the upsetting part" of the debriefing for the future English teachers encountering Riley Adler. She observed that many candidates were already resisting the unfamiliar teaching practices she encourages. And when, during the debriefs, she was the one disrupting their prior vision of teaching as simply sharing expertise, that resistance got even stronger. She has found that both the needed interruption and the reorientation to practice can occur more effectively when she is not the one shepherding both. As a result, that debriefing is regularly conducted by two instructors in a coordinated session.

Similarly, when future mathematics teachers encounter the Matthew Sloan and Luciana Ramirez simulation, they are faced with a problem of practice linked to ambitious mathematics teaching—how to create conditions in which students are empowered to work productively with one another in ways that honor their humanity and their relative (dis)comfort with mathematics. In what math literacies professor Teresa Dunleavy calls a "hot state" circumstance, teacher candidates are able to check themselves and their own immediate reactions when two students conflict while working together. In this simulation, candidates have opportunities to engage when Matthew, a white boy, attempts to dominate by speaking over groupmates and insisting that there is just "one way" to solve a problem. They are also pushed to note Luciana's use of Spanish in light of her (white) classmates' tendency to dismiss her by calling her "Lucy," a whitewashed version of her name that she does not claim. That power plays a critical role in mathematics students' interactions is new to most candidates in this field.

These approaches show how instructors have some autonomy in determining the format for the debriefing based on who the teacher candidates are and what the course content demands as long as they design the interaction so that candidates' own words and actions are central to the process of collaborative sense-making. This does not mean that there are not better or worse ways of debriefing simulations, but we do not yet have the data to be more specific about which is which. What we can say at present is that the primary goal of the SHIFT Project at Vanderbilt—to prompt the kind of pulled up short experience that opens candidates up to what they do not (yet) understand about the thoughts, feelings, and actions of those they will teach or work with—will likely be achieved no matter the specific strategies employed in the debriefing. So how facilitators organize the debriefing—how they group candidates, whether they or the candidates identify the target comments and observations, how the candidates' comments and observations are linked to course readings, and even how much time is invested in the debriefing—can be adapted to the specific course goals, simulation encounter, and instructor strength and is generally left up to instructors' pedagogical judgment.

Question 4: How/Where might I run into trouble?

Perhaps the most important constraint on any facilitator's planning and implementation is anticipating how a conversation *could* go awry. This possibility is not a function of potential student disagreement (after all, we want to foreground possible differences in interpretation and horizon) as much as the challenge of remembering the limitations of the facilitators' role.

Many, if not most, debriefings go quite smoothly as long as we remember our own guiding principle: allow the candidates to process their own and their peers' reactions and locutions in an atmosphere that encourages comparison, contrast, speculation, and even imagination but is not judgmental in tone. As facilitators, our job is stay out of the way and to allow what Kathleen Stewart calls "ordinary affects" to work their magic.[3] When we do enter the discussion, it is to encourage comparison and to "press on the sore spots compassionately," as our colleague Kara Krinks put it. But this is easier said than done.

The key is to keep questions concrete, specific, and targeted on the critical moment from the student's (or parent's) perspective. In debriefing the Daria Miller encounter, Liz likes to pull quotes of candidates' reactions immediately after Daria discloses that she feels racially targeted, and then she asks simply, "What do you think the student heard?" The same question can be asked about each of the comments curated for conversation. By staying focused on that moment, we redirect the teacher candidates away from their own feelings to the fact of the instance and the receptive and perceptive experience of the protagonist.

In some cases, especially when the critical incident invokes systemic racism, many candidates enter "so nervous," as Nicole Joseph characterized it, to take up the relevant issues. The question, as Jessica Watkins pointed out, is how much defensiveness and fear is too much. In her words, we want to "precipitate" a response, to prompt recognition of something new to learn, but to do so without shutting candidates down or pushing them behind a barrier of nonengagement. Kara Krinks noted that this is complicated by the fact that our students want to make everyone happy without compromising their personal or professional integrity. Many are more or less conflict averse (and in our experience that may vary by their level and subject area). It is disconcerting to them that conflict may well be the path they have to tread, that simple fixes are rarely available.

That teacher candidates are nervous is not a problem; it provides the energy to fuel a constructive debriefing. But it does have to be acknowledged and managed. That can be done by reiterating the nonjudgmental context for debriefing and by helping candidates understand that if they weren't aware of something important, if they weren't learning something about themselves, they wouldn't be experiencing these "nerves." In truth, it's a marker of self-awareness, a marker of being pulled up short (and one, based on feedback from graduates, that stays with them into the field). We need that to move forward.

As teacher candidates face their limitations, there is bound to be some defensiveness. Michael Neel reminded us that some candidates, when they realize that some of their peers were able to glean and understand more about the situation than they did, will initially make excuses for their insensitivity or inability to speak forthrightly. They might offer "I had a bad actor" who didn't give them all the information. They might complain about structures, about there being "not enough time." There will be "peaks and valleys of affective intensities," as Laura Carter-Stone put it. We can't control this, but we can hold space for it to spill out without valorizing or denigrating it. It is important that those affects and the accompanying rationalizations be expressed and then defused indirectly as the cumulative experience of the whole group is revealed. In the end, Neel noted, the students find it "bizarrely comforting" that others "messed up" just as they did. We agree that this is just the affective reasoning in play: *I may not have gotten this exactly right, but neither did anybody else, so I can simply relax and learn from it.*

Perhaps the greatest challenge is to identify those moments when the discussion is stalled by some obstruction of perception, affection, or expression; figure out what that obstruction is; and then find a way to help the teacher candidates let go of or see past that hurdle to take their speculation deeper. "Be prepared to shift gears!!" is the advice of our colleague Grace Chen, especially after listening carefully to teacher candidates' reactions and shared "difficult moments." Offer the candidates the space to say simply, without explanation, excuse, or even apology, "that was insensitive."

And they *will* say that given the opportunity. They will, as Carter-Stone put it, "break the seal of their self-protective silence." There will be aha moments as well as regrets and epiphanies. There will even be some utterly unnecessary self-flagellation. And they will invariably out themselves despite the fact that the SHIFT cycle is set up to preserve confidentiality. No one need own their mistakes or insensitivities publicly in the SHIFT cycle. Some never do. But most will find more than one opportunity to acknowledge to each other, to us facilitators, and even to the actors who participate in the debriefings, "that was me." While they may experience something akin to shame while watching their videos in the privacy of their own company, by the time we come together for a debriefing, and perhaps because of the shared experience of recognizing one's limitations, their affect is transformed from shame into something more constructive. There is a sense that "yes, I said/did that, but I can do better because now I *see* and understand what I have said or done."

Finally, be sure that you, as facilitator, are cognizant of and comfortable with the core issue(s) in the simulation scenario. Jessica Watkins noted the multilayered challenge associated with the science-specific SHIFT simulation. Teacher candidates are asked to react sensitively and sensibly when the situation integrates the nature of scientific inquiry and the power and epistemic privilege invested today in white Christianity. This particular simulation also challenges the pedagogical faith invested in student-centeredness. Candidates are forced to imagine the impact of cultural differences but are also asked to check their assumptions about teaching. Sometimes the best way to be "student-centered" might be to keep the student's focus on the demands of the discipline. Knowing in advance that all of this is coming at you will enable you to conduct a debriefing that maintains focus while allowing the teacher candidates' responses to be of primary importance.

Question 5: What is my responsibility when the SHIFT cycle is done?

The debriefing is not the end of the SHIFT simulation impact. In fact, nearly all the faculty members we spoke with suggested that if the candidates are still talking about the cycle when the class (and even the course) is over, then the simulation is successful and continuing to contribute to the reconstruction of horizons. A good rule of thumb for the debriefing is to keep the feelings and the ideas flowing, being careful not to prematurely stop the candidates from coming to a reconstructed self-understanding.[4]

There is always the possibility that our first attempt at debriefing will, like the teacher candidates' encounters, not live up to our visions of our own practice. One might ask, as Watkins did, "Have I done the identity work that *I* needed to do (myself and with my students) to make this simulation make sense?" Or, with respect to the content of the conflict, "Have I sequenced the semester to lay a groundwork in the kind of epistemic thinking the candidates will need *after* they have been pulled up short?"

You might wonder about the specifics of the debriefing tactic you employ. Carter-Stone wondered whether distributing quotes one at a time was better than distributing a whole list of quotes at once—Would the whole list overwhelm? Would it be too emotionally laden, preventing them from taking care with each one? Would the whole list at once provide the clear comparisons and contrasts needed to make new sense possible? When that happens, you may want to rethink tactics for next time. Or you may want to reposition the simulation within the course, or strengthen some aspect of the course content before, during, and after the scheduled encounter. That is a matter of pedagogical judgment. Indeed, the SHIFT process relies on *your* practice of anti-oppressive pedagogical judgment to move the teacher candidates toward their own practice of anti-oppressive teaching.

Coda

The Future of SHIFT

Equitable practice is not something teacher educators and teacher candidates can work toward incrementally. It requires a substantive shift in horizon, a shift that can only come from being pulled up short and then finding the way to new understanding. The SHIFT cycle represents both moments in this critical change process.

This book is intended to support two substantive yet modest claims. The first is that employing SHIFT simulations—live-actor, video-recorded, group-debriefed simulations constructed to highlight systemic social oppression and its impact in schools—moves teacher candidates of all identities and positionalities to actively take up systemic oppression that gets in the way of pedagogical responsibility. The second is that SHIFT simulations can be implemented with fidelity within any teacher education program as long as there is a commitment to preparing teacher candidates for anti-oppressive pedagogy.

We encourage you to follow our lead with respect to those principles that guide our practice but adapted, of course, to your faculty, candidates, and circumstances. These principles include building around "critical incidents," maintaining the complexity of teaching practice in each cycle, immersing candidates in richly specified contexts in which anti-oppressive practice is at stake, ensuring that situations are "usefully artificial," focusing on the development of dispositions that ground continuous learning, and locating your SHIFT simulations thoughtfully within the program. You do not need to use the same simulation scenarios, site them in the same courses, or offer them in the same sequence. Video-recording can involve iPads deployed in faculty offices or be done in dedicated simulation facilities. Actors may be formally paid or identified through a volunteer partner actors' company. The critical elements are (1) one or more challenging stories, (2) a live human encounter with a well-prepared actor, (3) a video-recording of that encounter for review (with care for privacy and security), and (4) one or more chances to co-reflect on the experience.

Seven years into the SHIFT Project at Vanderbilt, we are impressed with its impact on our teacher candidates in secondary education. But we are keenly aware of the work we still have to do. An immediate task is to fully implement SHIFT simulations for our undergraduate and graduate elementary education programs. While we have experimented with SHIFT simulations for in-service teachers, it is clear from these pilot efforts that the encounters look quite different for those whose visions of teaching have been hardened by the expectations of the particular system in which they find themselves. This is an important domain for practical experimentation and empirical research, especially in light of Bettina Love's recent call for "anti-racist therapy" for white teachers.[1] The fusion of feeling, thinking, and acting in SHIFT simulations evokes the kind of experience to which Love points.

While we and our colleagues have reported in journals and conference papers on the experiences of teacher candidates within the SHIFT cycle, more research is under way. We are attempting to determine how indicators of SHIFT are reflected in generally accepted measures of candidate adequacy (e.g., edTPA scores and student teaching evaluations). We are interested in tracking how SHIFT simulation experiences redirect candidates' interest in teaching underserved and minoritized students in disadvantaged settings. We are also exploring, with Deborah Kerdeman, whether a capacity to be pulled up short can be learned. Hans Georg Gadamer thought not, but Kerdeman is challenging that position, and our initial data and observations of our candidates suggest that the lasting impact of the SHIFT experience is precisely that: candidates are opened up, and remain open, to being pulled up short. That habit may well be a central element in the development of teachers who continually grow with their students.

We think of this work as a design study, where researchers and practitioners create and implement iterative solutions to practical and complex educational problems and then study those efforts through the careful and systematic gathering of data.² We invite you to participate in the ongoing design study that is SHIFT simulations. We invite you not just to follow our lead but to correct and enhance what we have done here. We invite you to join us in the learning community that the SHIFT focus enables, one where faculty are pressed to articulate and practice a vision of anti-oppressive pedagogy, where teacher candidates are challenged to expose their own thinking and feeling to criticism, and where programs are subject to reconstruction in the service of anti-oppressive goals. This is the real work to which we are called. We have much to learn.

Appendix

Sample Simulation Materials

Daria Miller Simulation

This simulation can be run as either Daria Miller or Darius Miller, depending on the availability of actors and/or the instructor's focus. Paired readings might emphasize stereotypes of "loud Black girls" or "dangerous Black boys" to deconstruct those biases, and their impact on Black youth, in the group debrief.

Teacher Interaction Protocol

STUDENT   Daria Miller
she/her, age 15, Black, tenth grade
unweighted GPA: 3.95

Daria Miller is one of twenty-six students in your tenth-grade honors class at McGavock High School in Nashville. During the first three weeks of the semester, you have gotten to know a little bit about Daria. In class, she is creative and hardworking. She gives thoughtful responses in her written work and makes meaningful contributions during class discussions. She seems to have a lot of friends in class who look up to her as a student leader. You have learned that she is the vice president of the sophomore class and that she plays on the JV basketball team, and you know from informal conversation with her that she has a younger brother in middle school. She seems well liked by other teachers.

The only problem you have had with Daria so far is that she is often talking when she is not supposed to be—when you are talking, another student is talking, or during individual work time. She is clearly an outgoing kid, and you know her talking is not malicious, but it seems disrespectful to you and the other students, and it is disruptive. You have tried to handle this without constantly calling out Daria for talking, both out of respect for her and to not further disrupt class. You often walk over near her desk to get her attention or just say her name and then pause to remind her that you have asked for quiet. She stops talking when you do this and seems to receive your efforts well. Daria is not the only student who talks when she is not supposed to, but it seems like you hear her voice more often and louder than anyone else's.

You called home last week to introduce yourself to her parents as part of your regular effort to communicate with home. You focused on all that Daria was doing well but also mentioned the talking when her mom asked if there was anything she could improve in class. Her mom seemed warm and receptive and said she would speak to Daria about the talking.

You are an experienced teacher and give a lot of thought to both content and classroom management. Daria is in your class after lunch, and you work extra hard to make that class interesting for the students and keep everyone energized. In general, you tend to do a lot of creative projects and group work and have found better structures this year to organize the students so they work productively with each other. Your students seem to enjoy their work for your class and are doing a better job of staying on task this year as a result of your efforts.

On Friday, you give the students the class period to finish working on a group project that will be presented on Monday. You begin by giving reminders about the project and then let the groups work for most of the period, moving from group to group to make sure the students are on task and to provide help where needed. Daria's group of five works hard for the whole period, calling you over just to ask a few clarifying questions about the project.

At the end of the period, with only a few minutes left, you call for the class's attention. The noise in the classroom slowly subsides, but several people around the room are still talking. Once again, you hear Daria's voice above the others as she talks to a student next to her. With the bell about to ring, you take a direct approach: "Daria, eyes up here. I need everyone listening." Before you can utter another word, Daria stands up, grabs her bag, and walks out of the room. She doesn't look at you but seems to be speaking to you when she says, "This is some bullshit. Why's it always gotta be me?" You try to call her back, but she does not seem to hear and keeps walking.

You have a large class coming in for the final period and so decide to delay speaking to Daria until after school. But since you do not want the weekend to go by with the situation unaddressed, you send a note to her last-period teacher asking Daria to come to your room before she goes home. You have hall duty after school but head back to your classroom quickly once it is done and find Daria waiting in the room for you.

Prereading Questions

Prior to the simulation, read the TIP and respond to the following questions:

1. Complete the following (one) sentence stem in your own words: "This simulation is mainly about . . . " Then make a list of the *three* most important words or phrases in the TIP.
2. What do you expect will happen during the simulation?
3. What does the TIP make you think of
   a. related to the content of this course? Connect to at least one reading or concept from this course.
   b. related to your own life? To what extent do you see your own lived experiences present, or not, in this scenario?
   c. related to US schools and society? Identify a current event or issue that this situation relates to.
4. If this situation happened in real life, what additional information do you think you would have? What information do you wish you had going into the simulation?

Actor Interaction Protocol

STUDENT Daria Miller
         she/her, age 15, Black, middle SES, 10th grade
         unweighted GPA 3.95

You are Daria Miller, a tenth-grade student at McGavock High School in Nashville. You are an honors student, captain of the JV basketball team, and vice president of the sophomore class. You are looked up to by other students and well-liked by your teachers. People describe you as smart, creative, and hardworking but also outgoing, friendly, and fun to hang out with.

Although you like your school, you have begun to feel repeatedly targeted as a Black girl by teachers and other staff members. Earlier in the week, in your history class, during the daily current events focus, your teacher, Ms. Walker, asked students to talk about their experiences with the local police. Ms. Walker then called on you specifically and asked, "How are Black people in the US feeling right now about all of these police shootings?" Later in the week, at lunch, you were sitting with a group of girls from the basketball team who are also in many of your classes. In talking about the game from the night before, the group got a little loud, and one of teaching assistants on duty in the cafeteria came over to tell you all to quiet down. But instead of addressing the whole group, she talked to you and one of your Black teammates sitting next to you. "Let's calm down, ladies," she said. "We don't need to be so loud in here. I would hate to have to separate you from your friends."

In the class following lunch, you tried to focus on your work. You are working with classmates in a group on a project that will be presented on Monday. The teacher begins by giving reminders about the project and then lets the groups work for most of the period. Your group stays on task and gets a lot done, with only a little work remaining to be finished over the weekend. At the end of the period, with just a few minutes left, your teacher calls for the class's attention. The noise in the classroom slowly subsides, but several people around the room are still talking. You are quietly talking to the student next to you about what needs to be done over the weekend when you hear the teacher say, "Daria, eyes up here. I need everyone listening." With the incidents in Ms. Walker's class and in the lunch room in the back of your mind, you stand up, grab your bag, and storm out of the room, saying half to yourself and half to your teacher, "This is some bullshit. Why's it always gotta be me?".

You go to your final class of the day, which is PE. You are angry but try not to let it show. Your friends notice but leave you alone. Toward the end of the period, you get a note that your teacher from the previous period has asked to see you before you go home. You head to her classroom after going by your locker and are waiting for her when she comes back from hall duty.

Important Characteristics and Background Information
- You have been in school for about three weeks and like your classes and teachers. You have begun taking more honors classes this year and are excited about them. All of your classes are honors level except for PE and Spanish II. You are one of only a few Black students in your honors classes, whereas your untracked classes are more representative of the school as a whole (~50 percent white, 30 percent Black, 15 percent Latinx).
- You really enjoy this class. The teacher makes it interesting and tries to keep everyone energized since it is right after lunch. You do a lot of creative projects and group work, which you usually enjoy. The teacher is pretty young but seems to manage the class well and isn't rude or mean when she calls people out for their behavior.
- You tend to be called out somewhat frequently for talking when you're not supposed to be. It isn't malicious on your part; it's usually related to class, and you are just interested in what you are working on. The teacher usually walks over near you to remind you to be quiet or says your name and pauses to wait for you to be quiet. She occasionally does this with other students too, but seemingly more with you than anyone else. She has also called home once, just to introduce herself to your parents, and she mentioned the talking to your mom, who told you to "straighten up" in class. It does not bother you too much because you *are* talking when you are not supposed to be. But by the third week, it also seems like you are getting called out more than other, usually white, classmates who are also talking.

Questions/Information to Present to the Teacher (Verbal Triggers)
- You feel that this teacher has been calling you out more often than others who are also talking when they're not supposed to be. You don't know if the teacher is doing it on purpose but don't really care whether it's intended or not. At some point during the simulation, you say to the teacher: *"I know I was talking when I wasn't supposed to be, and I'm sorry for that, but so were other kids, and you don't call them out like you did me. And it just seems I'm always being the one getting called out 'cause I'm one of the only Black kids in the room."*

- If the teacher asks about anything else that's bothering you, say: *"It's not just in here. Something happened at lunch, too, and it just seems like it's always the Black kids that are in trouble, even if other kids are doing the exact same thing."* If the teacher pursues outside-of-classroom concerns further, you also recount the incident earlier in the week in Ms. Walker's class.
- If the teacher is unwilling to accept your perspective on what is happening in the classroom ("I don't think I'm really calling on you more . . ." or "It's not because you're Black; it's just because you're the one I hear talking . . ."), resume a withdrawn posture. Do this if the teacher minimizes your assertion that race is at play or commits any form of racial microaggression. You never react by getting overtly angry; you withdraw, avoid eye contact, and placate the teacher (*"Yes, ma'm"*) to get the conversation over with.
- If the teacher responds by focusing on your role as a leader, simply point out that it seems unfair to hold you to a higher expectation than other students. Loop back around to language that points out that you are "one of the few" Black students in the class to try to engage the teacher in the conversation you are trying to have.
- If the teachers tries to compare themselves with you, use your judgment as to the reasonableness of their claims. If a teacher is not Black, and especially if the teacher is white, refute any of their attempts to tell you that they were "like you" or "know how you feel." Point out plainly that while they might have experienced some things similar to you, they are not Black. If the teacher is Black, respond as seems fitting to you, recognizing that Black teachers may still have racial bias in their discipline because of broader effects of racism in the school and society. This might include Black teachers who say they are holding you to a higher standard because they know you will have to work "twice as hard" to get the same respect in school and the workplace. You still don't like how it feels, but you may be more persuaded by the motivation.
- Redirect any attempts by the teacher to place the root of the issue anywhere other than her actions or incidents in the school. For example, if the teacher specifically asks about how things are going at home or uses language to suggest that something at home led to your outburst, say: *"Everything at home is fine. This has nothing to do with home."*

Additional Background Information
- Your father is Ray, who works as a building inspector for Sumner County. Your mom, Yvonne, stayed at home when you and your brother were little and now works as a part-time bookkeeper at Green's Exterminator Company. Your brother, Chris, is a seventh grader at Two Rivers Middle School. Your parents are both from Georgia, where your mother's parents still live. You have one aunt and some cousins who live in Murfreesboro, Tennessee.
- Your family attends church every Sunday at Trinity Baptist Church in Hendersonville, Tennessee.
- There are five Black students in this class of twenty-eight; all of them are girls.

Other Important Details for the Simulation
- Standard school attire at McGavock High School is a solid collared white or black shirt and khaki or black pants with a belt, with an optional solid-colored hoody. You should also have a book bag.

Rereading Questions

Following the simulation, reread the TIP and watch the video of your encounter to respond to the following questions:

1. Complete the following (one) sentence stem in your own words: "This simulation was mainly about . . ." Then make a list of the *three* most important words or phrases from your encounter with Daria.
2. Did the simulation unfold as you expected? Why or why not? Was there anything in the TIP that might have helped you anticipate something that was unexpected?
   a. To what extent did you change your original plan for the encounter based on what Daria said or did?
   b. Was there anything in the TIP that might have helped you anticipate something Daria said or did that you did not expect?
   c. Did you find yourself connecting to a class reading or topic during the encounter or while watching your video?

3. What was the main problem that Daria wanted to talk about? What was the main problem that you wanted to talk about? Whose problem did you spend the most time talking about in the interaction?
4. Based on your rereading of the simulation, what do you most want to focus on during the group debrief?

Alondra Correa Simulation

Teacher Interaction Protocol

STUDENT	Adrian Correa
	he/him, age 12, Hispanic, sixth grade
PARENTS	Alder and Alondra Correa
	ages 35 and 32, respectively
CONFERENCE TYPE	teacher initiated

Adrian Correa is one of twenty-three students in your sixth-grade class at Jere Baxter Middle School. During the first seven weeks of school, you have gotten to know Adrian as a student in both your first-period class and homeroom. In class, Adrian is quiet and hardworking. He is very polite, respectful of his classmates and of you, and he stays on task during independent and group work time. He rarely raises his hand to ask or answer a question, but he attempts an answer if called on directly. Adrian's fifth-grade scores on his Tennessee Comprehensive Assessment Program testing showed him as below grade level in English and social studies, near grade level in science, and on grade level in math.

Adrian is quiet, but he does seem to have a few close friends, mostly other boys in your homeroom, Jayden and Yadiel in particular. Adrian is an average student, with mostly Bs and Cs on his report card and occasional strong project-based performances in science and social studies. Outside the classroom, at lunch and recess, you have seen that Adrian is more talkative; he roughhouses with the other boys and seems more self-assured and joyful. You have also noticed a soft side to him, especially when he interacts with one of the older substitute teachers who is frequently in the building.

Adrian's teachers met last week to talk about him possibly needing support services in some of his classes. All his core teachers shared concerns around his reading and writing. Several teachers mentioned his difficulties reading aloud. He replaces words in the text with similar words that do not make sense or reads the words out of order. When he does read the word accurately, there is little fluency, which seems to affect his ability to comprehend. In passages with more difficult academic vocabulary, he has trouble recalling basic information and is seemingly distracted by the new terminology.

One teacher noted that he sometimes misspells the same word (often a new term for the unit) several different ways in the same assignment. One of the teachers who is fluent in Spanish mentioned that some of the Spanish vocabulary words Adrian uses in translation activities or when translanguaging are not words she recognizes in Spanish. He wrote prolifically in a mix of Spanish and English at the end of an ecology unit in science, for example, about the *jurakan* in Puerto Rico and referred to several animals the teacher did not recognize (*jicotea* and *cokí*, for example). Other teachers, including his elective teachers, note that Adrian has challenges following multistep directions. He appears to be listening when directions are given but then forgets the next step once he has completed the first one.

In general, Adrian seems to want to do what is he supposed to and tries his best, but he is struggling with reading comprehension and written assignments in multiple classes, suggesting that it goes beyond difficulty with a particular subject area. In the meeting, teachers reported trying similar things to support Adrian in their classrooms, like using Marzano's six steps for new academic vocabulary (something the faculty recently received professional development on), providing an option for partner work to support his reading comprehension, having him repeat back multistep directions as a reminder for the whole class, and just checking in on him more often during class. Thus far, only the partner work approach has resulted in much improvement. Conversations with Adrian's fifth grade team revealed similar patterns of challenges in the prior year, but not enough to warrant support services. The team plans to meet with the parents and then begin the referral process if needed.

From Adrian's file, you see that he lives with his mother in the Fallbrook Apartments on Dellway Villa Lane. His father's name is listed on the name for parents, but no address or phone number is provided for him under contact information. Adrian was enrolled at your school last fall, and you see no documentation from his prior schooling in his file. Prior to Nashville, the family lived in Union Park, Florida. His file indicates that English is spoken at home.

Your interactions with Adrian's mother prior to this meeting have been limited. Adrian returns schoolwide forms sent home the next day with a parent signature, and the one teacher on your team who sent home a personal note to his parents also got it back with a signature at the bottom, even though it was not specifically requested. You and two other teachers on the sixth-grade team have called home to share your concerns about Adrian's reading difficulties. There was no answer at the number provided, and an automated outgoing message meant you could not be sure if the number was correct, so you did not leave any details in the message other than to return the call. Despite calls by three different teachers, no one ever received a call back.

The sixth-grade team has begun meeting in person with parents whose students are having academic challenges in order to help develop teamwide plans to better support those students. As the homeroom teacher, you have been asked to hold a conference with Adrian's mother. You called to set up the meeting but did not get a return call, so you sent a note with Adrian detailing some of the concerns. Adrian came to school the next day and said his mom would be coming after school that afternoon to meet with you.

Today, you are meeting with Adrian's mother, Alondra.

Prereading Questions

Prior to the simulation, read the TIP and respond to the following questions:

1. Complete the following (one) sentence stem in your own words: "This simulation is mainly about . . ." Then make a list of the *three* most important words or phrases in the TIP.
2. What do you expect will happen during the simulation?
3. What does the TIP make you think of
   a. related to the content of this course? Connect to at least one reading or concept from this course.
   b. related to your own life? To what extent do you see your own lived experiences present, or not, in this scenario?
   c. related to US schools and society? Identify a current event or issue that this situation relates to.

4. If this situation happened in real life, what additional information do you think you would have? What information do you wish you had going into the simulation?

Actor Interaction Protocol

STUDENT	Adrian Correa
	he/him, age 12, Hispanic, sixth grade
PARENTS	Alder and Alondra Correa
	ages 35 and 32, respectively
CONFERENCE TYPE	teacher initiated

You are Alondra Correa, the thirty-two-year-old mother of Adrian, a sixth-grade student at Jere Baxter Middle School. You have lived in Nashville for approximately six months since moving from Union Park, Florida. You are involved in your child's education in the ways you know how to be—asking about homework on the nights you are home, checking his report cards, taking him to the library every other weekend, and communicating the importance of doing well in school. You also ask about his friends to make sure he is spending time with good influences. You feel hesitant to help when he asks you questions because you are unsure whether schools on the mainland are similar to the ones you attended in Puerto Rico. You are also timid about your own English skills, even though you learned English in school and have used it conversationally since leaving Puerto Rico. Adrian has never been held back, though, and so you do not worry too much. He stays out of trouble at school and is polite and respectful at home.

Adrian is a typical boy. He plays with other children in your apartment building, including Yadiel, who is in his class at school. He speaks Spanish in addition to English; he also knows some words and phrases (mostly for plants and animals) from Classic Taíno. He heard little English in Maricao, where you lived in Puerto Rico, but learned it in school starting in the first grade. He has now spent three years in mainland schools and communities that are either predominantly or exclusively English speaking. You speak Spanish at home and with friends and family in your community, but you write on school forms that you speak English at home. Shortly after arriving in Florida, a Puerto Rican *abuela* living next door told you that kids who speak Spanish at home are removed from their regular classes for extra help in English and so are viewed by their teachers as not as smart. You know your son is intelligent and do not want him to be seen as lacking by his teachers.

Adrian is fascinated by the natural world and was very excited by a class project he did on ecology. Because of the weather events that brought you to the mainland, and that recently affected Puerto Rico, he is also interested in weather and meteorology. He watches the weather report nearly every night you are home together. Adrian is a reluctant reader, but you have worked hard to get him to find books that keep his interest. When you take him to the library, you usually guide him to nonfiction books on plants, animals, and the weather. He reads them in short spurts, picking sections that look interesting and jumping around in the texts. He sometimes shares interesting tidbits from what he reads and then connects it to life back in Puerto Rico.

Adrian's interests in part result from his grandparents and his father, who still live in Maricao. He learned about the land from his grandparents, who taught Adrian about the secrets of coffee farming, and he also learned about plant and animal life from his father, Alder, who works at the fish hatchery in Maricao. Adrian would often go to work with him and loved to spend time with the fish. Alder made you take Adrian and move to the mainland after the fiscal crisis of 2016. He wanted to move with you all, but his elderly parents, coffee farmers, refused to leave their land. He stayed behind to care for them until he could convince them to leave, but you have now spent four years apart. It was especially difficult as you waited to hear whether they were safe after Hurricane Maria. Six weeks after the storm, you received word that they had survived, but the lack of electricity and strained communications since the storm have left you with little knowledge of what is happening. You are hopeful, though, that this event will convince Alder's parents to leave the island and join you and Adrian in Tennessee.

Several teachers from the school, including the homeroom teacher, have called home to talk to you about Adrian's reading. Each of the teachers who called said that they enjoyed having Adrian in class but had some concerns they wanted to talk about in person. Your work schedule has made it difficult to call them back during school hours, but you also wanted time to watch Adrian at home with his homework to make sure he was taking his schoolwork seriously. You hoped to avoid an in-person conference if possible, feeling that only children who were having trouble in school would have their parents called in to a meeting. Yesterday, though, Adrian brought a note home that included details about the teacher's concerns and a request to meet. You told Adrian to tell the teacher you would come in right after school.

Today, you are meeting with Adrian's homeroom teacher.

Important Characteristics and Background Information

- You speak Spanish and English but spend most of the day speaking Spanish, both at work and at home. You learned English in school in Puerto Rico, but you can read and write it better than you can speak it. You are timid about your English skills because you feel like some people perceive you as "not American" when they hear you talk.
- You work at an assisted-living facility, working with older adults who need various levels of home health support. You began working as a home health aide in Florida after moving there but worked for an employer you did not trust, and you earned a low wage because you lacked a credential. You worked for more than two years to get your home health aide certification. When you finished, you decided to move to Nashville with the hope of a lower cost of living and more opportunities as a credentialed aide. While your work is not always easy, and you work inconsistent hours, you think your work is valuable and are proud of it. You feel it also teaches your son the importance of caring for the older generation, which is an important part of your family's values. On the nights you cannot be home by dinnertime, Adrian goes next door to Yadiel's, where Yadiel's *abuela* cares for him. You try to return the favor whenever you can.
- You are a warm but shy person. You greet the teacher but sit hesitantly and engage only when asked a direct question or prompted, and then only after a short pause when you look away as though to gather your thoughts before speaking.

Questions/Information to Present to the Teacher (Verbal Triggers)

- When the teacher states that Adrian is having some challenges in school, you respond with a serious expression. You know that he always does his homework when you are home, and Yadiel's grandmother says the boys work on their homework together when he stays with them in the evening. Because Adrian talks about what he is studying at school, you think he understands the material. You do not dispute the teachers' observations that Adrian is having difficulties in his reading, but you want to make sure he is not being seen as less intelligent than his peers. If the teacher indicates that Adrian may need more support with his reading, say: *"Adrian is a smart boy. This I know. I do not want him taken out of the classroom for this. He needs to be learning what the other children are learning, not something different."*

- When the teacher shares that Adrian's other teachers think he needs extra help in school, ask for clarification: *"I know Adrian can read. He reads to me all the time. So why does he need extra help if he can already read?"* If the teacher asks you to talk about what he reads, talk about your biweekly visits to the library. Provide more details about the kinds of books he reads, how he reads, and what he tells you about only if prompted.
- If the teacher asks what language you speak at home, ask: *"Why do you need to know that?"* If they press further to know, simply say: *"My son and I can speak English fine."* If the teacher asks about Adrian's ability to read in Spanish, tell them that he mostly reads at home in English for school but that he can read in Spanish and has some children's books and comics in Spanish that he often looks at. You have not noticed any issue with his ability to comprehend what he reads in Spanish, but you also do not ask him comprehension questions after this kind of reading.
- If the teacher raises the issue of Adrian struggling to learn new vocabulary and using words in his writing that a Spanish-speaking teacher does not recognize, ask for specific examples: *"Like what?"* When the teacher provides examples of these words, translate them and explain they are Taíno that Adrian may have learned from children's books that were passed down from his grandparents.
- If at various points the teacher points to things that Adrian has done well or seems interested in, say simply: *"Well yes, that makes sense"* (or some variation). Only make the connection to Adrian's

grandparents and their farm, to his father's work, and so forth if the teacher prompts you.
- If the teacher asks about details of Adrian's father, answer the question. If the teacher suggests that he is an "absentee father," become indignant: *"How could you even think that about his father?"* If the teacher asks this in an indirect way, simply explain that he is still in Puerto Rico and provide further details only if prompted and if posed in a noninvasive way.

Other Important Details for the Simulation
- Prior to Hurricane Maria, you used to talk to your husband every weekend on Sunday night. Adrian would also send letters once a month to his grandparents, but, since the storm, you are not sure whether mail is consistently reaching the town. You and Adrian also went and visited in the summer of 2016. However, your job and the cost of travel has prevented you from returning since then. You miss your husband and the rest of your family, who live on the east side of Puerto Rico, but you see the opportunities for you and Adrian on the mainland. You also worry about your family's safety should another major hurricane hit.
- Your family is Roman Catholic.

Rereading Questions

Following the simulation, reread the TIP and watch the video of your encounter to respond to the following questions:

1. Complete the following (one) sentence stem in your own words: "This simulation was mainly about . . ." Then make a list of the *three* most important words or phrases from your encounter with Alondra.
2. What was your goal going into this encounter? Did anything in the encounter, whether in your interaction with Alondra or based on information you learned about Adrian, change your perception of this student, his family, or your goals for the encounter?

3. Watch your video encounter and make two lists:
   a. What did you tell Alondra about her son? Transcribe chunks of speech wherein you are telling. Note especially repeated words, phrases, or idioms/jargon you may have used.
   b. What did you learn from Alondra about her son? How did you learn it (asked a question, followed up on a statement, information volunteered by parent)?
4. Based on your rereading of the simulation, what do you most want to focus on during the debrief?

Phil Duncan Simulation

This simulation can be run as either Phil Duncan or Phyllis Duncan, depending on the availability of actors and the instructor's focus. We have only ever played the role with white actors, but the scenario could be played with a person of color to address combating stereotypes and biases in someone who is themselves discriminated against in society on the basis of their identity. Paired readings might then address the role of race, gender, age, and experience in how the narratives espoused in the interaction are formed and in how to respond so as to break them down.

Teacher Interaction Protocol

COWORKER Phil Duncan
he/him, age 62, 40 years' teaching experience

You are a first-year teacher at Hume-Fogg Academic Magnet High School in Nashville. You teach tenth grade and have been paired with your department chair as your mentor for the year since she teaches the other tenth-grade sections in your subject area. Two days before the first day of classes, you receive your class lists. Your mentor teacher, Ms. Wyatt, asks to see them and skims through them quickly with little comment. When she sees the list for your fourth-period class, though, she smiles, kind of laughs, and says, "You've got some characters in this class. You should go see Phil Duncan. He taught them last year and might have some useful things to tell you to get you off on the right foot with them." You met Mr. Duncan briefly, as he is in your department, but you have not spent much time with him. You find Mr. Duncan in the workroom, reintroduce yourself as a new member of his department, and share your class list in order to get some useful information on your students.

Hume-Fogg Academic Magnet High School

PERIOD 4

1. Bell, Cary E.
2. Connelly, Savannah E.
3. Cook, Davis P.
4. Cook, Emerson G.
5. Douglass, John Michael A., III
6. Dung, Phan T. A.
7. Garcia, James E.
8. Hernandez, Roxana Y.
9. Hixon, Janice J.
10. Hsing, Lian
11. Hunt, Dianne C.
12. Jackson, Sheila D.
13. Johnson, Cameron L.
14. Leither, William R.
15. Lugo, Ashley W.
16. Masood, Aadila D.
17. McGriff, Andrew J.
18. Miley, Alicia R.
19. Pauley, James S.
20. Remillard, Robert D.
21. Renfro, Douglas L.
22. Rodgers, Precious R.
23. Stinson, Jacqueline E.
24. Toupin, Marie G.

Prereading Questions

Prior to the simulation, read the TIP and respond to the following questions:

1. Complete the following (one) sentence stem in your own words: "This simulation is mainly about . . ." Then make a list of the *three* most important words or phrases in the TIP.
2. What do you expect will happen during the simulation?
3. What does the TIP make you think of
   a. related to the content of this course? Connect to at least one reading or concept from this course.
   b. related to your own life? To what extent do you see your own lived experiences present, or not, in this scenario?
   c. related to US schools and society? Identify a current event or issue that this situation relates to.
4. If this situation happened in real life, what additional information do you think you would have? What information do you wish you had going into the simulation?

Actor Interaction Protocol

COWORKER Phil Duncan
          he/him, age 62, 40 years' experience teaching

You are Phil Duncan, a sixty-two-year-old veteran high school teacher at Hume-Fogg Academic Magnet High School in Nashville. You have been teaching for forty years and will likely retire in the next five years. You have been teaching at Hume-Fogg for seventeen years and taught at John Overton High School prior to that. You know the Metro Nashville Public Schools well and have seen the system change a lot over the last thirty years, not necessarily for the better. You were excited when you got a job at Hume-Fogg because it allowed you to work with advanced students in a college-prep environment. You have come to be loved by your students and respected by your colleagues, even if they sometimes disagree with your more traditional teaching methods. For the last several years, you have taught ninth grade and so consider it your job to help the students adjust to high school.

You like teaching and see it as your calling. You enjoy your content area and teaching high school students in general. You are tired of the bureaucracy of public schooling and the constant pressures put on you and the other teachers to conform to certain reform efforts. By now you realize that the changes only last so long, and so you do not let it bother you. You know you are a good and caring teacher, and so you usually just shut your door and do what you know is best for the students.

This school year there is one new teacher in your department who is teaching tenth grade. You have met the new teacher briefly but have not spent any time with them. They arrive in your room while you are planning for the first week of school.

Important Characteristics and Background Information

- In general, you like all your students and care for them and their academic and personal well-being. They are all "good kids" in your mind; it's just that some lose their way or need a little more help than others. As Metro Nashville Public Schools have become more diverse over the years, you have seen that students do best when they just try to fit in with their peers so they do not stand out too much or get teased by the other students. Your general counsel to

students who are being teased or bullied is to just try to "blend in" with the other students.
- You like to be helpful to the new teachers and are willing to share your information about former students or to advise on teaching with those who ask. But in general, you let new teachers come to you rather than seek them out.

Questions/Information to Present to the Teacher (Verbal Triggers)

- Once the teacher enters the room, they will show you a list of student names and ask if you have any information to share about them. Take the list from the teacher so that it is in your hands. As you skim the list of names, smile, nod, laugh a little, and then say: *"Yes, you do have quite a crew here. I don't like to influence teachers' views of the kids too much, but I think I can give you some useful info to start with."*
- Go down the list and hit the target students listed below. After each student, look at the teacher and ask: *"Is that helpful?"* If they ask a question, respond to it and then keep moving without providing a chance for them to ask another question. If they just say "yes," keep moving down the list.
- If the teacher asks questions about the students' strengths and weaknesses related to their specific content area, you respond: *"Well, they're all honors kids here, so you don't have to worry too much about them doing well and acting right."*
- If the teacher asks about a student you don't have background on, you respond: *"S/He's a good kid. I don't remember anything really standing out about him/her. You shouldn't have any problems."*
- If the teacher ask questions or prompts you to talk about something outside of what is provided here (e.g., Did they do well with group work?), you respond: *"I usually find it's best to let new teachers try some things out for themselves and figure that out. We can talk more about that later on if you find you're having trouble."*

Information About the Target Students on the List

- *John Michael A. Douglass III*
  - All teachers get: "Great kid. I know his parents from church. His dad is a lawyer. John Michael is lucky to have them as parents. He

was adopted when he was little from somewhere in Africa—can't remember what country. But he's just a regular American now and probably doesn't even remember anything before here."
- If the teacher probes: "He's basically like a white kid who just looks Black. Really articulate. Focused on his studies. Last year some of the kids started calling him 'Shafi'—his middle name is something foreign like that—but I'm not sure what that's all about."

- *Roxana Y. Hernandez*
  - All teachers get: "Sweet girl. Really seemed to enjoy my class. Never missed a single class all year. The language thing can sometimes be an issue, but if you call her on it she'll stop."
  - If the teacher probes: "There's a couple of kids in the class who speak Spanish—like James, I think, spoke it growing up even. And when they get in groups they think it's cool to speak Spanish with each other. But of course, then I don't know what they're saying or if they're staying on task, so I make sure they stop and just speak English. This is school, after all."

- *Cameron L. Johnson*
  - All teachers get: "Ah, Cameron. He's a real creative type, you know. Kind of . . . flamboyant. The crazy hair that changes every week. Talks a little effeminate. Some days painted fingernails. That kind of thing. I talked to him last year about toning it down."
  - If the teacher probes: "He was getting bullied by some of the other kids, like the really guy-guys, and I didn't want anything to happen to him—'So just, tone it down and kind of blend in a little more.'"

- *Aadila D. Masood*
  - All the teachers get: "Really hard worker. Super focused. She had to leave my class every day last year to pray, which, you know, it's not ideal, of course, but the school says we have to let them go or we'll get in trouble. I tried to help her get used to how things are in America."
  - If the teacher probes: "Sometimes the kids give her a hard time about—what's the thing called she wears on her head? But she's quiet and keeps to herself. So I had to tell her, 'This is America. You've gotta stand up for yourself.'"

- *Marie G. Toupin*
  - All the teachers get: "I don't know if you've gotten her 504 paperwork yet, but Marie is in a wheelchair. Something happened when she was born and her limbs don't all work quite right. But her brain sure works well. Smart girl. And I just always told her, you know, 'I don't see a wheelchair. I just see Marie.'"
  - If the teacher probes: "Marie tells a lot of handicapped jokes, like she wants to make fun of herself so other people don't make fun of her. So I just try to help her realize that people aren't looking at her wheelchair; they're looking at her."

Additional Background Information

- You are a married parent of two. You married your spouse, Darlene, at age twenty, and you are both from Murfreesboro. She works for CSX railroad. Your children are Laurabeth and Wilson, ages 25 and 23 years old, respectively, both graduates of Overton High School and Middle Tennessee State University, which is also where you went to college and earned your teaching degree. Laurabeth is also a teacher in Cartersville, where she lives with her husband. Wilson has only recently graduated and is still looking for a full-time job.

Other Important Details for the Simulation

- This is a teacher planning day two days before the first day of classes. You are dressed casually but still professionally.

Rereading Questions

Following the simulation, reread the TIP and watch the video of your encounter to respond to the following questions:

1. Complete the following (one) sentence stem in your own words: "This simulation was mainly about . . ." Then make a list of the *three* most important words or phrases from your encounter with Phil.
2. Make a three-column chart with:
   a. in the first column, a list your desires for the simulation. What did you *want* to say or do, even if you didn't do it?

b. in the second column, list your fears during the simulation. What did you fear might happen if you gave in to your desires?
c. in the third column, note how you ultimately resolved any tension between your desires and fears. What decision did you make, and do you think it met more of your desires or guarded against your fears?
3. Watch your video encounter and look for two things:
    a. where did your facial expression or body language reveal what you were thinking about Mr. Duncan?
    b. what do you think Mr. Duncan thought about you by the end of the encounter?
4. Based on your rereading of the simulation, what do you most want to focus on during the group debrief?

Alexis Jimenez and Matthew Manning Simulation
Teacher Interaction Protocol

STUDENTS	Alexis "Lexi" Jimenez
she/her, age 16, Latina, eleventh grade
unweighted GPA: 3.25

Matthew Manning
he/him, age 16, white, eleventh grade
unweighted GPA: 3.8

You are an eleventh-grade AP US Government and Politics instructor at MLK Academic Magnet School in Nashville. The class has 28 students, with 17 males and 11 females. This is your first year teaching the AP course. Per the required topics in the course description, you have covered constitutional underpinnings, political beliefs and behaviors, political parties and interest groups, mass media, and institutions of national government. You are currently covering public policy, civil rights, and civil liberties.

Many of the students in the class tend to hold strong opinions on the topics you discuss. Most recently, for example, you discussed the First Amendment as it relates to athletes who speak out publicly against social injustice. You talked about Colin Kaepernick and why he chose to kneel during the national anthem, Sean King's call for a boycott of the NFL, and the decision by individual football teams to link arms, kneel, or remain off the field during the anthem. Some students also then brought up the decision by the NBA's Warriors and then the University of North Carolina–Chapel Hill not to visit the Trump White House following their championship wins. You also noted subsequent policies issued around the country by school districts regarding possible consequences for athletes who do not stand during the national anthem. The conversation was intended to get students talking about what the First Amendment does, and doesn't, protect against and what private individuals and businesses (e.g., NFL sponsors or companies that use athletes as spokespeople) can do in response to athletes speaking out.

One white student, Randy, argued that professional football players "aren't paid to give their opinion, just play football" and said players who do not stand should be fined or suspended for their actions. A few students, including Krista, the Black daughter of a Nashville Metro police officer, said that she agreed with Kaepernick's reasons for protesting but felt that his actions were disrespectful to those who had died to protect the US. Still another student, Alex, argued that the team-level protests were a coopting of Kaepernick's original message that deflected from the real issues. Some students, including Lexi Jimenez and Matthew Manning, were quiet through most of the discussion, listening but not speaking.

The whole-class discussion became fairly animated, with students just stating their ideas without actually listening to each other or responding. As a result, you have tried to develop norms for class discussion that promote listening and responding to others' ideas and often use structures to support that, from Padaeia seminars to fishbowl experiences.

Lexi and Matthew are solid students, but you don't have a clear sense of who they are as individuals because they seem to avoid sharing their personal views in class. They both have good attendance, are punctual, and come to class prepared. They seem to speak more in small groups than in large groups, especially with the students right around their desks. Matthew is fairly introverted and avoids engaging with the rowdier students in the class, who sometimes try to engage him in their clowning before or after class; he ignores them, and they back off. In his writing, Matthew takes a formal, academic tone and rarely makes evident his own opinion on a topic. Lexi seems to struggle when speaking in small groups that are otherwise all male students, which is part of why you have continued to have her work with those around her desk who seem to listen when she speaks. On barometer-type activities, she usually stands in the middle between agree and disagree and provides a vague response when prompted to elaborate on her position. Matthew is generally a high-B student, but recently he has received lower grades on a few smaller assignments and on the last free response writing assessment. Lexi has also seemed distracted on and off during class discussions.

On Friday, when you return to your classroom after hall duty, you find Lexi and Matthew in your classroom waiting to see you. Each asks to speak with you privately.

Prereading Questions

Prior to the simulation, read the TIP and respond to the following questions:

1. Complete the following (one) sentence stem in your own words: "This simulation is mainly about . . ." Then make a list of the *three* most important words or phrases in the TIP.
2. What do you expect will happen during the simulation?
3. What does the TIP make you think of
   a. related to the content of this course? Connect to at least one reading or concept from this course.
   b. related to your own life? To what extent do you see your own lived experiences present, or not, in this scenario?
   c. related to US schools and society? Identify a current event or issue that this situation relates to.
4. If this situation happened in real life, what additional information do you think you would have? What information do you wish you had going into the simulation?

Actor Interaction Protocol—Alexis Jimenez

STUDENT   Alexis "Lexi" Jimenez
                      she/her, age 16, Latina, eleventh grade
UNWEIGHTED GPA: 3.25

You are Alexis Jimenez, or Lexi, an eleventh-grade student at MLK Academic Magnet School in Nashville. You are a thoughtful and responsible student and have attended MLK since seventh grade. You have good attendance, are punctual, and come to class prepared. You complete homework assignments and turn in major assignments on time. You want to go to college after you graduate and are interested in pursuing a degree in either sociology or psychology. You are politically conservative and an evangelical Christian but tend to keep both your political and religious beliefs out of the classroom. You are part of a small but growing prayer group that meets before school and once a week at lunch to share fellowship.

You are currently enrolled in AP US Government and Politics. You like the class and the teacher, but the other students in the class hold strong opinions on the topics discussed, which is sometimes overwhelming for you. You are shy and introverted in general and especially so in large groups. The teacher often uses barometer-type activities, and you usually stand in the middle between "agree" and "disagree" so that you don't have to share your personal opinions with the whole class. You are friendly with two students near your desk, Samuel and Krista, and you have done several class projects with them in the fall. You find that you are more willing to discuss topics with them in small groups, especially as you get to know each other better. Krista is also in your prayer group, and you feel like she understands you even though you are not close friends.

You are generally a high-B student in this class, but recently you have been distracted in class and your grades have suffered. You find yourself turning over thoughts in your head during lectures and class discussions, trying to figure out how to say what you are thinking out loud, and then realize you are not paying attention to what is happening around you. Most recently, for example, your class discussed the First Amendment as it relates to athletes who speak out publicly against social injustice. The class talked about Colin Kaepernick and why he chose to kneel during the national anthem, plus his recently launched Nike campaign, as well as other outspoken athletes, both historically (like Curt Floyd and Mahmoud Abdul-Rauf) and currently (like Serena Williams and Aly Raisman). You discussed decisions by individual teams to link arms, kneel, or remain off the field during the anthem following comments by President Trump. Some students also brought up the decision by individual players (Tom

Brady under Presidents Obama and Trump) and teams (the Warriors and then UNC-Chapel Hill under President Trump) not to visit the White House following their championship wins. Your teacher also noted subsequent policies issued around the country by school districts regarding possible consequences for athletes who did not stand during the national anthem, including two students in Texas who were kicked off their team immediately after kneeling.

Your teacher kept trying to move the focus back on the First Amendment and what it does and doesn't protect against, especially when thinking about public versus private individuals and businesses, but most students just shared their opinions. One white student, Randy, argued that Kaepernick "isn't paid to give his opinion, just play football" and said he should be fined or suspended for his actions. A few students, including Krista, who is Black and the daughter of a Metro police officer, said that she agreed with his reasons for protesting but felt that his actions were disrespectful of those who had died to protect the US. Still another student, Alex, argued that the team-level protests were a coopting of Kaepernick's original message that deflected from the real issues.

The whole-class discussion became fairly animated, with students just stating their ideas without actually listening to each other or responding. You sat quietly listening but feeling really torn as to whether or not you should speak up. You actually supported Kaepernick's and others' right to peacefully protest, just as the Westboro Baptist Church does, and to infringe on his right to do so, or to threaten his job security because of it, seems unfair. At the same time, you feel that claims of racism are often overblown, especially by Black people, and feel the country would be more united and less divided if everyone followed the Bible's teachings that we are all God's children and made in his image.

You noticed the *Obergefell v. Hodges* Supreme Court decision on the syllabus and over the course of a few weeks have become increasingly worried about what it's going to involve in terms of class discussion. You are interested in learning about the decision, but you are nervous because you hold an opinion contrary to most of the other students and feel you cannot stay quiet in the discussion anymore. You have heard students in your school use terms like *fag* and *homo* when the faculty and staff aren't around, which you think are rude terms. You do not dislike gay and lesbian people and do not consider yourself homophobic. Mr. Jeffries, who teaches AP Biology, is gay and is one of your favorite teachers. He does not talk about his sexuality, but you have seen pictures of him with his partner on his desk, and his partner sometimes comes to school events like football games. Mr. Jeffries sponsors the Gay-Straight Alliance at the school but does not talk about that part of his job in the classroom, which is how you think it should be. You hold the opinion that teachers are there to teach content, not beliefs and values, and so they should be neutral, especially in a history class.

You decide to talk to your teacher, find out what will actually happen in class, and share your concerns. You go to their classroom after school on Friday.

Important Characteristics and Background Information

- Your parents are politically conservative and have raised you in the evangelical Christian faith. You have been attending Donelson View Baptist Church since you were an infant and were baptized in the church when you were nine. Your family attends church weekly and participates in a range of church-based activities. At home, your family prays before meals. Your parents often invoke scripture when they talk to you about values like honesty and when you talk about contemporary issues like gay marriage.
- You enjoy this class because it is challenging and connects to your interest in sociology. You took the class more for college applications than out of an interest in history, but you like how the teacher connects the content to current events. You are a solid, if formulaic, writer, though you don't especially enjoy free writing for this class.
- You know there are other students in the class who are Christians, but they have a more liberal stance on the gay marriage issue. Many of them also use scripture to support their opinion on the topic.

Questions/Information to Present to the Teacher (Verbal Triggers)

1. You want to find out how directly gay marriage and LGBT rights will be debated, but you don't want to share your opinion until you know where the teacher stands. Once the teacher comes into the room and greets you, say: *"Sorry to bother you after school like this. Do you have a minute to talk?"* After the teacher says yes and gives you a chance to speak again, say: *"I noticed the Supreme Court case*

on gay marriage on the syllabus for next week. What are we going to have to do in class?"
2. If the teacher tries to elicit the reason for your question (e.g., "Why do you ask?") or asks if you have concerns about what's going to happen in class (e.g., "It seems like you're worried about this. Can you tell me why?"), then say: *"I don't normally talk a lot in class, but this is an issue I feel really convicted about and want speak up about. But I'm not sure if I can do that without getting bashed by everyone for what I believe."*
3. If the teacher asks further probing questions, reveal your position on the decision, saying: *"I think the court made the wrong decision. I think it's just become more okay in the world to accept homosexual people, and so the court caved to that way of thinking."* (Pause before you use the word *homosexual*, like you're not sure if it is okay to say. Use this term consistently throughout the interaction in lieu of *gay*, *lesbian*, or *queer* unless the teacher explicitly addresses the terminology.)
4. If the teacher prompts you to say more, say: *"I have nothing against homosexual people. I'm not some bigot. I just do not think the Constitution guarantees them the right to marry each other. And I don't think I should have to be quiet about that in class because it might upset some people. Especially since they're allowed to talk about homosexual issues."* At some point, work in the fact that Mr. Jeffries is one of your favorite teachers as evidence that you are not homophobic.
5. If the teacher continues to probe your beliefs, say:
   a. *"I think the Bible teaches us to love the sinner but hate the sin. This decision makes a claim that the sin is okay as long as people get someone to marry them."*
   b. *"Marriage has always been a covenant between a man and a woman. So there's no way homosexual people have a right to that."*
   c. *"What comes after giving these people the right to marry? Then it's adopting kids, who then don't have either a mom or a dad. That's not fair to those kids."*
   d. *"Who's to say that once this becomes legal, there won't be a push from some group to make marriage between an adult and a child legal or some other thing? Just because some people are okay with it doesn't mean people have a right to it."*

6. If the teacher makes parallels to the history of civil rights for Black Americans, for example, say: *"But I don't have an issue with Black people. I mean, Krista is one of my friends in this class. I'm not talking about that."*
7. If the teacher focuses on your ability to speak freely in class, say:
   a. *"In recent history, we have started deciding that it is okay to let some people speak out—like Colin Kaepernick and the Black Lives Matter people who riot after police shootings—but not okay for others, like people who get fired for posting stuff on their Facebook page or on Twitter. Just look at what happened to some of the people at the Charlottesville protest. People might not like what they have to say, but don't they have the right to speak up for what they believe without retribution, just like the counterprotesters?"*
   b. *"If there is one thing that people in this country do have a right to, it's the right to free speech. I mean, that's in the very first amendment. Even the ACLU has supported people's rights to vocalize unpopular beliefs, like with Westboro."*
8. If the teacher points out that your shared opinion may silence other students, say: *"But that's their choice not to speak up. I'm not putting my hand over their mouth not letting them speak. They have the right to say what they think, just like I do."* If the teacher persists with the issue of silencing, say: *"It's clear that at this point in time, some people are given the right to say what they want because it's popular and others are told they have to stay quiet because it makes people uncomfortable. Just look at school prayer. But I think sometimes you have to make people uncomfortable in order to defend your beliefs."*
9. Respond to the teacher's plan based on what seems desirable given Lexi's personality and concerns, as described here. If the teacher describes a structure for discussion in which Lexi would be able to speak freely, respond positively to that. If the teacher asserts a need to privilege marginalized voices in the conversation, show some frustration and persist in arguing your points. If you are not sure, you can simply say: *"I guess."*
10. You are nervous about having this conversation. Stand near the door and fiddle with your bag until the teacher invites you to sit down. Once you sit down, sit back in the chair, keep your arms crossed or hands fiddling with something. If the teacher does not

invite you to sit down, remain standing and do not move physically closer to the teacher. Make eye contact on and off with the teacher when you first speak. Once you have disclosed the real reason for your question, you can react to what the teacher says. If the teacher continues to ask you questions and works to make you feel comfortable with the plan, you can sit up a bit, relax your hands and arms, and maintain better eye contact. If the teacher tries to formulate a plan without your input, continue to remain distant.

Additional Background Information
- Your father is Allen, who works as a manager at Lowes. Your mother is Rose, who works as a nurse at Skyline Medical Center. Your younger sister, Megan, is a seventh grader at Head Magnet Middle School. Your parents are both from southern Kentucky, where their families still live. Your house is in Madison, near where your parents work. This year you started driving to school and dropping off/picking up your sister at Head MS every day.

Other Important Details for the Simulation
- MLK Magnet's dress code can be found on the school's website. Please dress in accordance with these policies and also avoid any t-shirts with writing or images (e.g., sports teams, concerts/bands, etc.), as it may prompt conversation. You should also carry a book bag.

Actor Interaction Protocol—Matthew Manning

STUDENT   Matthew Manning
                   he/him, age 16, white, eleventh grade
UNWEIGHTED GPA: 3.25

You are Matthew Manning, an eleventh-grade student at MLK Academic Magnet School in Nashville. You are a thoughtful and responsible student and have attended MLK since seventh grade. You have good attendance, are punctual, and come to class prepared. You complete homework assignments and turn in major assignments on time. You want to go to college after you graduate and are interested in pursuing a degree in either law or nonprofit work related to reforming the criminal justice system.

You are currently enrolled in AP US Government and Politics. You like the class and the teacher, but the other students in the class hold strong opinions on the topics discussed in class, which is sometimes overwhelming for you. You are shy and introverted in general and especially so in large groups. When you complete assignments for class, you try to avoid sharing your own personal opinion and instead focus on analyzing primary and secondary sources for their contributions to a topic. You are friendly with two students near your desk, Alex and Xiomara, and you have done several class projects with them. You find that you are more willing to discuss topics with them in small groups, especially as you get to know each other better. The class has a lot of really rowdy male students who, earlier in the school year, harassed you as part of their clowning before and after class. You ignored them, though, and they mostly backed off.

You identify as gay but are not out, except to one close friend, who is not in your AP US Government and Politics class. You noticed the *Obergefell v. Hodges* Supreme Court decision on the syllabus and over the course of a few weeks have become increasingly worried about what it's going to involve in terms of class discussion. You are interested in learning about the decision, as it feels personally important to you, but you are nervous about students in the class making homophobic comments or expressing heterosexist sentiments. You have heard a lot of students talking about the decision already, and many of the students who were unhappy with the decision said they were opposed to gay marriage because of their religious beliefs. In addition, some of the male students in the class, as part of their clowning, call each other "fag" or "homo," so you know a class discussion would include at least a handful of students who would want to talk about sexuality specifically and not just civil rights.

You are generally a high-B student in this class, but recently you have been distracted in class and your grades have suffered. You considered faking an illness or skipping school the day the class discusses *Obergefell*, but you really want to participate in this discussion. You decide to talk to your teacher, find out what will actually happen in class, and share your concerns. You go to their classroom after school on Friday.

Important Characteristics and Background Information
- You have not come out to your family, but you think your lack of interest in girls or having a girlfriend has come to their attention

recently. Your sister has begun teasing you (unwittingly) about not dating. Your family is not openly homophobic, but you do not know how they will react to your coming out.
- You enjoy this class because it is challenging and connects to your interest in the law and social justice. You took the class more for college applications than out of an interest in history, but you like how the teacher connects the content to current events. You are a solid, if formulaic, writer, though you don't especially enjoy free writing for this class.
- You do not know if there are other gay students in your AP US Government and Politics class, but you do know there are other gay students in your grade at MLK. There is a Gay-Straight Alliance at the school, but you have never been a member.

Questions/Information to Present to the Teacher (Verbal Triggers)
- You want to find out how directly gay marriage and LGBT rights will be debated, but you don't want to out yourself until you know where the teacher stands. Once the teacher comes into the room and greets you, say: *"Sorry to bother you after school like this. Do you have a minute to talk?"* After the teacher says yes and gives you a chance to speak again, say: *"I noticed the Supreme Court case on gay marriage on the syllabus for next week. What are we going to have to do in class?"*
- If the teacher tries to elicit the reason for your question (e.g., "Why do you ask?") or asks if you have concerns about what's going to happen in class (e.g., "It seems like you're worried about this. Can you tell me why?"), then say: *"You may not know this, but I'm gay. The other kids in class don't know, but I'm guessing they wouldn't exactly be supportive. I don't want to feel uncomfortable listening to a bunch of gay-bashing."* If the teacher does not try to elicit the reason for your question or concerns, share this information at the two-minute warning.
- You are nervous about having this conversation. Stand near the door and fiddle with your book bag until the teacher invites you to sit down. Once you sit down, sit back in the chair, keep your arms crossed or hands fiddling with something. If the teacher does not invite you to sit down, remain standing and do not move physically closer to the teacher. Make eye contact on and off with the teacher

when you first speak. Once you have outed yourself and disclosed the real reason for your question, you can react to what the teacher says. If the teacher continues to ask you questions and works to make you feel comfortable with the plan, you can sit up a bit, relax your hands and arms, and maintain better eye contact. If the teacher tries to formulate a plan without your input, continue to remain distant.
- Respond to the teacher's plan based on what seems plausible given your personality and concerns. For example, if the teacher suggests a structure for class discussion that limits the number of people talking at once or a form of debate that randomly assigns a side to argue, you could say something like: *"I think that would help, but I'm still nervous about . . . [someone saying something offensive, having to take sides against the rights of gay Americans, etc., based on the suggestion]."* If the teacher removes responsibility from themself (e.g., "I can't censor what other students say") or puts the responsibility on you for managing your feelings (e.g., "This is just part of what you'll have to deal with"), you could simply say: *"Oh, ok"* or *"I guess so."* If the teacher says they plan to skip over the court case or not discuss it in class, sit up quickly and say: *"No, that's not what I want."*
- If the teacher asks about your recent drop in grades prior to coming out, say: *"I just have a lot on my mind right now and am having trouble focusing on my schoolwork."* If the teacher asks after you have outed yourself, say: *"I'm just worried that people are starting to notice and that I'm going to have to tell them. And in your class, because this was coming up on the syllabus, I was really focused just getting through next week."* If the teacher asks how long you've felt this way, say: *"A few weeks, I guess."*

Additional Background Information
- Your father is Paul, who works as a manager at an auto parts store. Your mother is Martha, who works as an aide at a preschool for exceptional ed students. Your younger sister, Laura, is a seventh grader at Head Magnet Middle School. Your parents are both from southern Kentucky, where their families still live. Your house is in Madison, near where your parents work. This year, you started driving to school and dropping off and picking up your sister at Head MS every day.

Other Important Details for the Simulation
- MLK Magnet's dress code can be found on the school website. Please dress in accordance with these policies and also avoid any t-shirts with writing or images (i.e., sports team, a concert/band, etc.) as it may prompt conversation. You should also have a book bag.

Rereading Questions

Following the simulation, reread the TIP and watch the video of your encounter to respond to the following questions:

1. Complete the following (one) sentence stem in your own words: "This simulation was mainly about . . ." Then make a list of the *three* most important words or phrases from your encounters with Lexi and Matthew.
2. After your first encounter was over, what did you anticipate in the second encounter? If you had no idea, what spectrum of possibilities did you consider?
3. After watching *both* of your videos, answer the following questions:
   a. To what extent were your responses to Lexi and Matthew similar or different? Were there certain phrases or ideas that existed in both?
   b. To what extent did your first encounter shape what you said or how you thought about your second encounter? To what extent do you think your first encounter would have differed had you seen the students in reverse order?
   c. To what extent did you activate ideas from course readings or discussions in how you responded to the students?
4. Based on your rereading of the simulation, what do you most want to focus on during the debrief?

Notes

Introduction

1. Hans Georg Gadamer, *Truth and Method* (2nd rev. ed.), trans. Joel Weinsheimer and Donald Marshall (New York: Continuum, 1998), 306.
2. Gloria Ladson-Billings, "It's Not the Culture of Poverty, It's the Poverty of Culture: The Problem with Teacher Education," *Anthropology and Education Quarterly* 37, no. 2 (2006): 104–09, doi:10.1525/aeq.2006.37.2.104; H. Richard Milner IV, *Start Where You Are, but Don't Stay There: Understanding Diversity, Opportunity Gaps, and Teaching in Today's Classrooms* (Cambridge, MA: Harvard Education Press, 2010).
3. Gary Orfield, Jongyeon Ee, Erica Frankenberg, and Genevieve Siegel-Hawley, *Brown at 62: School Segregation by Race, Poverty, and State* (Los Angeles: Civil Rights Project, UCLA, 2016); Charles T. Clotfelter, Helen F Ladd, and Jacob Vigdor, "Who Teaches Whom? Race and the Distribution of Novice Teachers," *Economics of Education Review* 24 (2005): 377–92, doi:10.1016/j.econedurev.2004.06.008; Russel J. Skiba and Natasha T Williams, *Are Black Kids Worse? Myths and Facts About Racial Differences in Behavior* (Bloomington: The Equity Project, Indiana University, 2014).
4. Hua-Yu Cherng, "Is All Classroom Conduct Equal? Teacher Contact with Parents of Racial/Ethnic Minority and Immigrant Adolescents," *Teachers College Record* 118, no. 11 (2016): 1–35, https://eric.ed.gov/?id=EJ1114995.
5. Dan Goldhaber, Lesley Lavery, and Roddy Theobald, "Uneven Playing Field? Assessing the Teacher Quality Gap Between Advantaged and Disadvantaged Students," *Educational Researcher* 44, no. 5 (2015): 293–307, doi:10.3102/0013189X15592622.
6. Joscha Legewie and Thomas A. DiPrete, "The High School Environment and the Gender Gap in Science and Engineering," *Sociology of Education* 87, no. 4 (2014): 259–80, doi:10.1177/0038040714547770; Alfredo J. Artiles, Janette K. Klingner, and William F. Tate, "Representation of Minority Students in Special Education: Complicating Traditional Explanations," *Educational Researcher* 35, no. 6 (2006): 3–5, doi:19.3102/0013189X035006003; Donna Y. Ford, "Recruiting and Retaining Black and Hispanic Students in Gifted Education: Equality versus Equity Schools," *Gifted Child Today* 38, no. 3 (2015): 187–91, doi:10.1177/1076217515583745
7. "Hate Crime Statistics, 2015," Pew Research Center, https://ucr.fbi.gov/hate-crime/2015.

8. Joel Mittleman, "Sexual Orientation and School Discipline: New Evidence from a Population-Based Sample," *Educational Researcher* 27, no. 3 (2018): 181–190, doi:10.3102/0013189X17753123.
9. Ibid.
10. Kevin K. Kumashiro, "Against Repetition: Addressing Resistance to Anti-Oppressive Change in the Practices of Learning, Teaching, Supervising, and Researching," *Harvard Educational Review* 72, no. 1 (2002): 67–92, doi:10.17763/haer.72.1.c11617526l7k46v6.
11. John Dewey, *Experience and Education*, in *The Later Works of John Dewey, 1925–1953* (vol. 13), ed. JoAnn Boydston (Carbondale: Southern Illinois University Press, 1988).
12. Kevin K. Kumashiro, "Towards a Theory of Anti-Oppressive Education," *Review of Educational Research* 70, no. 1 (2000): 25–53, doi:10.2307/1170593.
13. Ibram Kendi, *How to Be an Anti-Racist* (New York: One World, 2019). As the book title suggests, Kendi's focus is exclusively on racism, not other forms of oppression. However, the structure of his argument holds for our purposes.

Chapter 1

1. Howard Barrows, *Simulated (Standardized) Patients and Other Human Simulations: A Comprehensive Guide to their Training and Use in Teaching and Evaluation* (Chapel Hill, NC: Health Sciences Consortium, 1987).
2. Elizabeth Self, "Designing and Using Clinical Simulations to Prepare Teachers for Culturally Responsive Teaching" (PhD diss., Vanderbilt University, 2016).
3. Myron Moskovitz, "Beyond the Case Method: It's Time to Teach with Problems," *Journal of Legal Education* 42, no. 2 (1992): 241–70.
4. William T. Branch Jr., "Use of Critical Incident Reports in Medical Education," *Journal of General Internal Medicine* 20, no. 11 (2005): 1063–67, doi:10.1111/j.1525-1497.2005.0231.x; Robert E. Lee, Christie Eppler, Natasha Kendal, and Christopher Latty, "Critical Incidents in the Professional Lives of First Year MFT Students," *Contemporary Family Therapy* 23, no. 1 (2001): 51–61, doi:10.1023/A:1007872132292; Edana Minghella and Anne Benson, "Developing Reflective Practice in Mental Health Nursing Through Critical Incident Analysis," *Journal of Advanced Nursing* 21, no. 2 (1995): 205–13, doi:10.1111/j.1365-2648.1995.tb02516.x; Dawn Francis, "Critical Incident Analysis: A Strategy for Developing Reflective Practice," *Teachers and Teaching* 3, no. 2 (1997): 169–188, doi:10.1080/1354060970030201; Joanne E. Goodell, "Using Critical Incident Reflections: A Self-Study as a Mathematics Teacher Educator," *Journal of Mathematics Teacher Education* 9, no. 3 (2006): 221–48, doi:10.1007/s10857-006-9001-0; David Tripp, *Critical Incidents in Teaching: Developing Professional Judgement* (New York: Routledge, 1993).
5. Noah M. Collins and Alex L. Pieterse, "Critical Incident Analysis Based Training: An Approach for Developing Active Racial/Cultural Awareness," *Journal of Counseling and Development* 85, no. 1 (2007): 14–23, doi:10.1002/j.1556-6678.2007.tb00439.x; Teresa D. LaFromboise and Sandra L. Foster, "Cross-Cultural Training: Scientist-Practitioner Model and Methods," *The Counseling Psychologist* 20, no. 3 (1992): 472–89, doi:10.1177/0011000092203006; Venita W. Morell, Penny C. Sharp, and Sonia J. Crandall, "Creating Student Awareness to Improve Cultural Competence: Creating the Critical Incident," *Medical Teacher* 24, no. 5 (2002): 532–34, doi:10.1080/01421590210000125777.

6. Cory Wright-Maley, "Beyond the 'Babel Problem': Defining Simulations for the Social Studies," *Journal of Social Studies Research* 39, no. 2 (2015): 63–77, doi:10.1016/j.jssr.2014.10.001.
7. Pam Grossman, *Learning to Practice: The Design of Clinical Experience in Teacher Preparation* (New York: AACTE-NEA, 2010).
8. Hosun Kang and Elizabeth A. van Es, "Articulating Design Principles for Productive Use of Video in Preservice Education," *Journal of Teaching Education* 70, no. 3 (2019): 237–50, doi:10.1177/0022487118778549.
9. Magdalene Lampert, Megan Loef Franke, Elham Kazemi, Hala Ghousseini, Angela Chan Turrou, Heather Beasley, Adrian Cunard, and Kathleen Crowe, "Keeping It Complex: Using Rehearsals to Support Novice Teacher Learning of Ambitious Teaching," *Journal of Teacher Education* 64, no. 3 (2013): 226–43, doi:10.1177/0022487112473837.
10. Barrows, *Simulated (Standardized) Patients*.
11. Paulo Freire, *Pedagogy of the Oppressed*, trans. Myra Bergman Ramos (New York: Continuum, 1970).
12. Julie Cohen, Vivian Wong, Anandita Krishnamachari, and Rebekah Berlin, "Teaching Coaching in a Simulated Environment," *Educational Evaluation and Policy Analysis* (2020): 1–24, doi:10.3102/0162373720906217.
13. Meghan Shaughnessy and Timothy A. Boerst, "Uncovering the Skills That Preservice Teachers Bring to Teacher Education: The Practice of Eliciting a Student's Thinking," *Journal of Teacher Education* 69, no. 1 (2018): 40–55, doi:10.1177/002248711770257.
14. Melanie Rees Dawson and Benjamin Lignugaris/Kraft, "Meaningful Practice: Generalizing Foundation Teaching Skills from TLE TeachLivETM to the Classroom," *Teacher Education and Special Education* 40, no. 1 (2017): 26–50, doi:10.1177/0888406416664184.
15. This does not include steps that are specific to the teacher educator only and that precede the simulation, including assessing your program's readiness to use simulations (see chapter 5 this volume), writing or revising simulated encounters (chapter 6), or recruiting and training actors (chapter 7).
16. Zeus Leonardo and Ronald K. Porter, "Pedagogy of Fear: Toward a Fanonian Theory of 'Safety' in Race Dialogue," *Race Ethnicity and Education* 13, no. 2 (2010): 139–57, doi:10.1080/13613324.2010.482898; G. D. Shlasko, "Queer (v.) Pedagogy," *Equity & Excellence in Education* 38, no. 2 (2005): 123–34, doi:10.1080/10665680590935098; Kevin K. Kumashiro, "Uncertain Beginnings: Learning to Teach Paradoxically," *Theory into Practice* 43, no. 2 (2004): 111–15.
17. Audre Lorde, *Sister Outsider: Essays and Speeches* (Berkeley, CA: Crossing Press, 2007).
18. Richard O. Welsh and Shafiqua Little, "The School Discipline Dilemma: A Comprehensive Review of Disparities and Alternative Approaches," *Review of Educational Research* 88, no. 5 (2018): 752–94, doi:10.3102/0034654318791582
19. We describe our work with actors in chapter 7. For now, it's good to remember that actors are well prepared in advance of the encounters *and* that they have access to a full backstory that they may or may not reveal in the encounter, depending on the action of the teacher candidate.
20. W. E. B. DuBois, *The Souls of Black Folk* (Chicago: A. C. McClurg, 1903).
21. William Keener, "The Inductive Method in Legal Education," *Annual Report of the American Bar Association* 17 (1894): 473–90.

Chapter 2

1. H. Richard Milner IV, "Race, Culture, and Researcher Positionality: Working Through Dangers Seen, Unseen, and Unforeseen," *Educational Researcher* 36, no. 7 (2007): 388–400, doi:10.3102/0013189X07309471.
2. John Dewey, *Ethics,* in *The Later Works of John Dewey, 1925–1953* (vol. 7), ed. JoAnn Boydston (Carbondale: Southern Illinois University Press, 1985), 280.
3. Note that examples of more detailed teacher interaction protocols (TIPs) and actor interaction protocols (AIPs) are in the appendix.
4. Kevin K. Kumashiro, "Towards a Theory of Anti-Oppressive Education," *Review of Educational Research* 70 (2000): 25–53, doi:10.2307/1170593.
5. Gloria Ladson-Billings, "Yes, but How Do We Do It? Practicing Culturally Relevant Pedagogy," in *White Teachers/Diverse Classrooms: A Guide to Building Inclusive Schools, Promoting High Expectations, and Eliminating Racism,* ed. Julie Jandsman and Chance W. Lewis (Sterling, VA: Stylus, 2006), 29–42.
6. Deborah Helsin, "Regarding Uncertainty in Teachers and Teaching," *Teaching and Teacher Education* 23, no. 8 (2007): 1317–33, doi:10.1016/j.tate.2006.06.007; Kevin K. Kumashiro, "Uncertain Beginnings: Learning to Teach Paradoxically," *Theory into Practice* 43, no. 2 (2004): 111–15, https://www.jstor.org/stable/3701545; Deborah L. Ball and Francesca M. Forzani, "The Work of Teaching and the Challenge for Teacher Education," *Journal of Teacher Education* 60, no. 5 (2009): 497–511, doi:10.1177/0022487109348479.
7. Rudine Sims Bishop, "Mirrors, Windows, and Sliding Glass Doors," *Perspectives* 6, no. 3 (1990).
8. Barbara S. Stengel and Mary E. Casey, "'Grow by Looking': From Moral Perception to Pedagogical Responsibility," *National Society for the Study of Education* 112 (2013): 116–35, https://eric.ed.gov/?id=EJ1018420.
9. For an important discussion of the role of relation in educational and educative experience, see Charles Bingham and Alexander Sidorkin, eds., *No Education Without Relation* (New York: Peter Lang, 2004).
10. David Cohen, Stephen W. Raudenbush, and Deborah L. Ball, "Resources, Instruction, and Research," *Educational Evaluation and Policy Analysis* 25, no. 2 (2003): 119–42, doi:10.3102/01623737025002119.
11. It is true that instructors have access to the video recordings, but there is no evaluation or assessment involved. (In truth, the encounters run together in an instructor's mind. It's tough to remember who said what.) Instructors sample recordings looking for representative reactions or common verbal responses that might be interrogated in the group debrief as well as outliers worth further consideration.
12. It is worth noting that there is often a pattern in how teacher candidates encounter students, especially in their first SHIFT encounters. We often observe them trying out various "lines" that they have heard from former teachers, parents, teacher educators to see what will "stick" in the situation.
13. Robin DiAngelo, "White Fragility," *International Journal of Critical Pedagogy* 3, no. 3 (2011): 54–70, https://libjournal.uncg.edu/ijcp/article/view/249; Barbara Applebaum, "Comforting Discomfort as Complicity: White Fragility and the Pursuit of Invulnerability," *Hypatia* 32, no. 4 (2017): 862–75, doi:10.1111/hypa.12352.
14. This is discussed further in chapter 8, where we take up debriefing the encounters.
15. Thanks to our colleague Nicole Joseph for this phrase.
16. Sara Ahmed, *The Cultural Politics of Emotion* (New York: Routledge, 2004).

17. Dan C. Lortie, *Schoolteacher: A Sociological Study* (Chicago: University of Chicago Press, 1975), 55–81.
18. Charles Goodwin, "Professional Vision," *American Anthropologist* 96, no. 3 (1994): 606–33, doi:10.1525/aa.1994.96.3.02a00100; Gay, *Culturally Responsive Teaching*, 22–46.
19. W. E. B. DuBois, *The Souls of Black Folks* (New York: Penguin Books, 1903); Dorothy Hines-Datiri and Dorinda J. Carter Andrews, "The Effects of Zero Tolerance Policies on Black Girls: Using Critical Race Feminism and Figured Worlds to Examine School Discipline," *Urban Education* (2017): 1–22, doi:10.1177/0042085917690204; Eduardo Bonilla-Silva, *Racism Without Racists: Color-Blind Racism and the Persistence of Racial Inequality in America* (Lanham, MD: Rowman & Littlefield, 2013).
20. Mark R. Warren, Soo Hong, Carolyn Heang Rubin, and Phitsamay Sychitkokhong Uy, "Beyond the Bake Sale: A Community-Based Relational Approach to Parent Engagement in Schools," *Teachers College Record* 111, no. 9 (2009): 2209–54, https://eric.ed.gov/?id=EJ858252.
21. Henry A. Giroux, *Teachers as Intellectuals: Toward a Critical Pedagogy of Learning* (Boston: Bergin & Garvey, 1988): 121–28; Kumashiro, "Uncertain Beginnings"; Nicola Soekoe, "A More Possible Meeting: Initial Reflections on Engaging (As) the Oppressor," *Yale Human Rights & Development Law Journal* 20 (2019): 43–50, https://digitalcommons.law.yale.edu/yhrdlj/vol20/iss1/7/.
22. Cynthia Passmore and Jim Stewart, "A Modeling Approach to Teaching Evolutionary Biology in High Schools," *Journal of Research in Science Teaching* 39, no. 3 (2002): 185–204, doi:10.1002/tea.10020. In addition, before the encounter they read Beth Warren and Ann Rosebery, "Navigating Interculturality: African American Male Students and the Science Classroom," *Journal of African American Males in Education* 2, no. 1 (2011): 98–115, https://pdfs.semanticscholar.org/5ea1/64b3c7f7a6d805b2c8cde6eda2f30a11295d.pdf; and after the encounter they read Lisa Borgerding, "High School Biology Evolution Learning Experiences in a Rural Context: A Case of and for Cultural Border Crossing," *Cultural Studies of Science Education* 12, no. 1 (2017): 53–79, https://eric.ed.gov/?id=EJ1130857.
23. Rochelle Gutiérrez, "The Sociopolitical Turn in Mathematics Education," *Journal for Research in Mathematics Education* 44, no. 1 (2013): 37–68, https://www.nctm.org/Publications/journal-for-research-in-mathematics-education/2013/Vol44/Issue1/The-Sociopolitical-Turn-in-Mathematics-Education/; Nicole M. Joseph, Michael Hailu, and Denise Boston, "Black Women's and Girls' Persistence in the P–20 Mathematics Pipeline: Two Decades of Children, Youth, and Adult Education Research," *Review of Research in Education* 41 (2017): 203–27, doi:10.3102/0091732X16689045.
24. Diana Hess and Paula McAvoy, *The Political Classroom* (New York: Routledge, 2014); Barbara S. Stengel, "The Complex Case of Fear and Safe Space," *Studies in Philosophy and Education* 29 (2010): 523–40, doi:10.1007/s11217-010-9198-3.
25. At Lipscomb University in Nashville, Laura Delgado and Kara Krinks have begun a SHIFT program with this configuration.

Chapter 3

1. Hans Georg Gadamer, *Truth and Method* (2nd rev. ed.), trans. Joel Weinsheimer and Donald Marshall (New York: Continuum, 1998); Deborah Kerdeman, "Pulled Up Short: Exposing White Privilege," in *Philosophy of Education 2017*, ed. Ann Chinnery (Urbana, IL: Philosophy of Education Society, 2019), https://educationjournal.web.illinois.edu/ojs/index.php/pes/article/view/51/20. It is important to note that Gadamer

thinks that this experience cannot happen unless one is already open to the possibility of change. We appreciate Kerdeman pointing this out. However, our experience and that of our teacher candidates suggests that it may be possible to learn to be open. This is a claim Kerdeman is investigating in a forthcoming study.
2. "Pulled up short" is a term that appears in passing in Gadamer's *Truth and Method*. In "Pulled Up Short," Kerdeman highlights the importance of being pulled up short in Gadamer's philosophy and has extensively analyzed the centrality of this experience for education. We are indebted to Kerdeman for sharing her thinking with us about this critical moment in the fusion of horizons that, we argue, explains the power of SHIFT simulations.
3. Kerdeman, "Pulled Up Short."
4. Ibid., 1–3.
5. Gadamer, *Truth and Method*, 268.
6. Kerdeman, "Pulled Up Short," 6.
7. Ibid., 3.
8. Kerdeman makes a similar point in ibid. 9, 13–14.
9. For a discussion of a pedagogy of discomfort, see Megan Boler, *Feeling Power: Emotions and Education* (New York: Routledge, 1999); and for a pedagogy of interruption, see Gert Biesta, *Good Education in an Age of Measurement* (New York: Routledge, 2010).
10. Zeus Leonardo and Ronald Porter, "A Pedagogy of Fear: Toward a Fanonian Theory of 'Safety' in Race Dialogue," *Race Ethnicity and Education* 13, no. 2 (2010): 139–40, doi: 10.1080/13613324.2010.482898.
11. Thomas Philip, "An 'Ideology in Pieces' Approach to Studying Change in Teachers' Sensemaking About Race, Racism, and Racial Justice," *Cognition and Instruction* 29, no. 3 (2011): 297–329, doi:10.1080/07370008.2011.583369.
12. See, for example, John Dewey, *Human Nature and Conduct*, in *The Middle Works of John Dewey, 1899–1924* (vol. 14), ed. JoAnn Boydston (Carbondale: Southern Illinois University Press, 1979); and John Dewey, *Democracy and Education*, in ibid., vol. 9; H. Richard Niebuhr, *The Responsible Self* (New York: Harper & Row, 1963).
13. Dewey, *Human Nature and Conduct*, 132–34.
14. Barbara S. Stengel, "Making Use of the Method of Intelligence," *Educational Theory* 51, no. 1 (2001): 109–25.
15. See, for example, Barbara Stengel and Mary Casey, "'To Grow by Looking': From Moral Perception to Pedagogical Responsibility," in *NSSE Yearbook: A Moral Critique of American Education*, ed. Hugh Sockett and Robert Boostrom (New York: Teachers College Press, 2013), 116–35.
16. In describing this process, we seek to avoid the hard distinction between epistemological agency that Gadamer wants to challenge and the ontological agency he is defending. Because we view the SHIFT experience from a critical pragmatist perspective, we hope to preserve both Gadamer's view that one's horizon is constitutive of self (and being pulled up short prompts a shift of self in the world) and arguments like that of Andrea R. English, which view the fusion of horizons as an epistemological rather than ontological experience. See Andrea R. English, *Discontinuity in Learning: Dewey, Herbart, and Education as Transformation* (Cambridge, UK: Cambridge University Press, 2013). While we cannot fully engage this question here, we

appreciate Deborah Kerdeman's clarifying this difference of interpretation in private conversation.
17. bell hooks, *Teaching to Transgress* (New York: Routledge, 1994).
18. Dewey, *Human Nature and Conduct*; Kevin Kumashiro, "Toward a Theory of Anti-Oppressive Education," *Review of Educational Research* 70, no. 1 (2000): 25–53, doi:10.3102/00346543070001025; Dan Lortie, *Schoolteacher: A Sociological Study* (Chicago: University of Chicago Press, 1975).
19. We note that Kerdeman makes this point about her own experience ("Pulled Up Short," 10–11).
20. Gadamer, *Truth and Method,* 270, 271.
21. Ibid., 305.
22. As Gadamer puts it, "Understanding is not a resigned ideal of human experience... Understanding is the original characteristic of the being of human life itself" (ibid., 259.)
23. Ibid., 276 (italics added), 270.
24. Kerdeman, "Pulled Up Short," 4.
25. Deborah Kerdeman, "Preparing Educational Researchers," *Educational Theory* 65, no. 6 (2015): 723.
26. "The purpose of my investigation is... to discover what is common to all modes of understanding and to show that understanding is never a subjective element to a given 'object' but to the history of its effect; in other words, understanding belongs to the being of that which is understood" (Gadamer, *Truth and Method*, xxxi).
27. Ibid., xxxii.
28. Kerdeman, "Pulled Up Short," 5.
29. Gadamer, *Truth and Method*, 269.
30. Ibid.
31. Kerdeman, "Pulled Up Short," 5.
32. Gadamer, *Truth and Method*, 306.
33. Kerdeman, D., "Pulled Up Short: Challenges for Education," in Philosophy of Education 2003, ed. Kal Alston, (Urbana, IL: Philosophy of Education Society, 2004), 209–210, https://educationjournal.web.illinois.edu/archive/index.php/pes/article/view/1735.pdf.
34. Gadamer, *Truth and Method*, 355.
35. Kerdeman, "Pulled Up Short: Challenges," 211.
36. Warnke, in ibid., 211.
37. Kerdeman, "Pulled Up Short: Challenges," 214.
38. Gadamer, *Truth and Method*, xxxviii.
39. Kerdeman, "Pulled Up Short," 8–11.
40. We have done limited work with in-service teachers in schools using the simulated encounters but with different outcomes. We believe that this idea of letting go all at once may be a partial explanation for the different outcomes. Teacher candidates are being asked to let go of personal understanding of the world, which subjects their actions in private life to further scrutiny in a way only they can fully do. When teachers in schools are asked to let go of these understandings, it calls into question personal and professional understandings of the world, which then subjects both their personal and professional lives and actions to scrutiny in ways that may have implications for their employment or standing in the school community.

41. John Dewey, "The Theory of Emotion: (I) Emotional Attitudes," *Psychological Review* 1 (1894): 553–69; John Dewey, "The Theory of Emotion: (II) The Significance of Emotions," *Psychological Review* 2 (1895): 13–32.
42. Sara Ahmed, *The Cultural Politics of Emotion* (New York: Routledge, 2003).
43. Ibid., 62–63, 68.
44. Ibid., 64, 69.
45. William James, "On a Certain Blindness in Human Beings," in *Talks to Teachers on Psychology and to Students on Some of Life's Ideals* (New York: Harry Holt, 2012).
46. See, for example, Teaching Works, http://www.teachingworks.org; and Teacher Education by Design, https://tedd.org/learning-labs/.

Chapter 4

1. David Stroupe and Amelia Wenk Gotwals, "'It's 1000 Degrees in Here When I Teach': Providing Preservice Teachers with an Extended Opportunity to Approximate Ambitious Instruction," *Journal of Teacher Education* 69, no. 3 (2017): 294–306, doi:10.1177/0022487117709742.
2. David Cohen, "Professions of Human Improvement: Predicaments of Teaching," in *Educational Deliberations*, ed. M. Nisan and O. Schremer (Jerusalem: Keter, 2005).
3. D. Sumara and B. Davis, "Enlarging the Space of the Possible: Complexity, Complicity, and Action Research Practices," in *Action Research as a Living Practice*, ed. T. Carson and D. Sumara (New York: Peter Lang, 1997).
4. Elizabeth Self, "Designing and Using Clinical Simulations to Prepare Teachers for Culturally Responsive Teaching" (PhD diss., Vanderbilt University, 2016).
5. George Saunders, "The New Mecca," in *The Braindead Megaphone: Essays* (New York: Riverhead Books, 2007), 55. For a discussion of this notion applied to education, see Barbara Stengel, "'So Open It Hurts': Enabling 'Therefore, We Can . . .' in the Dangerous Secure World of Education," in *Philosophy of Education*, ed. Cris Mayo (Urbana, IL: Philosophy of Education Society, 2013), 1–15.

Chapter 5

1. John Dewey, *Human Nature and Conduct*, in *The Middle Works of John Dewey, 1899–1924* (vol. 14), ed. JoAnn Boydston (Carbondale: Southern Illinois University Press, 1979); John Dewey, *Democracy and Education*, in ibid., vol. 9; Gloria Ladson-Billings and William F. Tate IV, "Toward a Critical Race Theory of Education," *Teachers College Record* 97, no. 1 (1995): 47–68; William F. Tate IV, "Critical Race Theory and Education: History, Theory, and Implications," *Review of Research in Education* 22 (1997): 195–247; Gloria Ladson-Billings, "Culturally Relevant Pedagogy 2.0: a.k.a. the Remix," *Harvard Educational Review* 84, no. 1 (2014): 74–84; Geneva Gay, *Culturally Responsive Teaching: Theory, Research, and Practice* (New York: Teachers College Press, 2010); Jean Lave and Etienne Wenger, *Situated Learning: Legitimate Peripheral Participation* (Cambridge, UK: Cambridge University Press, 1991).
2. Ben Dotger, *"I Had No Idea": Clinical Simulations for Teacher Development* (Charlotte, NC: Information Age, 2013).
3. Stephen Sawchuck, "For Preservice Teachers: Lessons on Cultural Sensitivity," *Education Week*, February 16, 2016, https://www.edweek.org/ew/articles/2016/02/17/for-preservice-teachers-lessons-on-cultural-sensitivity.html.

4. Kara Krinks and Laura Delgado have begun a very interesting iteration of SHIFT simulations at Lipscomb University based in part on Krink's experience teaching the science literacies simulation as a doctoral student at Vanderbilt. What is especially compelling about their work is the way they have maintained the SHIFT cycle but adapted the content to the students and structures at Lipscomb.
5. Readers who are interested in materials for simulations not provided in this manuscript can email the authors to inquire about encounters referenced in the text or on topics of interest.
6. Ibram Kendi, *How to Be an Anti-Racist* (New York: One World, 2019).
7. Jean Lave and Etienne Wenger, *Situated Learning*; Maggie Lambert, *Teaching Problems and the Problems of Teaching* (New Haven, CT: Yale University Press, 2001).
8. Ibid.
9. Peter Senge, *The Fifth Discipline: The Art and Practice of the Learning Organization* (New York: Doubleday, 1990).

Chapter 6
1. Carla Shalaby, *Troublemakers: Lessons in Freedom from Young Children at School* (New York: New Press, 2017); Mica Pollock, Sherry Deckman, Meredith Mira, and Carla Shalaby, "'But What Can I Do?' Three Necessary Tensions in Teaching Teachers About Race," *Journal of Teacher Education* 61, no. 3 (2010): 211–24, doi:10.1177/0022487109354089.
2. Robin DiAngelo, *White Fragility: Why It's So Hard for White People to Talk About Racism* (Cambridge, MA: Beacon Press, 2018).
3. Audre Lorde, *Sister Outsider: Essays and Speeches* (Berkeley, CA: Crossing Press, 2007).
4. We are willing to share Vanderbilt SHIFT TIPs, AIPs, and pre/rereading questions under a Creative Commons Copyright (Attribution-NonCommercial-ShareAlike). We ask only that you acknowledge the source and adapt/use these materials for the benefit of teacher education and teacher candidates. Please contact the authors.

Chapter 7
1. In this simulation we used faculty children as actors because we knew that these children (some siblings) had prior experience discussing similar topics and that they would have support at home after their SHIFT experience. We have also talked productively with local youth theater companies, including social justice groups.
2. We do not pay the youngest actors in cash or at the same rate as adult actors. We do thank them by giving them gift cards to bookstores.

Chapter 8
1. We acknowledge the engagement, support, and wisdom of the colleagues we quote and cite here. This chapter is a testament to their willingness to take the SHIFT Project and purposes seriously and to share their insights with us.
2. Prudence Carter, "'A Shade Less Offensive': School Integration as Radical Inclusion in the Pursuit of Educational Equity" (Brown Lecture in Educational Research presented at American Educational Research Association, Washington, DC, October 24, 2019).
3. Kathleen Stewart, *Ordinary Affects* (Durham, NC: Duke University Press, 2007).
4. We note that this is the same direction provided to the actors in preparation for the encounters.

Coda

1. Bettina Love, "Dear White Teachers: You Can't Love Your Black Students If You Don't Know Them," *Education Week*, March 18, 2019, https://www.edweek.org/ew/articles/2019/03/20/dear-white-teachers-you-cant-love-your.html.
2. Paul Cobb, Jere Confrey, Andrea diSessa, Richard Lehrer, and Leona Schauble, "Design Experiments in Educational Research," *Educational Researcher* 32, no. 1 (2003): 9–13, doi:10.3102/0013189X032001009; Sepehr Vakil, Maxine McKinney de Royston, Na'ilah Suad Nasir, and Ben Kirshner, "Rethinking Race and Power in Design-Based Research: Reflections from the Field," *Cognition and Instruction* 34, no. 3 (2016): 194–209, doi:10.1080/07370008.2016.1169817.

Acknowledgments

The SHIFT Project at Vanderbilt University—and this book—would not be what it is without the support, commitment, and thoughtful engagement of colleagues. We thank Justine Bruyère, Grace Chen, Laura Carter-Stone, Teresa Dunleavy, Mariah Harmon, Andy Hostetler, Melanie Hundley, Heather Johnson, Nicole Joseph, Kara Krinks, Michael Neel, Emily Pendergrass, Rebecca Peterson, Dan Reynolds, Marcy Singer-Gabella, and Anita Wager for both encouraging and challenging us in the development of the SHIFT cycle and for being willing to step into the fray by incorporating SHIFT simulations into their courses and programs. Several master's students have provided this project with logistical support over the past several years, and we thank them: Marie Artap, Rebecca McKnight, and Karen Sun. We offer special thanks to Karen Sun for their assistance in the preparation of this manuscript and their encouragement toward its completion.

SHIFT simulations can be run with modest expenditures, but there *are* costs involved. Peabody College dean Camilla Benbow has been supportive of this work since its inception, both financially and professionally. We appreciate her commitment to anti-oppressive pedagogy in the long tradition of Peabody College, acknowledge her material support for our work, and look forward to moving SHIFT simulations into a newly developed lab on campus. We also acknowledge past internal funding from the Bonsal Applied Education Research Award and external funding from a subcontract of a grant from the Arthur Vining Davis Foundation.

We have developed SHIFT simulations within our practice of teacher education over the past seven years, but that development has required both praxis and theoretical reflection. We acknowledge those who have challenged our thinking, shared their ideas, and urged us onward. We are particularly grateful to Ilana Horn at Vanderbilt University, Ben Dotger at Syracuse University, Justin Reich at the Massachusetts Institute of Technology, Deborah Kerdeman at the University of Washington, and Audrey Thompson at the University of Utah. In addition to the contributions of these scholars, whose work we know quite well, we appreciate those colleagues who have helped us fine-tune both practice and theory by responding with interest and intelligence to various conference and workshop presentations. We cannot name all of them, but their feedback is represented in our work.

The preparation of this manuscript was enriched by a number of scholars who read chapters and responded with helpful comments. These include Deborah Kerdeman (University of Washington); Grace Chen, Teresa Dunleavy, Ilana Horn, Nicole Joseph, Michael Neel, Marcy Singer-Gabella, and Jessica Watkins (Vanderbilt), and Dan Reynolds (John Carroll University). This book would be weaker without their willingness to share their time and responses.

We acknowledge as well the kind and thoughtful guidance provided by our editor at Harvard Education Press, Nancy Walser. From the prospectus to the final submission, she was an important presence in bringing this book to reality.

The teacher candidates who have learned and developed through SHIFT simulations have generously shared their insights about the experience with us, and we acknowledge especially those whose words we quote in chapter 4: Tianling Feng, Lizzie Hinton, Josh Knight, Lindsey Lieck, Minta Ray, Josh Rosen, Ashley Seiss, Karen Sun, Emily Waltman, Daniel Wilson, and Luis Zoniga. Thanks to them and to all who have taught us as they participated with open hearts and minds, growing through the process into anti-oppressive educators.

Finally, on a personal note, Barb thanks Monica and Libby, who provided her with space and support for writing, and Henry, Will, Maggie, and Fran, who provided regular and oh-so-rich distractions from the work. Liz thanks Wes and her kids, Oliver, Emmeline, and Zola, for giving her plentiful distractions from writing, and her students past and present, who make the work interesting always.

About the Authors

ELIZABETH A. SELF is an assistant professor of the practice in the Department of Teaching and Learning at Vanderbilt University's Peabody College. With an interest in the social foundations of education, she teaches courses in the elementary and secondary licensure programs that focus on philosophies of education, critical pedagogy, and the practice of teaching as situational and contextual. Her current research focuses on designing and using live-actor simulations to prepare teachers for anti-oppressive education. Her work on simulated encounters has been featured in *Education Week*, *Chalkbeat*, and on the *TeachLab* podcast series. Self earned her MEd in the Learning, Diversity, and Urban Studies program and her PhD in the Learning, Teaching, and Diversity program at Vanderbilt University's Peabody College.

BARBARA S. STENGEL is a professor emerita of education at Vanderbilt University's Peabody College. A teacher educator since 1980, she is the author of *Just Education: The Right to Education in Context and Conversation* (Loyola University Press, 1991) and coauthor (with Alan Tom) *Moral Matters: Five Ways to Develop the Moral Life of Schools* (Teachers College Press, 2006). She has published her work related to teacher knowing, the moral dimensions of teaching and teacher education, and affect in educational interaction in various journals and handbooks, including *Teaching Education*, *Educational Theory*, *Studies in Philosophy and Education*, and *The Handbook of Research on Teaching* (5th ed., American Educational Research Association, 2016). Stengel is past president of the Philosophy of Education Society, has served on the executive board of the John Dewey Society, and is currently an associate editor of *Educational Theory*.

Index

actions/feelings interaction, 68–69
actor interaction protocols (AIPs), 106, 121–122, 126
actors
 overview, 133
 calls for, 137–138
 during encounters, 145–148
 feedback from, 146–148
 finding, 133–136
 history of use of, 99
 honoring involvement of, 148–151
 importance of, 76
 payment of, 105–106
 training of, 138–145
affect versus emotion, 68, 70
age of actors, 134–136
Ahmed, Sara, 69–70, 72
AIPs (actor interaction protocols), 106, 121–122, 126
anonymity, 47, 73, 170
anti-oppressive educators, 6, 37, 107
assessment, 19–20, 73
avatars, 20–21

business school education, 15–16

capacity, 103–107
case method of education, 15
classroom culture, 160
classroom management, 79
class time, 106
cognition and emotion, 67–68
compensation of actors, 150–151

conference presentations, 149–150
confidentiality, 47, 73, 170
contingent thinking, 87–88
critical incidents, 12, 16, 37, 37–39. *See also* encounters
The Cultural Politics of Emotion (Ahmed), 70

Daria Miller simulation example, 27–32
debriefing. *See* group debriefs; raw debriefs
defensiveness, 46–48, 121, 156–157, 170
deliberate practice, 18
Dewey, John, 68–69, 72
difficult conversations, comfort with, 157–158
disruption. *See also* pulled up short phenomenon
 allowing of, 49, 158
 discomfort for, 46
 encounter choice and, 113–114
 as inherent in teaching, 40
 restoration needed after, 65
dissatisfaction, 118
Dotger, Benjamin, 18–19
dramatic rehearsal, 60

educational outcomes, 4
emotion and cognition, 67–68
emotion versus affect, 68, 70
encounters
 overview, 24, 113
 actors influence on, 142–143

225

encounters, *continued*
  choice of, 113–117, 132
  elements of, 117–126
  feedback on, 126–127
  goals of, 116
  location and sequence of, 51–54, 110–111, 127–128
  realistic nature of, 76–78
  revision of, 123, 126–127, 129–132
  engagement, 102–103. *See also* raw debriefs
ethic of responsibility, 60
ethics, 134–136
excitement, 69–70

facilitation
  overview, 153–155
  end of, 171–172
  for generative debriefing, 160–163
  preparation for, 155–160
  problem prevention, 168–171
  sample debriefing plans, 163–168
fear, 68, 71–72, 169–170
feedback, 146–148, 160
feelings/actions interaction, 68–69
fidelity, 154
fight/flight, 71
funding, 105–106, 150–151
fusion of horizons concept, 64–65

Gadamer, Hans Georg, 62–63, 64, 66
generative versus obstructive interactions, 165
goal alignment, 102–103, 158–159
group debriefs. *See also* facilitation
  actor involvement in, 148–149
  example of, 31–32
  privacy in, 47, 73, 170
  revision of, 130–132, 172
  in SHIFT cycle, 26–27
  white fragility and, 47
guiding principles of SHIFT
  overview, 35–36
  complexity of teaching practice, 39–42
  context and narrative as richly specified, 42–45, 120–122
  critical incidents, 37–39
  dispositions grounding continuous learning, 48–50
  location and sequence of cycles, 51–54
  situation selection, 45–48

habits, 62
hermeneutically trained consciousness, 64–65
horizon shifts
  fusion of horizons concept, 64–65
  need for, 4–5, 59
  SHIFT cycle for, 3, 61, 63
  time needed for, 166–167

identities
  facilitation and, 162
  guiding principles of SHIFT and, 37–39
  simulations to account for, 22, 61
  surfacing in critical incidents, 38–39
immersion, 47–48
impacts of SHIFT. *See also* group debriefs; pulled up short phenomenon
  overview, 75, 92–93
  on faculty, 91–92
  learning as unfolding over time, 83–86
  openness stance and, 88–91
  realistic nature of encounters and, 76–78, 117–119
  recognition of simulation moments in future, 91
  should to could shift, 86–88
  staying power of, 78–83
information gathering, 165
infrastructure requirements
  overview, 97–98
  questions to ask about, 101–112
  SHIFT Project and, 98–101
insecurity, 65
instructors, defined, 6
interact stage of SHIFT cycle. *See* encounters
interruption. *See* pulled up short phenomenon

Kerdeman, Deborah, 57–58, 63, 65, 66–67, 174

legal education, 15
literacies courses, 52–53, 125–126, 167
live actors. *See* actors
loss, 65–66

medical education simulations, 15
methods courses, 163, 167
microteaching, 17–18
mind-body dichotomy, 68–69
minoritized students, educational outcomes for, 4
money issues, 105–106, 150–151

negative learning, 123, 127
Niebuhr, H. Richard, 60
nonjudgmental atmosphere, 169–170

obstructions, 170
obstructive versus generative interactions, 165
oppression, 4–5

parent-teacher conferences, 114
past histories, 69–70
Peabody College (Vanderbilt), 107–108
pedagogical responsibility, 59–62
peer feedback, 160
plausibility of narrative, 119–122
positionalities, 22, 37–39, 61, 162
prejudice, 67–68
prejudices, 63, 64
prepare stage of SHIFT cycle, 23–24, 28–29
prereadings, 19, 23–24, 28–29
presuppositions, 38
principles of SHIFT. *See* guiding principles of SHIFT
problem-based education method, 15–16
productive discomfort, 46
program capacity, 103–107
program change, readiness for, 111–112
project coordinators, 106–107
pulled up short phenomenon
    overview, 55–57
    encounter design for, 129–130
    need for, 67–72
    pedagogical responsibility and, 59–62
    power of, 57–59, 62–66, 67
    in SHIFT cycle, 66–67, 72–74
    teacher educator experience of, 156–157

quality control, 154
questioning, 169

raw debriefs, 25, 30–31, 78–79
react stage of SHIFT cycle. *See* raw debriefs
reconsider stage of SHIFT cycle. *See* group debriefs
rehearsal, 17–18
relational quality, 44
relational systems, 71–72
remuneration of actors, 150–151
rereadings, 19, 25–26
resolution, 118
The Responsible Self (Niebuhr), 60
review stage of SHIFT cycle, 25–26, 30–31, 47
revision
    of encounters, 123, 126–127, 129–132
    of group debriefs, 130–132, 172
role-play, 17–18
rules versus principles, 36

safety, 157
Self, Elizabeth, 11–13, 98–100
self-understanding, 62–63, 64, 170–171
sequencing of simulations, 51–54, 110–111, 127–128, 158–159
SHIFT cycle. *See also* encounters; facilitation; group debriefs; raw debriefs; review stage of SHIFT cycle
    example of, 27–32
    horizon shift due to, 3, 4–5, 59, 61, 63, 64–65, 166–167
    instructor clarity on, 159–160
    location and sequence of, 51–54, 110–111, 127–128, 158–159
    pulled up short phenomenon in, 66–67, 72–74
    steps in, 23–27, 100, 174

SHIFT Project, 2, 59, 98–101
SHIFT simulations. *See also* encounters; guiding principles of SHIFT; pulled up short phenomenon
  assessment and, 20, 73
  authors' paths to, 11–14
  benefits of, 2, 14, 65
  customization of, 173
  described, 3
  differences from other simulations, 15, 21–22
  emotion and behavior and, 70, 72
  future of, 173–175
  immersion and, 47–48
  microteaching and rehearsal and, 18
  multiplicative impacts of, 32–33
  problem-based education method and, 16
  purposes of, 55
  research on, 174
  safety in, 6, 31, 47, 73, 157, 170
  selection of, 108–109
  simulated interaction model and, 19
  structure of, 72–73
  teaching concepts versus experiences of, 73–74
  virtual simulations, 21
should to could shift, 86–88
simulated interaction model (SIM), 18–19
simulations. *See also* SHIFT simulations
  in non-teaching education, 14–16
  other uses for, 16–21

theory as needing enactment, 57
  as tool to support learning, 61, 104
social foundations courses, 51–52, 111, 116
socialization, 77
social practice, teaching as, 109–110
standardized patient encounters, 15
Stengel, Barbara, 13–14, 99–100
stereotypes in simulations, 122–123
subject-specific courses, 52–53, 125–126, 167
systemic oppression, 4–5, 12, 58

teacher candidates, 5, 115–116
teacher educators, 6
teacher interaction protocols (TIPs), 23, 106, 120–121, 126
teacher preparation programs, 5
teaching as social practice, 109–110
TIPs (teacher interaction protocols), 23, 106, 120–121, 126

unintended learnings, 82–83

Vanderbilt University, 107–108
videotapes, 105. *See also* review stage of SHIFT cycle
virtual simulations, 20–21

Warnke, Georgia, 65–66
wedge theory, 112
white fragility, 47
white privilege, 57–58